ABOUT THE AUTHOR

Jenny Randles has investigated scientific anomalies for 25 years and has engaged in research for many leading organisations, including the British UFO Research Association – for whom she served as Director of Investigations for 12 years – the Dr J Allen Hynek Center for UFO Studies, the Association for the Scientific Study of Anomalous Phenomena and the UFO Investigators Network. She has lectured and participated in research at various universities, including Massachusetts Institute of Technology (MIT) and Manchester University. Her articles have appeared in many sources such as *New Scientist*, *Omni*, *The Times* and the *Guardian*. She has written and presented several radio documentaries, was the story consultant on all series of the hit ITV programme *Strange But True?* and in 1996 scripted and presented the BBC TV documentary *Britain's Secret UFO Files*, which gained a record audience. Jenny has a diploma in Media and Audio Visual Communications and is the author of 45 books, with over one million copies sold in 27 countries. She lives in the north Derbyshire Peak District.

Other books by the author

The Complete Book of Aliens and Abductions
The Paranormal Sourcebook
The Truth Behind the Men in Black
Truly Weird
Something in the Air
Strange But True? Casebook

with Peter Hough

The Complete Book of UFOs
Strange But True?
Life After Death and the World Beyond
The Afterlife
Psychic Detectives

with Dr David Clarke & Andy Roberts

The UFOs That Never Were

TIME
STORMS

JENNY RANDLES

TIME STORMS

Amazing evidence for Time Warps, Space Rifts and Time Travel

PIATKUS

First published in 2001 by
Judy Piatkus (Publishers) Limited
5 Windmill Street
London W1T 2JA
e-mail: info@piatkus.co.uk

For the latest news and information on all our titles,
visit our website at www.piatkus.co.uk

A catalogue record for this book is available
from the British Library

ISBN 0 7499 2159 5

This book has been printed on paper manufactured with respect for
the environment, using wood from managed sustainable resources

Typeset by Palimpsest Book Production Limited,
Polmont, Stirlingshire
Printed and bound in Great Britain by
Butler & Tanner Ltd, Frome, Somerset

Contents

Introduction

FOR THE YOUNG WIFE OF A COLONEL IN THE ROYAL ENGINEERS, THE YEARS AFTER World War II in India were living history. Dawn watched as the British Empire was handed back in pieces and as the certainties of the old world gave way to the tensions and opportunities of the new. In a culture where women were still subservient, it was an extraordinary experience.

As events of global significance unfolded, they left Dawn with a passionate concern for the teeming masses of the region. Her deeply held Christian faith led her to organise and remain committed to relief work, despite her later bereavement, failing eyesight and deteriorating health. She was an inspiration to all who knew her. My conversations and recorded interviews with her impressed me absolutely as to her sincerity.

Despite all the colourful colonial pomp, it was a strange incident in the autumn of 1947 that turned out to be the most incredible event she ever experienced. When she first told me about it, decades later, neither of us had any idea what had happened to her and to ten others on that long-gone day. It was, as she said modestly, 'just one of those things that nobody can comprehend. Perhaps we are not meant to do so.'

As I listened to her words in her smart Cheshire home, with the distant hum of an electric train blocked from my mind by her mesmerising recall, it was easy to agree with her. I could not offer any rational explanation for the things that she was telling me. They did not fit into the commonly accepted understanding of science that I had been taught as a student. It seemed like an intractable mystery so weird that it might never find resolution.

I was wrong. What happened to Dawn was a chance meeting with

what I have come to call a time storm. It may be one of the most fascinating phenomena in science today, yet it has attracted hardly any
meaningful investigation. This is not a supernatural fantasy. It is completely real. These occurrences set a major challenge to current scientific
awareness, and in this book we will see just why.

That October Dawn and her husband, then living in Nepal, to the
north of India, were to take part in an expedition to visit the Dalai Lama
– a revolutionary experience for a refined Englishwoman of thirty. To reach
the home of the spiritual leader involved a journey that even today would
be hazardous – crossing desert plains and then climbing foothills in order
to enter the vast Himalayan ranges of Tibet. It would be a long, slow drive
of at least two weeks' duration in antiquated wartime vehicles, and because
of the risk from bandits and mercenaries major security precautions had
to be taken.

Dawn and her husband travelled in a heavy army truck. A Gurkha
rode with them as shotgun protection. Other jeeps and trucks in the
convoy were also manned by armed Gurkhas and carried possessions,
supplies, gifts for the Dalai Lama and various other necessities for an epic
journey through inhospitable terrain. Several religious leaders, including
two Plymouth Brethren, were in the party. Dawn's husband, the colonel,
was in charge of everyone's welfare.

They had been travelling for about a week and the scenery was growing
more spectacular by the day. Late in the afternoon they stopped near a
tiny village that consisted of little more than a handful of huts. As the
sun slid towards the dusty horizon, Dawn asked the Gurkha sergeant,
who was on guard duty in case of danger, which of the vast peaks towards
which they were now heading was the famous Mount Everest. He smiled
as he replied: 'My lady, those are just hills!'

The heat had been relentless for days, so when an icy coldness suddenly struck Dawn – as if a fridge door had been swung open – she knew
immediately that something was wrong. But she did not know precisely
what.

'I was sitting on the tailboard of the truck,' she told me. 'As soon as this strange sensation struck I looked up. It was apparent that the others were feeling it, too. Then I felt as if something was touching me. The Gurkha nearest to me reacted. My skin was tingling. It was like a prickling sensation growing stronger.'

Many things now happened in what must have been only a short space of time.

'We saw a strange red object. It was coming towards us across the plateau,' Dawn recalls.

Some villagers hovering near the trucks, intrigued by this rare visit from Westerners, fled in terror at the sudden sight. From the expressions on their faces it was clear they knew what was coming. Later they confirmed that such a floating 'apparition' had struck before. It was to be feared, and the only thing to do when it appeared was to hide.

Dawn was stunned and terrified, and even the Gurkhas were paralysed with shock for a few moments. But her husband's army training must have over-ridden his own fear. Reaching for his weapon, he ran towards the front of the truck in an attempt to intercept the unidentified intruder. But as if he had run into an invisible brick wall, the colonel took only a few steps before crashing to the ground motionless.

'It did not seem to have any particular shape,' she adds. 'It was a very strange cloud. It was moving just above the surface – but definitely moving. I would say that it was as big as a large house.'

By now Dawn was unable to take her eyes from the apparition. She too was incapable of movement, and just sat on the side of the truck, her muscles rigid.

'It did not seem to have any particular shape,' she adds. 'It was a very strange cloud. It was moving just above the surface – but definitely moving. I would say that it was as big as a large house.'

As the 'cloud' approached their truck, it passed near the place where her husband lay sprawled on the ground. Its motion scattered villagers and Gurkha guards, many of whom leaped into the trucks in the hope that these would provide sanctuary. But the thing seemed to home in on Dawn's truck and moved around it as if performing a military inspection.

'There was an extraordinary pressure in the air. The truck was actually vibrating,' she says.

The other vehicles nearby were shaking and rattling, and their noise pierced the silence left by the menacing form. The air surrounding the party felt alive in an electric manner that none of them had ever experienced before.

'It was very peculiar. I cannot explain it. The prickling sensation had grown in power, and it felt as if my hair was standing on end. Almost like an electric shock, but not quite so severe. It went on for some time. In fact I couldn't say how long. Time just seemed to lose all importance.'

Although Dawn had no way of knowing it, she was describing a set of symptoms frequently reported in such encounters: ambient sounds that just seem to disappear; an eerie stillness and silence; the flow of time stopping inexplicably and leaving a numbing timelessness. Researchers call these symptoms collectively the Oz Factor and later you will see just why. They recur so regularly in time storm encounters that they must represent a clue to the science that is involved.

One of Dawn's last concrete memories is of the strange 'storm-like' mass that induced this sense of 'timelessness' (hence 'time storm') moving past and leaving the victinity of the truck. 'It floated about and seemed to change shape,' she says. 'It seemed solid in the middle, but the outside was like fog or vapour. It was not a hard object. Not some sort of craft. It was sort of woolly-edged. The redness from the distance was now gone [possibly it had been catching the rays of the setting sun from the direction it arrived: JR]. It was now a grey, floating mass.'

She has an image in her mind of the final moment that she saw this thing, still virtually on top of her. The grey mass was floating there. The guards were frozen in mid-flight, as if time had stopped or vanished. Her husband was lying on the ground in front of jeep, quite possibly dead. There was this strange pressure in the air and the terrible electrical tingling. There was silence, stillness and timelessness.

Then reality changed in an instant.

Dawn's next memory was of what seemed to be moments later. But night was falling fast. There was no prospect of continuing their journey now. Gradually things returned to normal and she stooped to help a Gurkha lift her husband to his feet. The colonel had little recall of what had happened. He felt dizzy and sick, but was not permanently disabled. There was no way to know if the events that had taken place before them had lasted seconds or days. Subjectively, there was no discontinuity. Yet in reality everything had altered in the blink of an eye. There had been some sort of space–time dislocation.

We all take the ticking clock for granted, as an immutable reality. But for Dawn it had shattered.

It was well into the night before the party began to discuss these amazing events. All had experienced some part of them. Nearly everyone had felt the prickling sensation and the downward pressure. Several were also beginning to feel its legacy of sickness.

Dawn told me, 'Nobody spoke for a very long time. I don't know how long. There was just this silence. When we did talk, at first we thought we had imagined it. But we all had seen and felt the same things, so we knew that it had happened. Then my colleagues and I started to come out in a rash: an itchy, red rash on all the places where I felt that I had been touched – my arms, legs, face and neck. I felt sick – and indeed within minutes I *was* sick. Several of the others were equally stricken. None of us could eat anything until the next day. The rash lasted throughout the following day, but gradually subsided on the second day, as did the nausea.'

The three who were worst affected by illness, vomiting and the rash were Dawn, her husband and the Gurkha sergeant. Interestingly, it was they who had been closest to the floating cloud. The next day, still camped outside the village, the party had to decide what to do next. The villagers refused to be drawn into discussing what had happened. The Gurkhas seemed less than keen to go on into the mountains and the isolation that lay ahead. By mutual consent it was decided to turn round and make the six-day journey back to Nepal.

Dawn says she was sad to miss out on the visit to the Dalai Lama, although some time later she did meet him – in less trying circumstances. But when the decision was taken to abandon the trip to Tibet that day, 'I was quite glad to be getting out of there.'

Dawn's amazing story fascinated me because I had no doubt she was describing a real event. The only question I could not answer was what on earth it was.

I considered the obvious options, such as a sandstorm or fair weather whirlwind that can create a cloudy mass in hot weather and set up pressure changes. Tornadoes can even possess electrical charges that they vent as lightning bolts. But whilst both of these options explain some of the features, they ultimately fail to account for all of them. It might be tempting to dismiss the odder parts as the result of imagination or memory distortion built around a mundane storm. If this case were an isolated incident, that would be a reasonable deduction. But I soon learned that it was not.

Dawn's story inspired me to dig deep and look for comparisons, and to my considerable surprise I found them everywhere. Moreover, they are part of a pattern that has sat undiscovered within the archives of science and the more shady realms of the supernatural, often wrongly ascribed to some dubious phenomenon such as UFO (unidentified flying object). It is clear to me that what struck that day and caused such fear even amongst battle-hardened soldiers was no alien visitation. It is a phenomenon of this earth, and will in time have a scientific resolution.

As I hope this book will demonstrate, Dawn's encounter in the foothills of Tibet was just a typical time storm. It has many features that recur. Once we realise that we are seeing a newly recognised and consistent phenomenon and then seek the patterns revealed within the unfolding evidence, we can start to look for answers.

It is clear to me that what struck that day and caused such fear even amongst battle-hardened soldiers was no alien visitation. It is a phenomenon of this earth, and will in time have a scientific resolution.

But first we need to follow the trail of evidence from case to case and see just why the accepted scientific basis of time is put into question as a result. There will be some answers and plenty of surprises in the stories that follow. There will be startling ideas and very strange concepts. But as I hope you will appreciate, it will be the trail of evidence that will lead us towards many startling possibilities.

Amazingly, one reasonable deduction is so bizarre that it will read like science fiction. Yet our journey is through the real world of temporal physics, human experience and documented cases. If the destination appears hard to believe, it can only be said that fact, logic and science will have taken us there.

Be prepared. For the evidence to be assessed in this book harbours proof that time travel is not merely possible but may be happening all around us right now. If so, then research into time storms may become one of the most exciting areas for new scientific exploration.

PART ONE

·

THE EVIDENCE

Extraordinary Case Histories

1
Very Strange Clouds

WHEN A SCIENTIST IS CONFRONTED WITH A POSSIBLE NEW ANOMALY, IT IS important to start by collecting the evidence. To emulate this sensible and trusted method we must establish the parameters of the time storm experience, bearing two essential points in mind.

Firstly, witness reports can be mistaken. This requires us to consider more mundane solutions for these sightings and not jump to conclusions from individual, and initially merely alleged, encounters. Only if clear patterns emerge can we start to feel confident that something is being uncovered.

Secondly, these reports are likely to be sensationalised and distorted by the global fascination with reputedly paranormal happenings. This may well have transformed a mystery of nature into something that it never really was. We will have to strip away talk of aliens or the supernatural and cut to the heart of the evidence to find the raw facts, the physiological and physical properties. So you will not find paranormal interpretations in this book. What will be presented is simply the evidence that has been documented.

Unfortunately, that has to be done almost from scratch because this is a new mystery about which little has been written. Cases, reports and ideas lie scattered in many sources – often misleading ones such as UFO files. I must emphasise that what follows are best considered to be encounters with a novel but down-to-earth phenomenon.

Happily, there is no shortage of examples to define what we are talking about. In this chapter I shall set out a cross-section from all over the world to help build a portrait of the time storm. Then we can move on to define its nature in more detail and consider how it affects our scientific assessment of time itself.

EXPLORERS

The first case is a low-level incident but with impressive witnesses.

Adelaide Island (Antarctica), 1966

It occurred early on the morning of 22 May 1966 to the British Antarctic Survey then located close to Mount Gundrey on Adelaide Island in this frozen wasteland. The man who reported the event was Irish explorer Eric Wilkinson. Then senior meteorologist with the team, he was well placed to know that the cloud that he and colleagues saw that day was a very strange one indeed.

What appeared to be a dense white mass appeared in the south and rose vertically from near ground level beside a small hill, floating at what was estimated as about 600 feet in altitude. The mass was approximately 100 feet across and was largely homogeneous during the forty-five minutes that it remained in view. It was moving only very slowly and seemed to pulsate, expand and contract in density. As it did so, a noise was emitted across the silent, snowcovered landscape. It sounded like the buzzing of a huge swarm of bees or the hum generated by an electricity transformer.

At one point, a dark 'tube' emerged from the cloud and struck the snow on the ground below. The tube came out at a 45-degree angle and created a second 'reflected' ray or beam at a 75-degree angle in the opposite direction, rising from the point where the first tubular beam had struck the earth. The snow too was also affected by this impact, rising upwards in a spiral as if tossed by a whirlwind. O

Before the cloud was lost to view Wilkinson took several photographs of the phenomenon, including some that showed the 'tube' and its effect on the snow. These have failed to explain what the phenomenon was, other than the general inference that it must have been some very rare form of atmospheric disturbance of unknown origin.[1]

INCIDENT AT MINEHEAD

Minehead (UK), 1977

At 7.36 a.m. on 26 September 1977, Patricia Cater, a Bristol-based computer programmer, was driving a van towards Minehead on the A39 near Kilve in Somerset when she saw a strange floating mass north of the road. It was near ground level, just above a hedge, so Patricia stopped and got out for a better view. As she reached the gate leading into the field, she saw some cows huddled together in one corner and apparently disturbed by something.

The form that hovered behind the bushes was like a large grey egg. Still more curious than frightened, Patricia walked across the field to get a closer view, but as she put it, 'I entered a region where my skin prickled and my hair stood on end.' It seems clear that she was encountering a zone of electrostatic charge that was presumably associated with the cloud.

Recalling a school experiment with a Van der Graaf generator – a device that creates a large static field – Patricia knew that there was a powerful energy here. She heard a humming noise emanating from the floating mist and decided not to risk going closer. As she backtracked, she realised that there was a sharp 'cut-off' where the energy field ended and the prickling sensation suddenly ceased.

When Patricia returned to the van the floating cloud had not moved. She noticed that it was now twelve minutes later than when the experience began – perhaps no more than a failure to note the normal flow of time during the incident, although this was never measured.[2] ○

THE BLACK CLOUD

Engineer Sten Ceder was driving home along the E4 route in northern Sweden after visiting some friends near the town of Ojebyn.

'Everything became black around me. The blackness seemed to be a dense, floating mass of smoke that lay around me so that it was impossible to see anything.'

Ojebyn (Sweden), 1971

The date was 20 September 1971 and it was 10.45 p.m. – a cool evening, with many stars in the sky. Ceder reports that as he neared a crossroads, the sky lightened in a curious way, not unlike the polar region aurora caused by atmospheric ionisation. But the curtain of light that shone down on to the road ahead was in the form of vertical beams that did not quite touch the ground. Within seconds the car was encircled by them.

This light show was accompanied by a strong force – a form of gravity push that Sten could not properly define. He says it gave a 'sense of discomfort' and was 'a kind of atmospheric pressure.' He put his foot hard on the brakes, but the car failed to respond and was propelled onward.

Then, Ceder reports, 'Everything became black around me. The blackness seemed to be a dense, floating mass of smoke that lay around me so that it was impossible to see anything.' Moreover, the black cloud created another strange effect. It was as if all the light was being absorbed into it – not just from the air, but from the vehicle too. The headlights (which were on full beam and later found still to be operating) seemed to have ceased emitting any perceptible illumination.

Ceder swung around sharply to the left, hoping to escape down the turn-off at the crossroads – though nothing was actually visible through the black void that had engulfed him. Then, suddenly, he emerged into the light again and some distance from where he expected to be. He blinked, looked around and saw the dark, cloud-shaped mass rising from the road into the sky. As it moved, it was so black that it seemed to erode all ambient light in its vicinity.

He later returned to the crossroads to look for the skid marks that he was certain his car must have left – but, to his bafflement, there were none. ○

There are many features here – such as the gravity anomaly and 'black hole' effect on light – to file away for discussion later in this book.[3]

CARS AND MISTS

My records include a number of cases of cars being 'accosted' by glowing mists that appear out of nowhere with humming/buzzing noises and that cause electrical disturbance.[4]

A disturbing example of this type comes from Australia, from where industrial chemist Bill Chalker reports on his findings.

Nemingha (Australia), 1976

At 5.45 a.m. on 22 March 1976, a couple driving home to Murrurundi in New South Wales had a bizarre experience, according to a letter they sent to the *Northern Daily Leader* newspaper a few days later. They had stopped just outside Tamworth at the settlement of Nemingha

– a small crossroads consisting of little more than a hotel, a petrol station and a railway halt. They had parked and were consulting a road map, trying to decide the best route to take.

On the otherwise deserted early morning highway a white car now appeared, coming from the road that led to Tamworth. The couple got out, hoping to flag it down and ask the driver's advice. However, at that moment something weird happened. A hazy yellow-green light seemed to fall from nowhere and in moments it engulfed the white car. As if its driver had lost control, the vehicle crossed to the wrong side of the road where it was surrounded by a very localised small patch of white haze or mist. The car coasted to a stop in the middle of the road. It had seemingly lost all power and its lights were off.

According to the stunned onlookers, after about a minute or two 'the white haze disappeared. A lady dressed in blue stepped from the car and with a yellow cloth proceeded to wipe the windscreen, which seemed to be covered in a white substance.' After she did so, the car's lights suddenly returned – apparently without anybody inside to switch them on. The woman looked shocked, threw away the 'duster', jumped into the car and drove off. Simultaneously, the discarded cloth burst into flames.

The startled couple had now been joined by a pick-up truck that had stopped beside them. Its driver was staring at the events in amazement, and all three witnesses watched as the white car drove slowly away towards Nundle. Its windscreen wipers were clearing the forward view, whilst the rest of the vehicle was covered by a white layer that had not been there before the strange haze appeared. Unsurprisingly, the couple were concerned and eventually returned home by a roundabout route that they felt was 'safer' than the one from which the mist had arrived. ○

Bill Chalker's visit to Nemingha failed to resolve this case although he attempted to assess the possible ways by which chemical changes in the atmosphere might leave a white deposit that would spontaneously combust in this manner. No obvious sources were found – although he did note that the car was travelling close to electricity power lines at the time. As we look at further cases from around the world, you will notice other reference to a strange powdery white substance. It is one of the clues that stand out.[5]

DEFYING GRAVITY

Whilst strange, the Nemingha case is not unique.

Barnard Castle (UK), 1977

On 6 June 1977, Mark Henshall, then a sixteen-year-old farm worker, was riding his motorcycle late at night on the rural B6278 north of Barnard Castle in Co. Durham, near the village of Lartington. The weather was unseasonal for midsummer – cold and very wet. Luckily, in these conditions, there was not much traffic on the isolated, narrow, winding road. But at 11.30 p.m. Mark noticed two purple glows behind him and, thinking they were the lights of a vehicle, kept glancing back to keep a check on them. After about thirty seconds he noticed that a Jaguar car was about to overtake, so he pulled over slightly to let it pass. The purple glows had been forgotten for the moment.

But just as the car overtook him, a blinding, hazy glow swamped both vehicles. It was a vivid, fuzzy purple colour with a pinkish tinge – possibly suggestive of ultra-violet radiation. Simultaneously with this sudden 'assault', Mark noticed the power drain away from his motorcycle. He reports, 'I could not understand what was happening at first. Then I moved the throttle and there was no response. I felt my back and legs becoming hot and as I looked at my [leather] jacket it was beginning to steam.'

Despite losing power, the bike was 'pulled' up the hill and the Jaguar also seemed to move on (its driver later reported that he too lost power and yet moved forward against gravity – he assumed via momentum). Whatever the case, both vehicles travelled uphill about 300 feet with the fuzzy glow engulfing them, but with no actual power by which to do so. Indeed, a site reconstruction later showed that both vehicles were tugged right over the top of a small hill. Then the misty mass just disappeared.

Mark instinctively applied his brakes, but this only caused his motor-cycle to lurch forward and still be pulled ahead. Previously in good order, the brakes were found next day to be so worn as to require resetting. Mark describes at one point taking off his glove after the brakes had finally worked (by now the glow had vanished). He reports that he touched the metal side tank and it was extremely hot. He also noticed that, despite the heavy rain that had left him soaking, his riding suit was bone dry. Later it was found to be 'stiffened' on the back by the heat. There was also not a trace of surface water on the motorcycle in the immediate aftermath of this event – it was as if it had been instantly evaporated.

> *'I felt my back and legs becoming hot and as I looked at my jacket it was beginning to steam.'*

The driver of the Jaguar stopped and got out, and he and Mark Henshall discussed what had happened. The car engine had 'faded away' for about thirty seconds. Although the driver did confirm the details of this incident to investigators, he was so shaken that he requested anonymity, and preferred not to discuss the matter beyond giving a basic account of what had happened. ○

When her son arrived home at about midnight, Mrs Henshall commented that his hands and face seemed very red, as if sunburnt. They were also hot to the touch, although this effect quickly faded. Some days later Mark developed a severe stomach upset, but it is not clear whether this was connected with the incident.[6]

A RED SUN

This next case was reported in 1969 to the aviation journal *Wings over Africa* by a South African rancher and private pilot.[7]

Natal (South Africa), 1969

Anton Fitzgerald was walking with his farm manager towards the airstrip on his central Natal ranch. This was a June morning, just after dawn. His Zulu tractor driver had pulled the light plane from its hangar, and they were heading down a slope to meet him so that Anton could fly to Durban.

As he then reports, some 600 feet away near the plane he saw an 'eerie reddish glow'. It resembled a pocket of marsh gas or swamp mist, but formed a bubble shape and was clearly luminous. As the two men stared at this phenomenon, they saw a flock of sheep beside the airstrip acting very curiously. The animals were surrounding the mist in half circles and were all attracted to it. He describes the pattern they formed as like 'iron filings on a piece of paper around a magnet' – possibly a very significant remark.

As the two men drew closer, the reddish-pink mist started to climb upwards. There was no sound. But what was truly weird was that sheep were being attracted upwards along with it, as if being pulled by some force. They were practically airborne and standing vertical (Anton likens them to ballet dancers on tiptoe), with only the points of their back feet keeping them earthbound.

Now, as Anton and his manager closed in on the rising mass, they too felt a curious weightlessness. Anton reports how the saliva was sucked up to the roof of his mouth, and how the morning dew that soaked into his socks as they crossed the field was rising from his calves and up his legs.

Then the mist had gone, the sheep were back on the ground (although one had vanished and was never found) and the excited tractor driver was babbling in Zulu. He said that this was the confirmation of a long-standing tribal legend about a 'red sun' that had been seen in this area and that 'ate cattle'.

A few minutes later, as he taxied through the spot on the runway where the mist had been, the aircraft took off on its own, Anton reports. It was rising rapidly in a way he had never experienced before, as if defying gravity and without creating the expected g forces. Before he knew what was happening, he was at 10,000 feet, with his ears popping repeatedly due to pressure changes, but the effect seems to have quickly faded. But he had to contact Durban control and ask to be allowed to descend to his allotted height, explaining to them that some freak 'updraft' was to blame. ○

THE LOST DOG

This next case ties together a number of features from previous events. It was described first hand to Roy Sandbach and myself.

Oswestry (UK), 1988

On 9 February 1988, John, a former army man, had been looking for farm labouring work near Oswestry in Shropshire. He had got up early on a sunny day but had not been successful, and at about 8 a.m. was walking home on a road about two miles south-east of the town. As he approached a parked car, just off the quiet road, he saw a woman exercising her spaniel. The dog was off its lead and running about, barking merrily, playing on the grass verge bordering a field.

Then suddenly it went 'berserk' and ran across the road, oblivious to its safety, barking furiously at something. John followed the dog and saw what he termed 'a yellow fog' about 45 feet in diameter and glowing brightly. It straddled the hedgerow and the path at the side of the road. It was producing a noise 'like the wind rushing', and indeed the mist was whirling in a spiral, causing the leaves around it to rotate as if the victims of a mini-tornado. Apparently unafraid, the dog ran straight into the fog and promptly disappeared. It is not clear if it literally vanished or was simply obscured by the mist.

Seeing this 'abduction' of her pet, the owner began to scream hysterically and John attempted to calm her. They both noticed a 'terrible musky smell – vile, horrible and sulphurous' and an eerie stillness. They also felt a strange sensation like an electric tingling, and saw that their hair was standing on end as if filled with static.

In what can only have been moments (although nobody was watching the time) the fog vanished 'like smoke disappearing'. They saw the dog lying flat on the ground, with its body on the path and its head on the kerb. It looked dead. Rushing over, John found that the animal was alive, though apparently unconscious. He also noticed that its body was soaking wet and extremely warm – the heat was causing the water to evaporate rapidly. He notes that 'it was steaming like it had just come out of a bath.' The dog's eyes were red and bloodshot. Its chest was rising and falling in heavy panting movements, but otherwise it seemed close to death. O

John placed the spaniel on the passenger seat of the car and covered it with a blanket. The woman, apparently in total shock, drove away without saying a word. But John noted the details of her car as she sped away and was therefore able to trace her. She later confirmed that the dog did recover within an hour or so and seemed none the worse for the experience.

But a few weeks later it died. However, it was quite elderly and its death was probably not suspicious.[8]

LITTLE HOUGHTON

Little Houghton (UK), 1973

One night in September 1973, Paul, then twenty-one, was driving through the village of Little Houghton in the English Midlands. As he passed the church clock, he noted it was about 2 a.m. Because of his long drive home from a dance he had drunk very little. But after passing the clock, he lost all sense of time until he found himself wandering on foot at Bromham – sixteen miles closer to Bedford. He was soaking wet, although it was not then raining. There was no sign of his car and he had no obvious injuries. What is more, it was now daylight – around 7 a.m.

Paul found a friend who lived not far away, and told him that he had no memory of the past few hours, but could only assume he had had a car accident whilst driving home. His friend drove him along the A428, retracing his route towards his last recalled location – (Little Houghton). They found the car about five miles from Bromham, near a village called Turvey.

The car was in the middle of a muddy field yet there was no sign of tyre tracks leading from the closed gate. It was locked (Paul had the keys in his pocket) and appeared undamaged. It was not possible to drive it out through the thick mud caused by heavy rain that Paul later discovered had fallen during the five hours that are lost to his memory. The farmer had to tow it out with his tractor, but there was nothing wrong with the vehicle itself.

Two years after this strange event Paul recalled a little more about it during a sudden flashback. He now recalled driving out of Little

Houghton and seeing a fuzzy white glow heading towards the windscreen. Then there was blackness until he 'came to' five hours later, wandering on foot near Bromham.[9] ○

This story has a remarkable sequel.

Little Houghton (UK), 1983

In February 1983 an unrelated witness, forty-four-year-old Peter Rainbow, was visiting his sick mother in the same village of Little Houghton. With no knowledge of Paul's previous encounter, he left Northampton at 6.45 p.m. on his motorcycle to travel along the A428. As he rounded the bend at Great Houghton his engine and lights cut out. Peter used an old biker's trick to correct what he assumed to be a blown fuse – he wrapped silver foil around it to facilitate conduction. When this made no difference he took out a spare fuse, and was just about to fit this when he saw that a white, egg-like glow was clinging to the ground in the field next to him.

> *'Everything was quiet. There was no noise at all. No birds. No cars. Nothing. I felt almost in a trance.'*

The entire area had been plunged into silence. As he put it, 'Everything was quiet. There was no noise at all. No birds. No cars. Nothing. I felt almost in a trance.'

This is the same effect reported by Dawn in Nepal in 1947 (see p. 4).

The white mist wobbled and gyrated like a spinning top. Then in a blur it was gone. This acted like the breaking of a magic spell. Peter now realised that he was no longer holding the fuse. It had gone. He was grasping the ignition key – although it had been in the lock. The engine now fired normally. Peter drove the short distance to Little Houghton, where the church clock showed 8.30 p.m. An hour-and-a-half had apparently disappeared in just moments.[10] ○

THE TRABANT

I discovered this next incident on a trip to Hungary.

Lake Balaton (Hungary), 1992

It involved a young woman driving her Trabant car home west of the town of Szekszard one evening in January 1992. A fuzzy white light appeared ahead of her on the road towards Lake Balaton and swooped towards her windscreen. She recalled her engine and lights fading. Then there was blackness and she regained her senses an unknown time later (but it appears to have been at least several hours, as it was now the early hours of the following morning). The car was inside a field totally surrounded by snow, which had not fallen since some days previously. Yet there were no track marks to indicate how the car could possibly have got into this position – something that stunned those who retrieved the vehicle, especially as the nearest road was some distance away. The similarity with the Turvey case should be apparent.

Somewhat groggy, and with a painful leg injury, the woman stumbled out of her car and staggered across the field towards a distant light. It turned out to be a security light at an industrial complex. By now she was feeling dizzy and sick and her leg was covered in blood, so one of the security guards drove her to hospital. Hearing only her confused words, he assumed she had been in an accident. At the hospital it was discovered that she had several small marks that resembled electric burns. She also had a red rash not unlike sunburn over the exposed part of her body (normal sunburn was impossible given the weather). ○

She recovered quite quickly – suffering only a spotting of blood as noted by a gynaecologist (she was not pregnant). The police followed her directions and went to the field. Here they found her Trabant, and were astounded to discover that the door handle was almost welded shut and had been subjected to intense heat. However, there was no trace of any actual fire or fire damage to the rest of the vehicle.[11]

PICLINEN LAKE

You would be forgiven for thinking that these time storms happen only to cars on lonely roads. In fact, whilst car-bound encounters are common, other types of transport can be involved too.

Piclinen Lake (Finland), 1987

At about 8.40 p.m. on 31 July 1981, two male holidaymakers in their mid-thirties were out in a motorboat on Lake Piclinen in Finland. They had taken the vessel out in the Cape Vaaraniemi region and were heading back to shore near Lieska when something strange happened.

As they told astronomers Juhani Kyrolainen and Pekka Terrikorpi, to whom they reported the incident, a black floating mass appeared above them in the sky. It headed towards the boat, and at closer view looked like a ball of fog or mist. Two glowing lights were seen within it.

. . . a black floating mass appeared above them in the sky. It headed towards the boat, and at closer view looked like a ball of fog or mist. Two glowing lights were seen within it.

One of the men reports that as it grew nearer he felt paralysed, either by fear or some force being emitted. He began to cry out, when suddenly there was a 'reality jump'. As both men attest, the black mist had gone. They were still sitting in the boat, but seemed to have shifted position within it and had no memory of how this had occurred.

Worse was to follow. The sky looked different (it was lighter than they recalled), and once they got their bearings they could tell that they were still off the Cape and had not drifted as they should have done with the strong local currents. The trouble was that – as their watches indicated and as was later proved – it was now 4.10 a.m. on the following day. Seven hours had disappeared in the blink of an eye. Both men also suffered interesting after-effects that are, as you will see, consistent with many other severe encounters involving a time storm. They describe these as a serious disruption of bodily co-ordination, with symptoms, which lasted about a week, such as shaking hands, inability to walk properly and lack of balance. Their nervous systems had been severely affected in some way by the associated energy field.[12] ○

NIGHT MANOEUVRES

To close this opening review, here is one of the most remarkable cases yet studied.

Putre (Chile), 1977

On 24 April 1977, a small unit of army conscripts was sent on a two-day exercise into the inhospitable terrain above the small town of Putre in Chile. The intention was to harden the inexperienced young troops for the rigours of military life. That night they camped on a windswept, arid plateau at Pampa Lluscuma, at a height of 12,000 feet. In charge of the raw recruits was Corporal Armando Valdes.

At 3.50 a.m., Pedro Rosales, the recruit on guard duty, saw something very odd. He called out to Valdes, who came immediately. What appeared to be two fuzzy violet lights were descending from the mountains and heading their way. The ground below was filled with an eerie glow. (Note the links with the Durham case just six weeks later – see p. 17)

Unsure if these were flares being used in a mock attack, Valdes sprang quickly into action. He ordered some of the men to screen the camp fire light with blankets in the hope that they might escape detection in the dark. He told the others to secure and prepare their weapons just in case. By now there was just one large fuzzy glow on the hill a few hundred yards away. It sat there immobile for some minutes.

Ignoring protests from his frightened charges, at 4.15 a.m. Valdes advised them to cover him with their weapons whilst he went to investigate. He told them to crouch behind a nearby wall, rifles poised. Then, uttering a plea for God to protect him – and with, they reported later, a conviction in his eyes – the corporal clambered over the wall and headed into the darkness towards the purple glow.

Within seconds the inky night had swallowed him up. Moments later, the violet glow below them disappeared too. The conscripts fell into stunned silence before debating what to do next. They decided to wait and hope that their commander might return – which at 4.30 a.m. he duly did. But he approached them from behind – not from the direction in which he had just walked. Moreover, he was clearly less than well.

The startled soldiers saw him wandering as if in a trance, his voice uttering words that sounded like those of sleepwalker. 'You do not know who we are or where we come from,' he said in a monotone, although he never consciously recalled saying this. He reached the camp site, looking barely able to stand, and collapsed on to the ground apparently unconscious.

Having cared for him as best they could, the men waited for a cold dawn to rise over the mountains. It was then that they noticed several very strange things about their stricken leader. Although they had seen him shave only hours earlier, he was now sporting several days' growth of beard. His watch had stopped at about 4.30 a.m., the approximate time of his return to the camp, but the date display – which had to be wound on manually through twenty-four hours at a time to alter it – read 30 April. It was as if Valdes had lived through five days in under fifteen minutes.

At about 7 a.m. the corporal regained consciousness, but he was still far from lucid. He appeared to be in a state of shock, with massive memory loss and no proper body co-ordination. The troops took the decision to abandon their exercise and get him to the nearest town, a difficult two-hour trek.

At Putre, the local schoolteacher, Pedro Araneda, was the closest to an expert on hand and he taped an interview with the still only semi-coherent officer and some of the men. This was to prove important, because when the Chilean military arrived they put a block on the tape's release and the military governor of Arica province ordered Valdes to keep silent about his experience. However, Araneda was eventually allowed to release his transcripts. O

The army command would only confirm that the story was true but was completely inexplicable to them. They refused permission for Valdes to make further public comment. In any event, from what he told Araneda the corporal was little wiser than anybody else. He recalled walking towards the glow, then nothing until he was recovering consciousness beside the camp fire.

I have learned much from Antonio Huneeus, a Chilean-born journalist resident in the USA, who has pursued this case. The military do appear to have investigated. But details of the outcome are unknown aside from hints that other unexplained events may have occurred around the same time in the Tarapaca region that surrounds Putre. Despite obvious interest in the story for a few days, the inability of the main witness to talk quickly killed any prospect of widespread publicity. But it is known that Valdes asked for a transfer away from this part of Chile soon afterwards, and his request was granted. He and his wife moved to a place called Temuco. Then in 1983 – though the request had to be approved by the then Chilean leader General Pinochet – one journalist was granted the opportunity of talking to Valdes. Unfortunately, he was still very reticent and did not have much to add.

All that Valdes could do was confirm that the basic details reported were true; he had recovered no memory of his missing fifteen minutes (or five days) in the intervening years. 'They are a void in my mind,' he commented. However, some circumstantial evidence did surface: in 1980 Valdes may have been forced to undergo psychiatric treatment in a Santiago hospital, since his bizarre encounter had left him debilitated and traumatised. He displayed no evidence of prior mental abnormality.[13]

As you can see from numerous cases such as these, glowing mists and clouds with remarkable properties are appearing all over the world. Witnesses reporting them are generally unaware that others have already done so. This enhances the impression of a true anomaly, because there is little pattern of expectation.

These seemingly reflect a type of atmospheric anomaly with intriguing physical and physiological effects. From its appearance and its effects, I refer to this as a time storm.

2
The Nature of the Beast

THE CASES SURVEYED IN CHAPTER 1 SUGGEST A REAL AND CURIOUS PHENOMENON. It has consistent features, such as a fuzzy glow or misty cloud, electrical fields and associated physiological effects. It has been occurring for many years and examples have been reported from several continents. Any real scientific anomaly should indeed be widespread.

Whilst time storms often get reported in a spurious context, that is a consequence of how people interpret strange experiences today. It should not diminish the basic evidence. Rarely is there any good reason to assume that aliens or mystical phenomena are involved. Yet the promotion of these incidents in bizarre ways often cloaks them in needless fantasy. It is also a deterrent to scientific investigation, which is why time storms are under-explored.

Of course, we are dealing with apparent gravity anomalies and fundamental issues of time and space where things occur that seem impossible according to how most people understand the universe. Yet by removing this anomaly from the dubious context of paranormal happenings, illumination can follow, for what we see then are independent stories that are really just variations on one theme. Indeed, it is clear that time storms are far more globally consistent and scientifically credible than most odd events that get far more public attention.

AN UNRECOGNISED MYSTERY

The unrecognised nature of the time storm is significantly in its favour. Nobody has been investing these stories with objectivity, so there is little public awareness of what they are supposed to be about. It is unfortunately true that alien abduction yarns, for example, are well known. Most people could invent an alien contact story that would superficially convince – thanks to books, TV shows and movies.

It is hard to envisage this arising with a time storm. The incidents appear in sources with relatively little access, and it is difficult to imagine how they could be consistently fabricated or imagined, so we have a decided rarity in today's culture, in which multiple TV channels saturate us with supernatural mythology. We can identify a *new* mystery which has reached the twenty-first century virtually untainted by not being given a name, invested with a history and turned into the subject of a popular legend.

KEY FEATURES

Let's review the key features of the time storm.

Firstly, there are strange clouds, or mists reported close to ground level. Although these can appear dark at night, typically they have illumination – presumably from some generated energy. Colours vary, but green/yellow and red/purple are common. Fuzzy, grey masses that can be mistaken for solid objects are reported, although clues as to their vaporous nature are usually apparent. Witnesses may, for example, say that a shape emerges within fog or they might describe how the amorphous nature of what they saw changed shape. These are all hints of a time storm at work, even within cases that do not at first seem obvious.

Similarly, when witnesses refer to lights or glows, it is important not to assume too much. Witnesses to anomalies often deduce that lights and misty shapes are part of an otherwise unseen object, and simply 'join the dots' in their minds to create a structure that is not really present. Nearly every unexplained phenomenon through the ages has been invested with intelligence in this way. It is why lightning was initially considered to be a weapon of the gods. Likewise today, time storms gather structure that is not actually present. We always need to take one step back from the words that the observers use to see nature at work within.[1]

There are also the physiological effects associated with the time storm. These are not always present. They may depend upon the strength of any energy fields involved, or on the closeness of the witness to the phenomenon. Other factors, such as shielding by car bodies or the simple decision of a witness not to subsequently report how they felt during an experience, can be relevant. This lack of knowledge can also cause an investigator not to ask specific questions, and may lead to an apparent lack of such evidence described in a case. But when these physiological effects *are* reported, they prove to be stunningly consistent. You will see countless references to tingling sensations, hair standing on end, goose pimples, (actually the skin literally 'crawling' in the presence of the electrical charge), a sense of being watched and in more extreme cases body rashes, sunburn effects, pounding headaches, watering eyes and nausea. All of this directs us towards a genuine electromagnetic (EM) field that accompanies the time storm.

This energy field marks its presence in other ways. It clearly has considerable power and, as we have already seen, often interferes with electrical systems (such as a car engine) and adapts into another form (such as heat). Vehicles in close proximity to a powerful time storm seem vulnerable to some form of impedance effect. Engines are drained of power, lights are temporarily extinguished and the flow of energy through mechanical components is blocked. The radiation emitted can also follow the normal rules of physics and be detected. There are frequent references by witnesses to feeling hot or, as in the Durham case (see p. 17), to a large amount of water being evaporated.

Studying the physical processes at work will tell science a great deal about the nature of a time storm. But these processes are important for another reason too. Few witnesses understand physics to the extent that they could make up the scientifically credible stories. These cases make sense in terms of real physics, and as a consequence infer the presence of actual energy fields. For supporting statistical analysis see the research compiled by BUFORA.[2]

A more difficult aspect of the time storm is the apparent subsequent change in the psychological state of a witness. There are many references to feelings of isolation, the reduction of sensory input ('all sounds just disappeared') and a detached state of mind in which people almost drift into unconsciousness. The woozy, drowsy Oz Factor state is trance-like in its manifestation, with definite properties of an altered sense of awareness. It does seem to act as the gateway to some of the deeper levels of the experience, and is nearly always present in cases where truly fantastic things are reported.

Whilst we must consider the role of human psychology and its reaction to trauma – perhaps inducing a state of mental dissociation – I believe this may mean that the altered state induces visions (like waking dreams), and that some of the fantastic features of the time storm may be happening within such a vision. If so, these elements are not of course real, but images triggered by physically real energies behind the time storm. What we can say is that the most profoundly strange time storms induce an altered state of consciousness – the Oz Factor – that is central to the weirder experiences described by a witness.[3]

Straddling the border between effects possibly induced by real physical forces and those that may be visionary in nature is the surprisingly common report of changes to the nature of gravity. We are all used to the idea that on earth objects fall downwards. It is hard to take seriously claims that sheep, cars or even humans might reverse that trend and float upwards. Yet we have all seen shots from the NASA shuttle or the Mir Space Station which show astronauts escaping gravity. It is perfectly commensurate with science. We just don't expect to find it happening on a back road to Bedford. But if witnesses say that it does happen, we need not consider ghosts, spaceships or the supernatural as possible causes. Physics can still provide the key.

Somewhat more problematic are the rare but none the less significant cases that invoke spatial distortions. A witness literally moves some distance with no explicable means by which to do so. Often the switch is slight. But the implication of such instant transfer is that it happens by some means not consistent with ordinary science. In fact, this staple of science fiction, known as teleportation, is a disturbing feature of some time storms.

However, the strangest aspect must be the temporal disruption. Even discussing such a thing as a dislocation in time, where a witness moves forward by hours or sometimes even days, seems tantamount to submitting to the *Star Trek* school of scientific nonsense. But we cannot deny cases simply because we do not like what the evidence is telling us. These reports are undeniably fantastic, and if they are in any sense literally true they challenge our understanding of time.

These effects – some simple, others less so, some modestly strange, others akin to science fiction – are what make the time storm one of the most extraordinary phenomena on earth. They are a real puzzle and test our analysis of the data. These cases require the skills of many people, be they sceptical or open-minded. But challenges should be met head on, not run away from as seemingly absurd. And, as we will discover, there are reasonable answers to be found when we explore each aspect in detail.

3
Mists That Glow

STORIES OF GLOWING MISTS OR FOGS HAVE BEEN TOLD FOR CENTURIES. SOME care is needed because natural phenomena such as marsh gas (a floating, sometimes luminous emission) were for a time considered supernatural and appear in many old stories. It was associated with evil spirits leading travellers astray, usually literally into the marsh. Bad luck did follow the encounter, but as a perfectly natural consequence because the phenomenon tended to occur in dangerous locations and lured the unwary towards them. It is interesting that a mundane event was wrongly imbued with assumptions of intelligence. However, we can trace stories in old records that seem relevant.

Song-Zi Xian county (China), 1880
The annals of Song-Zi Xian county in China relate how on 8 May 1880 a local farmer, Ju Tan, came upon a misty light in some bushes. He described feeling very strange, including a tingling paralysis, and that there was a humming/rushing noise. He then found himself floating upwards and lost all sense of time and space. His very next recall – as if it had been a moment later – was of being found in a dazed state by a forester in Guizhou province. This was 300 miles from his farm, and two weeks had simply gone by 'in a blink'.[1] ○

This case has nearly every key feature of the time storm and yet precedes any modern tale that might be considered an influence. Its obscurity also makes it an unlikely trigger for today's encounters, as few modern witnesses can have heard of it. Indeed, one can just imagine that, if Ju Tan had been driving past that bush in his car a hundred years later, it would resemble other time storms even more closely.

But let's now concentrate on the physical descriptions of these misty glows and lights.

SNOW IN MAY

A typical nocturnal case is reported by Norman James from Surrey.

Dartmoor (UK), 1994

In May 1994 he and his wife were on a caravanning holiday in Chagford, Devon, in the heart of Dartmoor. At about 3 a.m., Norman got up to go to the toilet and noticed how the clear, moonlit night was being disturbed by a strange mist, which formed a 'white, vertical, oblong blanket, phosphorescent but giving off no light.' Even more peculiar was the fact that it seemed to have deposited what he terms 'scatterings' of a white powder, not unlike snow, on the grass immediately beneath. Actual snow is most unlikely, given the weather. The mist was so solid that it hid objects just feet behind it, but was only about fifteen feet long and some five feet high.

When Norman returned to the caravan he told his wife, who came to the door and saw it too. By dawn it had gone. Nor was there any trace of the white powder. Neither the farmer on whose land they were staying nor the local weather centre which they consulted, had ever heard of a phenomenon like this.[2] O

Of course, we have. The similarity to the case at Nemingha in Australia, where a white mist left deposits on a car, is evident (see p. 16). We shall come upon this effect later in other cases. So it is an important clue as to the physical forces involved.

Secondly, the witness made the interesting comment that no shadows seemed to be cast by the caravan, despite the bright moonlight. You will come across other references to light distortion effects of this type in the presence of these mists. It may again be a useful clue.

It is possible that the white powder is localised condensation of water vapour, just like real frost or snow. In late spring, this would quickly melt. Remember the frequent reference in time storm cases to the puzzling wetness that soaks the body in the immediate aftermath (see, for instance, p. 22). If these people are covered in a layer of frost during the encounter, and if that layer melts before they regain full awareness (that is, after the phenomenon has gone and normal temperatures return), they might find themselves inexplicably damp.

The question is: what sudden cooling process could generate such a frost during a time storm?

THE FLORIDA INCIDENT

Pilot Martin Caidin told me of his own encounter with a strange cloud in mid-air. It was to prove baffling for a man noted for his daredevil exploits and whose novel *Cyborg* was the basis for the TV show *The Six Million Dollar Man*.

Atlantic Ocean (USA), 1986

In 1986 Caidin was piloting a Catalina flying boat back to the naval air station at Jacksonville, Florida, after a tour of Europe that had included a landing in Plymouth harbour. They had crossed the Atlantic and on 11 June were on the final leg from Bermuda. The plane was packed with some of the most skilled aviators imaginable, including a US navy captain, a USAF flight engineer and a captain who flew heavy commercial jets – a total of seven witnesses to what happened next. They also had ultra-sophisticated navigation equipment, including direct links to a weather satellite that was printing out continual photographic images of the route ahead, to back up their claims.

Flying conditions were perfect, Caidin told me, as they flew towards the north Florida coast. He was in the cockpit between two other pilots who were taking a turn at the controls. As he idly looked down through the crystal-clear atmosphere to the blue sea in which dolphins had been cavorting, the aircraft's wings suddenly disappeared. The satellite photo moments earlier had shown the nearest cloud to be over 200 miles away, near Melbourne Beach. As Caidin puzzled over this, the other wing vanished. The sky, too, had changed. They were flying through what he calls 'eggnog' – a uniform creamy yellow substance that was clinging to the Catalina.

> *. . . the crew found that all their navigational aids had failed. Nothing was working properly. Millions of dollars of communications equipment, electronics and radios had dissolved into randomly flashing lights and meaningless displays of digits.*

Worse followed, as the crew found that all their navigational aids had failed. Nothing was working properly. Millions of dollars of communications equipment, electronics and radios had dissolved into randomly flashing lights and meaningless displays of digits. Even stranger, the fog that was immersing the aircraft had a narrow range. Through the top the sky was visible, and underneath in a hole was the sea. It was as if a long vortex tube was attached to the Catalina and flying with it. Meantime the gyros and compasses were spinning wildly. Only due to the expertise of those on board was it possible to survive this frightening situation.

After at least an hour (time too lost any pattern) they suddenly came out of the fog. At that instant the instruments all came back on line. The pilots did a circle back to look at the amazing 'fog' that they had just flown through, seemingly interminably. There was nothing – only perfect weather all around, as there had been immediately before the wings had vanished. Soon afterwards, they landed safely at Jacksonville. ○

What clearly did not happen is that the Catalina flew *into* a very large cloud mass, however unusual. If it had done so, the crew would have seen it after exiting and the weather, radar and satellite instruments would have shown it. The key may be in the funnel effect, which made the sky and sea visible in a narrow vortex above and below that travelled with them. It is reasonable to argue that the yellow cloud with electromagnetic properties formed *around* the aircraft and clung to it as it moved – rather as we have already seen in cases where the mist seems to home in on cars and travel with them.

You may wonder why the crew of the Catalina felt no strange physiological effects as other people have described. Caidin does refer to a strange sense of calmness, possibly the Oz Factor. But it is worth remembering that cars (and aircraft) act like giant Faraday cages and insulate the occupants from the most severe effects of any charged fields outside. During a thunderstorm, inside a car is just about the safest place to be.

This effect, discovered by noted pioneer in electromagnetic theory, Michael Faraday, is partly explained by the cocooning of the bodyshell that diffuses the charge. Witnesses to a time storm often report the strongest physical sensations only after they step *outside* their vehicle. Perhaps this basic law of physics was the salvation of the Catalina crew: electric shocks, nausea or paralysis could have proved catastrophic when skilful flying was essential.[3]

THE BENDIGO LIGHT

Martin Caidin and his colleagues were fortunate, but fate is not always with the witness. Disaster struck, for instance, during an extraordinary incident that took place near Bendigo in the state of Victoria, Australia.

Bendigo (Australia), 1966

Around 8 p.m. on 4 April 1966, Ron Sullivan, a businessman in the steel industry, was driving along a quiet road close to Burke's Flat. Off to the right in a field he noticed a curious glow – a fuzzy, phosphorescent mass perhaps fifteen feet across and shining white. This sounds very like the Dartmoor mist (see p. 36). As Sullivan moved towards it, a strange phenomenon developed – an oval appeared above the phosphorescence and a cone formed between the two. Lights like a rainbow ran down the side. Then the two parts of the mass moved towards each other, the whole thing contracted to a point and disappeared.

This remarkable light show has features of a prismatic mirage which can form within refracting mists when bright lights shine through. It was extremely alluring, and Sullivan had great difficulty keeping his mind on the unlit country road.

A far more serious and fantastic problem was the effect on his car headlights. As Sullivan drove towards the mass, the beams began to bend. The closer he got, the more the beams were deflected towards it. This is, of course, logically impossible. Light cannot be pulled off a straight path if space–time physics is behaving as expected. The influence of a massive gravity field, such as theorised by physicists in the presence of a black hole, could perhaps provoke such an effect. But black holes are believed to exist only in deep space. Moreover, the enormous gravity effects they induce ought to be destructive to all physical matter in their immediate vicinity.

The apparent pulling of the car headlights sideways into the field on the right led Sullivan to compensate by forcing his car to the left. This is an instinctive response, similar to the illusion that you get on a moving train. If you stare at the rails as you travel, they appear to flow in the opposite direction once the train stops at a station. This is because the mind compensates for the sudden lack of motion by assuming that the tracks must still be moving but going in the reverse direction.

Unfortunately, while Sullivan was struggling to control his car, he was really driving off the left side of the road, straight towards a roadside tree. Luckily, he spotted it just in time and swerved back on to the highway. If light rays can be deflected near time storms, is that why shadows were absent in the Dartmoor case?

Several days later, when he arrived back home from his business trip, Sullivan heard that a young man called Gary Taylor had died in a car crash on the same road at Burke's Flat. This was on the night of 6 April, forty-eight hours after his own sighting. Sullivan decided to tell the police what he had experienced in case it helped their accident investigation. The police told him that no other vehicle had been involved in the crash and that Taylor had seemingly just driven straight off the road into a tree. It was the same tree that Ron Sullivan had almost hit.[4] ○

4
Bodies That Tingle

WE CAN NOW LOOK IN MORE DETAIL AT CASES WHERE PHYSIOLOGICAL sensations are described. In my database, they feature in as many as 70 per cent of the three hundred time storm reports that I have logged. Notice how closely linked these symptoms are, despite coming independently from all over the world.

THE TICKLE

An interesting case was reported to me by a Mr Roberts of Kent.

St Margaret's Bay (UK), 1966

In July 1966 he was driving near St Margaret's Bay on the Dover road when a sudden rainstorm caused him to stop for a while. On his seaward side was a field containing cattle. As he waited for the heavy rain to subside, Mr Roberts heard a peculiar hissing noise and began to feel a strange but indefinable sensation, not unlike a tingle or tickle in the air. He suspected an imminent lightning strike (although there was no electrical storm) and watched in trepidation. Instead, the air began to swirl in a misty flow that seemed connected with the hissing. This resolved into a vertical tube that was surrounded by the opaque swirls, although inside was clear and calm. There is a similarity here with the funnel effect noted by those on board the Catalina flying boat (see p. 38).

Mr Roberts says the effect was like a giant perspex beaker placed over the field. The oddest part was that the rain struck the misty wall at its edge and seemed to defy gravity. Rather than falling straight down like the other rain, it was deflected like the Bendigo car headlights, running down to earth at a steep angle. Inside the clear central area beyond the swirling mist no rain fell at all. Moments later the rain eased and Mr Roberts drove away at speed. He told me he had a perfect view of this weird phenomenon from only ten feet away.[1] ○

> *. . . the effect was like a giant perspex beaker placed over the field. The oddest part was that the rain struck the misty wall at its edge and seemed to defy gravity.*

A similar physiological description comes from a witness in Ski, Norway in November 1953. As he drove home near Lake Gjersjoen, a green glow encircled his car. He felt a tickling not unlike 'pins and needles' all over his body. Later the driver noticed that his watch had stopped. The car was also found to have taken on a shiny cast, as if its dull beige colour had been scrubbed clean.

A jeweller found that the man's watch had to be demagnetised, and the car's metal body reverted to its normal dullness within days. A logical suggestion is that surface rust was removed – perhaps the iron oxide was attracted off by the same strong electromagnetic field that created the tingling sensation.[2]

SIZEWELL BEACH

Sizewell Beach (UK), 1975

Postman Thomas Meyer had a frightening experience on 24 February 1975. At the time he was walking his dog, Titus, on Sizewell beach in Suffolk. It was a clear evening, and at 6.55 p.m. something headed in near ground level from the North Sea. Within seconds it was hovering over the sands about fifty feet away. Described as resembling a floating pumpkin, this was a misty oval that glowed a vivid greenish yellow with what seemed like a fluorescent emission. As it hovered, it made his skin feel warm, as if he was being exposed to a sun lamp. The air also smelled pungently of acid drops, probably a consequence of ionisation taking place due to the strong EM field that was breaking down the chemicals in the atmosphere. Meyer stood transfixed as this thing revolved in front of him; his terrified dog fled and was later found about a mile away, cowering by the security fence at the edge of the nearby nuclear power plant. The pumpkin sped back out to sea without making any noise. O

Two interesting postscripts occurred. Afterwards the witness felt aching sensations in his joints. There were also reports in the villages of Leiston and Sizewell of high levels of interference on TV pictures that night – possible symptoms of the EM field and the resulting atmospheric ionisation.[3]

PHYSIOLOGICAL EFFECTS

There are many reports like those above. But in a few extreme cases the effects outlast the encounter itself by up to several days. These effects can range from a reddish skin coloration lasting hours (as with Dawn in Tibet) to longer-term nausea and muscle pains (as experienced by the Suffolk postman). Or there can be another consequence, as hinted at by this next case from the USA.

Leominster (USA), 1967
At 1.05 a.m. on 8 March 1967, William Wallace and his wife were driving home. Passing the outskirts of Leominster, Massachusetts, they

encountered a strange, isolated patch of mist and a glowing egg shape. Baffled, William got out to take a closer look; at that moment the car engine, lights and radio faded. He was pointing to the object and describing it to his wife, who was still in the car. Then he felt his arm tugged, as if by some massive force, and it was slammed against the metal body of the vehicle where it was held as if in a vice. At the same time, his body felt numb and tingling as electric shocks coursed through his arm. Possibly the EM field was scrambling electrical impulses from his brain that would normally control muscle movements, so disrupting the functioning of his body parts. The misty egg shape began to wobble and emit a humming noise, then climbed into the sky. Wallace's paralysis effect gradually faded, and within a minute or so the car was working perfectly again. However, for some days Wallace suffered extreme physical disability. He noted in particular that his muscle co-ordination and nervous response were unusually restricted. ◯

In cases like this – and especially those where nausea also results – it is possible that the reported rapid temperature changes from extreme heat to great cold in the vicinity of the time storm are relevant. Not only might these 'freeze' the air, causing white snow- or frost-like deposits, as seen, but the changes may provoke body chills that induce what is effectively a cold.[4]

Hook (UK), 1967

An even more detailed description comes from a British van driver who was travelling on the A32 at Hook, Hampshire on 26 October 1967. At 4.30 a.m. he encountered a rotating mass and experienced a power drain on his engine, lights and radio. Physical effects included intense pressure on his eardrums that could only be relieved by the traditional method of holding his nose and blowing. This infers that atmospheric pressure was altering. Indeed, the fluctuations were so rapid that they produced a clicking sound as his eardrums were pushed in and out. There was also an all-pervading smell like electric arcing (probably due to ionisation of the surrounding air). It was accompanied by a heavy sensation that he likened to the oppression created by a thunderstorm.

When driving away, the witness had a struggle to co-ordinate the movements of his hands and feet. He was so clumsy that he says it was almost like learning to drive all over again. For days afterwards he felt a tingling sensation in the ends of his fingers. O

A medical doctor, Bernard Finch, who interviewed the witness, finds this information of great importance.

Dr Finch argues that the energy field associated with these phenomena may damage the nervous system and its connection to the spinal cord, producing temporary paralysis and electric shock sensations. Because the nervous system is affected, problems with body co-ordination may persist for days. Gradually, the nerve links will regenerate, resulting in the 'pins and needles' sensations as neurones transmit impulses again via the regenerated pathways channelling bodily electrical signals. The everyday pins and needles that we all occasionally experience occurs when the flow of blood is cut off to body extremities (for instance, if you sit on your fingers). Then, as the nerves fire up when the blood flows again, tingling results. If such an effect generated by an EM field is only mild, recovery could occur within seconds. But if it is stronger, it could take days or even weeks to get the body realigned.[5]

The substantial physiological effects reported in cases like these offer an obvious pattern. They are medically assessable and logical. They are predictable consequences of exposure to strong EM fields. Many of the disruptions are of a kind that ordinary people are unlikely to understand, and their recurrence is excellent evidence for a physically real phenomenon.

5
Cars That Stop

ONE OF THE MOST COMMON FEATURES OF TIME STORM CASES IS THAT NEARBY electrical systems can be compromised. As many cases happen when people are driving cars, motorcycles or trucks, the presence of a time storm is usually apparent from the puzzling effects on their vehicles. Here are some descriptions of what takes place.

THE TASMANIAN LIGHT

Lawitta (Tasmania), 1979

On 5 February 1979, a man had a terrifying experience on the island of Tasmania. He was driving the fifty miles from Hamilton to Hobart in his Ford Cortina. It was 9.50 p.m., and he was close to the small settlement of Lawitta. He had his radio on, but suddenly it went dead. Looking up bemused, he found his car swallowed up by a murky white light which swamped everything so that he could not even see beyond the windscreen. At that instant the vehicle lost all power and his memory faded out. What seemed like moments later, he shook his head and found himself driving on

He had his radio on, but suddenly it went dead. Looking up bemused, he found his car swallowed up by a murky white light which swamped everything so that he could not even see beyond the windscreen. At that instant the vehicle lost all power and his memory faded out.

the same highway but at a point further along, nearer to Granton. His mind was fuzzy, his memory dulled and he had almost no recall of who he was or how he had got there.

Moments later a passing police car flagged him down to caution him because his lights were not on. Seeing his distressed condition, the police officers took him to hospital, where he was diagnosed as suffering from traumatic amnesia brought on by shock. When a bright light was shone into his eyes to test his visual acuity he reacted in sheer terror, but could not explain why. Although this witness did slowly recover, the electrical wiring in his car had burnt out (hence the non-functioning lights), the battery was flat and most of the water had evaporated from the radiator.[1] O

RIVERSIDE ENCOUNTERS

Two related cases that offer useful information occurred within forty-eight hours of each other though three thousand miles apart.

Grenoble (France), 1958

French computer scientist Dr Jacques Vallée followed up one incident that took place on 28 October 1958, witnessed by Jean Boyer, who was driving on a mountain road some forty miles from Grenoble in the gorge formed by the Grand Buech River. It was 7.55 p.m. and Boyer was near the Pont-la-Dame area, where metal road and rail bridges cross the river close together. Above the iron rail bridge he saw a lens shape with a central glowing area seething with energy and of a predominantly reddish hue. Indeed, what resembled electric sparks were being expelled. Boyer says they were very bright but dispersed into the air before falling to earth. He drove his station wagon directly beneath the bridge but without any effect on the engine, the lights or himself (probably because the object remained several hundred feet above him). However, he could see the object swaying gently like a leaf in a breeze, and as it departed there was a clear blast of air displacement that rocked his vehicle, which he had now stopped and parked.[2] ◯

Circumstances had been different (yet interestingly similar) two days earlier across the Atlantic.

Baltimore (USA), 1958

At 10.30 p.m. on 26 October 1958, Alvin Cohen and Phillip Small were driving on a road by the bridge that crossed Loch Raven Dam near Baltimore, Maryland. They too saw a lens-shaped mass ahead that was low down between the bridge and the dammed lake. When they got to within about seventy-five feet (considerably closer than Boyer in France) their car engine and lights failed. Cohen, the passenger, reports how at first there was no effect as they drove towards the floating mass. Then as they closed in 'the dash lights went out, the headlights went out and the motor went dead.' He felt that from this sequence it was an electrical disruption rather than a mechanical one.

Small reports how they jumped out of the now stalled car, but there was nowhere to run. They were on a narrow road with a cliff on one side and the lake on the other. So they stood with the car between themselves and the oval mass and watched. After about forty seconds, it suddenly became very bright and seemed surrounded by a diffuse vapour. Then it shot upwards and disappeared.

Coincident with this illumination there was a loud bang or blast of air that was heard by witnesses in a restaurant a mile away. The men also felt a heat on their faces that Small describes thus: 'It didn't seem like the heat of a burning object but something like an ultra-violet light or some kind of radiation.' Their faces felt flushed as they drove off, and eventually a police patrol was called out and they were taken to a local hospital. They were released after a check-up, but their faces remained slightly reddened over the next day or so.[3] O

Again there are consistent features between different cases. These two very similar reports also imply that physical proximity may be the key to whether car stops occur. The strength of the EM field probably falls according to an inverse square law, as does most physical radiation: the further from its origin, the weaker the effects. Tests have been carried out on motor vehicles to see what kind of field strength is necessary to induce the reported effects on engine and lights. The size of the required EM field is huge and would result in physiological effects on witnesses. It would also permanently distort the magnetic signature (the mapping of the magnetic field installed in a car's body structure on construction – and unique to each vehicle). A few experiments have been conducted to try to find hard evidence of this effect, but not enough to produce conclusive results. The difficulty is finding an identical car as a comparison – one with sufficiently similar signature due to virtually contemporary construction at the same factory – in order to judge magnetic signature changes on the body of an affected vehicle.[4]

GOOD NEWS

Here is a watery variation on the car stop theme.

Western Atlantic, 1963

In 1963 The American ship *Good News*, commanded by Captain Don Henry, was in the Tongue of the Ocean, part of the western Atlantic. It was mid-afternoon and the crew were involved in a routine towing operation, pulling an unmanned barge of waste. This 2500-ton vessel was attached to the *Good News* by a line. Henry reports that he was called out on deck by his crew as the ship's compasses suddenly began to spin frantically around. At the same time a strange, uniform fog had appeared out of nowhere on an otherwise fine day and surrounded the ship. This had caused the sea and the sky to blend into one grey-white mass with no sign of the horizon. Moreover, after a few feet the line towards the barge disappeared and faded into nothingness. Checks revealed that the barge was still there (tension was felt when the tow was pulled manually), but visually it had disappeared.

Determined to escape this mystery, Henry ordered his crew to move into clearer air (assuming there was some) but the *Good News* would not respond. There was no power to the motors or any of the electrical equipment. After about ten minutes, they got the motors to fire but the tug, still hidden in the cloud or mist, resisted their pull and the *Good News* remained stationary. Then, as if some hold had been suddenly released, the ship lurched forward, towing the barge out of the fog that now rapidly dissipated. Henry sent a launch to check the barge. The crew noted that all was well but that the surface of the vessel was unexpectedly hot. ○

We have noted anomalous temperature changes before, of course, during time storm incidents (see p. 21). They probably occur when EM energy generated by the cloud transforms into heat by established physical principles such as the law of conservation of energy.

Another interesting aftermath was that a large number of flashlights on the *Good News* were found not be working. In addition, all the batteries were drained of power and could not be recharged.[5]

ALMIRANTE SALDANHA

Trindade Island (Brazil), 1958

A related case offers permanent evidence. It occurred on 6 January 1958 to forty-eight crew aboard the Brazilian naval vessel *Almirante Saldanha*. The ship had for some days been in the vicinity of Trindade Island, a rocky outcrop 600 miles off the Brazilian coast. The previous October, as part of a global science project called the International Geophysical Year, a small meteorological station had been set up on the otherwise uninhabited Atlantic landmass. It was operated by this team of naval and scientific personnel.

. . . virtually everyone on deck had seen something approach, circle, then do a loop around the island and disappear out to sea again.

At about 9 a.m. that day a radio sonde balloon had been released from the island to take weather readings, and its progress was being supervised by naval commander Carlos Bacellar. The balloon transmitted radio signals to feed back information on weather conditions in the sky above the island. Everything was going perfectly, until just after noon the radio emissions stopped. Going outside to investigate, Bacellar saw the balloon below a single cloud in an otherwise clear sky. The balloon was being sucked upwards fast, directly into the cloud. Here it remained, obscured for ten minutes, then reappeared with its radio equipment no longer attached. This was never found.

On board the *Almirante Saldanha* virtually everyone on deck had seen something approach, circle, then do a loop around the island and disappear out to sea again. It was at very low height. The witnesses included air force and naval personnel and the expedition's photographer, Almiro Barauna, who had a Rolleiflex camera. Barauna was able to take six photographs while the object was visible, though unhappily two were spoiled (they show only ocean and rock) because he was constantly jostled by fascinated sailors peering over the side.

The photographs were immediately processed in the darkroom under Bacellar's supervision. What had circled the *Almirante Saldanha* and the island was a fuzzy mass rather like an image of a galaxy in space. It appeared to rotate as it moved and was greyish, although with a greenish tinge to the haze or mist that surrounded the dark centre. Some witnesses thought it was a strange aircraft surrounded by a localised fog (reminiscent of the Catalina flying boat incident). Others considered that it was no more than a misty form and that the shape was simply an illusion formed by the darker parts in the middle. The photographs support both impressions. O

On arrival back at Rio de Janeiro, a major investigation of the incident was set in motion. Extensive tests at a Cruzeiro do Sul photographic laboratory found no evidence of trickery. The baffling story was taken to the head of state, President Kubitschek, who ordered full public disclosure with a carefully worded statement supporting the witnesses but professing no opinion as to what they had observed. During the two or three minutes that the object was near the ship, an electric winch was winding on board the launch that had brought the meteorology crew from the island after their problematic balloon experiment. During this time the electrical power failed; the winch only operated again after the cloudy mass had flown back out to sea.[6]

6

States That Alter

ALTHOUGH THE TIME STORM IS NOT YET RECOGNISED BY SCIENCE, IT DESERVES to be studied professionally as an anomaly of nature and not as a piece of sensationalism. These ionised phenomena can be photographed if you have a camera and the presence of mind to use it. It is no different from, say, a bright meteor or a bolt of lightning – both difficult to capture on film because of their transient nature, but none the less real.

Now we head into more contentious waters. But it is still wise to recall that altered states of consciousness arise through scientific means. They do not reflect anything mystical, and are probably a consequence of what happens when the human brain is 'assaulted' by an energy field. This view is the result of research in Canada by brain specialist Dr Michael Persinger, who established that EM fields can affect the temporal lobe in the brain and induce altered states of awareness which provoke hallucinatory visions. Physical and visual effects triggered by EM radiation can invoke experiences reported as paranormal. In fact, the triggering energy is absolutely real; only the resulting visions are not.[1]

Psychologists are researching the role played by the temporal lobe in generating effects such as migraines, hallucinations, feelings of mystical contact and apparent supernatural visions. Swiss neuroscientist Peter Brugger reported in June 2000 that 'excitability of the temporal lobes seems to be a plausible explanation' for false visual signals where the person sees themself 'out of the body' and in a dissociated state.[2] Chemical changes, too, can create various mystic states of consciousness.[3]

Bristol psychologist Dr Sue Blackmore, a leading researcher into alleged near-death visions, in which people on the brink of dying claim to see heavenly lights, has worked with Persinger and experienced his induced altered states. She thinks they may also stimulate near-death visions by a similar process.[4]

This field appears similar to the forces described during time storms. The only difference may be that the field strength in time storms is much stronger than that created by Persinger's lab tests, as he restricts the output during experiments. So we ought not to be surprised if witnesses to time storms relate weird visionary experiences that result from the severely altered states that may be induced in their brains.

THE OZ FACTOR

For many years witnesses have claimed to experience a series of curious sensations in close proximity to glowing lights. These symptoms, as already explained, are called the Oz Factor.

Colchester (UK), 1971/2

Roy Wilkinson from Essex told me what happened to him on the evening of 10 November 1971 at Hythe Hill in Colchester. As he walked towards a factory where he then worked, he saw an egg shape low over a nearby building. Milky white in colour, it was surrounded by some sort of aura or haze that made the whole thing seem fuzzy and opaque. As he came within a few feet of it, he stood mesmerised as it changed colours in sequence. Then time suddenly lost meaning. Roy found himself walking in a

. . . time suddenly lost meaning. He found himself walking in a vacuum and was aware that what should be a busy area was in fact now deserted. There was an eerie silence as if every sound in the world had stopped.

vacuum and was aware that what should be a busy area was in fact now deserted. There was an eerie silence as if every sound in the world had stopped. When this sensation vanished, so did the glowing mass. Roy says, 'I turned the corner and it was like opening a door and entering a party.' The world was back, and all its sounds and the flow of time had returned. But during those timeless moments when he was close to the glowing mass he was experiencing the classic symptoms of the Oz Factor, as if he had been utterly extracted from living inside normal reality. ○

The problem with such cases is in deciding from three possibilities. Perhaps this is a psychological state in which the sense of timelessness and isolation is purely subjective – altered consciousness, much as Persinger suggests. Some of these sensations might, however, be tied to the physiological energy emissions that we have seen in other cases. Witnesses may misread physical processes within their bodies as subjective states of minds. For example, tickling sensations on the skin caused by contact with the electrostatic charge may infer to someone that they are being watched by an unseen 'presence'. Indeed, witnesses subjected to EM fields who feel this 'tickle' do often describe the effect in this way. Or, thirdly, we must ask is there any literal reality behind the alleged distortions within the flow of time? This is something we will gradually find ourselves having to consider as the cases we confront grow in strangeness.

One possible clue here is that Roy Wilkinson had two other experiences to relate. In one of these episodes, which took place on 25 January 1972, he had seen a glowing light above him undulating across the sky like a snake. When it passed directly above him, he felt the ground under his feet become 'alive with electricity. It was like receiving a mild electric shock.' His body was tingling.

You will recognise some of the physical symptoms of an EM field here. But what of his third strange encounter, which befell him when he was seventeen? He describes walking along an alleyway in the centre of

Evidence that strange clouds can generate both unusual light and physical effects is demonstrated by this photo. Taken by Eric Wilkinson during an Antarctic survey in 1966, it shows an isolated cloud producing an angled light tube that churned up snow with forces akin to many time storm cases described in this book (see p.12).
© ERIC WILKINSON

One of the photographs taken from the decks of Brazilian naval survey vessel the *Almirante Saldanha*, moored in the south Atlantic off an uninhabited island whilst conducting a scientific survey. The misty cloud with a dark central rim was associated with strange suction forces and electrical interference (see p. 52).
© A. BARAUNA

One of several strange light phenomena captured by researchers with the scientific survey team, known as Project Hessdalen, that has operated since 1982. These, as yet poorly understood, atmospheric plasmas recur frequently in this remote Scandinavian valley near Trondheim and demonstrate that reported 'UFO' sightings often have an explanation in terms of cutting edge physics (p. 57).
© PROJECT HESSDALEN

On December 7th,1980-The nuclear carrier USS Nimitz disappeared in the Pacific...and reappeared December 7th,1941...off Pearl Harbour

THE FINAL COUNTDOWN

RICHARD R. ST JOHNS PRESENTS
KIRK DOUGLAS   MARTIN SHEEN   KATHARINE ROSS
JAMES FARENTINO
in THE BRYNA COMPANY'S PRODUCTION of
THE FINAL COUNTDOWN featuring RON O'NEAL
and CHARLES DURNING as Senator Chapman Directed by DON TAYLOR
Produced by PETER VINCENT DOUGLAS Executive Producer RICHARD R. ST JOHNS
Screenplay by DAVID AMBROSE & GERRY DAVIS and THOMAS HUNTER & PETER POWELL
Story by THOMAS HUNTER & PETER POWELL and DAVID AMBROSE
Director of Photography VICTOR J. KEMPER Music by JOHN SCOTT
Associate Producer LLOYD KAUFMAN Edited by ROBERT K. LAMBERT

The movie *The Final Countdown* is a modern spin on the legend of the Philadelphia Experiment. It includes an exciting story alongside elements that tally remarkably closely with true-life cases in this book – notably the electric storm, glowing mist and the ability to travel through time as a consequence (see p. 236).
© MGM/UNITED ARTISTS

In science fiction, time travel often produces entertaining paradoxes. The movie series *Back to the Future* sets out what might happen if someone travels through time (in this case by way of a modified car!) and meets their family before their own birth (see p.124).
© JENNY RANDLES

Colchester one November evening when a small 'glow' appeared, moving towards him. Stepping back, he expected someone to pass him in the narrow passage. But as the glow approached it was clear there was nobody – just this floating light. Then there was what he terms 'a blackout' and he was inexplicably standing some yards away at the end of the alley, with no recall of how he got there. Moreover, Roy was absolutely soaked – as he put it, 'like I had stepped in the bath with all my clothes on.' You will no doubt immediately recall other cases where glows and mists have provoked a blackout, a discontinuity in space and time, and left the witness inexplicably wet (see p. 22).

That all of these different – but to us familiar – occurrences should be reported by one person in three separate events seems beyond coincidence. Does it infer that there may be something special about the way certain people's brains (or temporal lobes) can work, and if so, does it make them somehow more susceptible?[5]

THE SATER CASE

Frightening physical effects occurred in a case from Sater in Sweden that took place on 31 December 1987.

Sater (Sweden), 1987

Mrs Bensson, a retired nurse, was concerned about her pet cat and dog who at 2 a.m. were very restless, but when put outside they seemed to want to return. Then, to her horror, she saw her dog shaking beside an ice-blue mass surrounded by a grey-orange mist. From the base large sparks or miniature lightning bolts were entering the soil. Concerned for her pet, Mrs Bensson went towards the floating mass and began to feel very strange.

The physiological sensations will be familiar. She spoke of a 'wash' of electrical charge that came over her, causing her skin to tingle and prickle, her head to start pounding as if it was about to explode and her jaw to ache very badly. Mrs Bensson tried to call out to her husband, but was paralysed. There was also a massive change in her state of consciousness. She likened this to 'my mind being sucked out' and seriously felt that she was dying. It was as if all her consciousness was being extracted.

Mr Bensson had been awoken by his wife's movements and the opening and closing of the front door. He could hear a strange humming/buzzing sound and went to investigate. His wife was barely aware of his arrival, but recalls having just felt a sharp pain in the base of her neck/top of her spine. It was as if someone was sticking a needle in that place. This seems to have coincided with the misty globe suddenly vanishing. As Mr Bensson walked outside, there was a pungent smell in the air which he likened to sulphur (later this mellowed, and after about half an hour he said there was just a tang of ozone in the cold night air). Stranger still, both the cat and the dog were sitting on the ground, staring into space as if hypnotised. His wife was following their gaze and appeared to be in a deep catatonic trance, from which it took several minutes for her to be awoken.

Mrs Bensson was taken to bed where she remained for several days suffering from a severe migraine and deep nausea. Her jumper had melted, and tests following a police investigation (Mr Bensson reported that his wife had been inexplicably assaulted) revealed only that a powerful electrical discharge had struck her body and heated the jumper's fibres.[6] ○

THE VIEW FROM WITHIN

One final instructive case provides an insider's view of being literally encased within one of these phenomena, and poses disturbing hints about the potential reality of time distortion effects that we must start to consider.

Kent (UK), 1966

David from Kent told me about an experience he had in 1966: 'I was about eighteen and I had been out with a girlfriend. It was around midnight and we were going to her house. We regularly took a short cut through a large open space that had a wooded area and stream with an arched bridge.' He adds that it was a muggy summer night and there was moonlight to guide them, so they sat on the bridge enjoying the solitude. Then they were startled by a group of teenage lads and at first feared trouble – but the boys were evidently terrified by something that was chasing them.

As David says: 'Suddenly everything appeared abnormally quiet – even for night-time. My ears felt as if they had been closed – like when you fit your fingers in them. Then it was a numb feeling. Then a strange depression set in. It was a feeling of heaviness and I had a sense of moving my head in slow motion. I turned to look at my girlfriend, who also seemed concerned . . . she felt giddy . . . the voices [of the running teenagers] sounded as if they were coming from a valley that caused them to echo.'

These sensations were accompanied by a visual apparition: 'I then noticed a white mist about six inches off the ground . . . it had definitely not been there a few minutes before.' This 'swirled around' them, and as it did so something stunning occurred. Time slowed down. David's body movements seemed to take for ever. His cigarette smoke was spiralling upwards far too slowly. It was as if he had been dislocated from the flow of time and reality. The effect on sounds, causing them to slow and seem 'hollow', was very odd.

'It was like a record being played at a slower speed, and we could not understand what we were trying to say to one another. I would have got up and run, but I felt so heavy and my girlfriend was now clinging to me in hysterics.' The teenage motorcycle gang that fled past 'with a look of pure horror on their faces' were moving 'in a slow-motion fashion – like a man on the moon.'

Time had lost meaning, but eventually 'the feeling of heaviness and depression lifted and then our ears began to pop like they do when on an aeroplane.' He added that, although some minutes had passed (it was unclear how many, but it seemed like hours), his cigarette had inexplicably not burned down – as if the physical processes involved had been suspended in time.[7] O

> 'It was like a record being played at a slower speed, and we could not understand what we were trying to say to one another. I would have got up and run, but I felt so heavy and my girlfriend was now clinging to me in hysterics.'

In this particular case many phenomena come together and pose a real challenge to our thinking. The physical sensations of ears popping and heavy pressure surely relate to the alterations in atmospheric pressure caused by the energy field. The Oz Factor sensations are in evidence, indicating an altered state of consciousness. But what of how time itself just did not behave as it ought to have done?

This may be the key to the whole time storm mystery.

7
Things That Float

IT IS RELATIVELY SIMPLE TO ACCEPT THAT SOME KIND OF NATURAL ENERGY SOURCE might create misty glows in the sky, induce electrical charges or affect the chemical computer inside the human brain. But we must now cross the borders of credibility.

It helps to consider the forces of nature involved in a tornado as it sucks up a tree or the magnetic levitation propulsion techniques now being developed for high-speed trains under test in Japan and Germany. These create a cushion of energy that causes the locomotive to hover above the tracks in apparent rejection of physical laws. What may appear to be gravity-defying phenomena can have scientific explanations. We might seem to have taken a U-turn into the twilight zone, but incredible phenomena only seem incredible if we fail to find scientific rules that define them.

MARPLE RIDGE

Peak District (UK), 1988

On 15 June 1988 a series of separate events occurred which were only pieced together when my colleague Roy Sandbach and I conducted our investigation on site. They began at about 11 a.m. when Graeme Brock, headmaster of a primary school at Marple Ridge on the edge of the Peak District, saw what looked like hay rising from a field nearby. Suspecting a prank by youngsters, he went to investigate – but found no one there. At 12.45 Brock was supervising a game of rounders in the school field when more hay began to float up from adjacent land, defying gravity and floating skywards on its own. The game was forgotten and everyone watched in awe as the hay spiralled to condense into a solid-looking lens shape. Within moments this had turned into something like the dark grey oval clouds frequently reported in time storm cases. Then – as if the upward (presumably it was air flow) forces that were causing the hay to rise were now balanced by a downward force (no doubt gravity) – the mass stopped, to hover at 150 feet.

It then began to move horizontally across the sky and cross the corner of the school field, heading towards the town of Stockport. If the thing had been seen only at this point, it is likely that it would have appeared to any innocent witnesses as a passing 'flying saucer'. The mass was evidently rotating as a result of further forces (anti-clockwise if viewed from above).

When it was hovering briefly above the startled crowd, just starting to move off at a sedate pace above their heads, several people felt an odd sensation. Brock described a 'soft pressure' pushing down on his shoulders – an almost identical comment to that made by other time storm witnesses. Some of the children also felt a 'tingling' as it passed above, suggesting that electrostatic fields were involved in this complex of interacting forces and energy.

When the 'misty' mass had vanished beyond the school, several witnesses later told me it crossed a housing estate. They had no idea of what had happened at the school. The cloud had now thinned and was breaking into pieces in a manner likened to a spiral galaxy. Indeed, much of the hay lost cohesion and was dumped on a golf course, while the remainder drifted away as a 'strange cloud'.[1] O

The history of this area is fascinating. During my researches I found a 1968 car stop event at Chisworth, and a place called the Devil's Elbow with a record of folk tales about spooky glows. Folklorist Dr David Clarke has reported on numerous local events – for instance, blue glows which created tingling sensations on witnesses walking in this beautiful hill country. These hint at the way in which air draughts (similar to fair weather whirlwinds), counterbalancing pressure forces, gravity anomalies and electrostatic energies might all somehow coalesce as part of these phenomena.[2]

THE NULL G EFFECT

Palm Beach (USA), 1970

A different account of these balancing energy forces is provided by Bruce Gernon, who on 4 December 1970 was flying with his father in a light aircraft on the 300-mile run into Palm Beach, Florida. As he ascended for the routine seventy-five-minute flight, Gernon describes entering a strange lens-shaped cloud that quickly encircled the plane. They were almost lost within this expanse except for what he terms a 'tunnel' that seemed to reach all the way up to the sky above. This is another effect we have heard described before – indeed, this case is remarkably similar to the Catalina flying boat case (p. 37).

Gernon also reports that the circular walls of this tunnel seemed to rotate and glow (possibly due to ionisation). As the plane emerged from the tunnel and escaped the cloud, its wings touched the edge of this glowing tube. At that moment both occupants say they felt a total loss of gravity, as if they were in a space capsule and weightless. Their seat belts kept them in place, but the powerful forces were very obvious. As they broke free, the null g (nullified gravity) effect ceased. However, they had not emerged into clear sky. Instead, a strange green mist was now clinging to the plane and all their instruments were malfunctioning. When the mist cleared, moments later long parallel slits of mist appeared in the sky before they plunged into clear air. Not that this immediately ended the confusion. For they were now seen to be passing Miami on the final leg of their flight. Yet this was impossible. They had covered the distance far too fast (at a speed nearly twice what the aircraft could achieve), and checks later revealed that they had used only two-thirds of the fuel that they should have done. ○

Here we see how the mysterious gravity distortions appear to have led almost unnoticed to major anomalies of time and space as well. This is going to be a recurring theme.[3]

THE TOULON INCIDENT

Cuers (France), 1971

Renard was a French naval technician working in the Mediterranean port of Toulon. In 1971 he was regularly driving the eighty miles to Nice to visit his girlfriend. He always left for the homeward trip around midnight, taking two hours to reach Toulon. Checks on driving the route show this to be a reasonable estimate.

On this particular night, at 1.30 a.m. he was on the final leg near Cuers, listening to the radio to pass the time. Suddenly, the transmission began to fill with static and then faded away. Then he noticed an orange glow low down and almost on the bonnet of his Citroën. Renard knew that the road ran close to a military base, and assumed the orange blob was from there. But then his engine began to fail and he lost speed as the orange glow grew closer. Fearful that a plane had mistaken the road for a runway, he instinctively pressed on the brakes – even though the engine had now stopped completely. Nothing happened. Indeed, to his utter astonishment Renard could see that the orange glow was illuminating everything around him and he was floating off the road some ten or fifteen feet up. Almost as soon as he became aware of this impossibility, the orange glow vanished and there was a heavy thud as the Citroën was dumped back on to the RN 97.

Staggering from the car, dazed but not injured, Renard gaped in shock at the damage. The boot had been thrown open and the spare wheel tossed on to the road, the driver's seat had collapsed and the back seat was deformed. The car bodywork was crumpled and the vehicle was set at an angle across the normally busy road. Although at that late hour traffic was moderate and no cars had been in his immediate vicinity – that is none were close enough to see anything – it took only moments for other vehicles to start arriving. Already other traffic was coming to a halt, thinking he had been in a crash. One driver stopped to offer Renard a tow, since his Citroën was now apparently dead and devoid of electrical power. In this way, the battery was recharged sufficiently to restart his engine. He continued on his way home, driving the final fifteen miles cautiously. Then he noticed the bigger mystery. The encounter had happened at around 1.30 a.m. He was dumped back on to the road no later than 1.35. Other traffic arrived almost immediately, and even with the tow he should have been home by 3 a.m. In fact it was now 6 a.m. He had somehow 'jumped' three hours forward in time during what appeared to be the brief moments during which he was floating above the road in the grip of this orange glow. ○

We can be fairly sure that Renard left Nice when he says he did (his girl-friend confirmed his departure time as 11.45 p.m., as she could not get back into her building after midnight). Renard cannot have been uncon-scious after the car crashed down on to the road as his vehicle was blocking both lanes of traffic and there would have been a major hold-up. Yet if he had been floating for hours above the road in the grip of this gravity-defying glow, how could it have escaped the attention of countless passing motorists – not one of whom reported seeing a hovering car? Worrying as the conclusion is, we have to wonder whether Renard floated through *time* as well as space that night.[4]

THE EYRE HIGHWAY

A remarkable episode of this same type made headlines thanks to an accident of the calendar.

Mundrabilla (Australia), 1988

It occurred on 20 January 1988, when Australia was celebrating its bicentennial. Forget the silly media hype – consider only the verifiable facts.

Faye Knowles and her three sons, aged between eighteen and twenty-four, were driving from their home in Perth, Western Australia, to pay a surprise visit to her family who lived in Melbourne in the east. The vast size of the continent meant that the journey would take a couple of days of practically round-the-clock driving, so everyone would be taking their turn at the wheel of the 1984 Ford Telstar. Their route along the Eyre Highway passed between the Nullarbor Plain to the north and the ocean to the south; at the time of the incident they were approaching a coastal mountain range near the South Australian border.

Traffic was relatively light as there are only scattered settlements along the highway. Although the Knowles family were unaware of other vehicles on the road with them, later research (to which I am indebted to Keith Basterfield and Bill Chalker) has revealed the full picture. The drivers of two long-haul trucks recall leaving the township of Caiguna around 1.30 a.m. (South Australia time) when what was clearly the Knowles Ford also set off eastwards. But by about 4 a.m. this group of vehicles had become separated, with the Knowleses unaware of the two trucks and neither of these vehicles knowing the whereabouts of the other.

The first truck, driven by Graham Henley, was heading for Victoria and was some miles ahead of the Ford. The other truck was on a run from Perth to Adelaide. Its driver, John de Jong, had stopped at Madura to get some sleep and his co-driver, Anne, had taken over for the next leg. This had caused them to fall behind both Henley's truck and the Knowleses' car by some minutes. These witnesses were traced and interviewed, and their stories prove consistent. A fourth vehicle (a car and caravan heading in the opposite direction to the others, towards Perth) has never been located despite strenuous efforts.

At 4 a.m. Graham Henley, then twenty miles from the small town of Mundrabilla, noticed something odd in his rear view mirror. He described it as 'a big fried egg hanging upside down' – a floating white mass with a glowing yellow centre. He saw it 'juddering' about the road, appearing and disappearing several times. It was clearly in the air and not simply vehicle headlights. Henley watched the thing for about five minutes, then lost it. At 4.30 a.m. he arrived in Mundrabilla and stopped for a rest. Soon after his arrival, the Knowles' Ford screeched to a halt by the roadhouse where he had parked, and four very distressed people scrambled out.

Anne's story is less dramatic. About thirty miles west of Mundrabilla she passed two people standing at the roadside. A few yards further on a car was off the road pointing back towards Perth. Finding drivers in trouble in a remote area usually calls for an offer of assistance, so Anne woke John de Jong to ask if they should stop. But as there was no sign of an accident, he said no. A few minutes later what appears to have been the same car (the Knowleses' Ford) screamed past the truck heading towards Mundrabilla. Its lights were off, even though dawn was still an hour away. When they reached the town, Anne and John found a gathering by the roadhouse, which turned out to be the Knowleses talking to Graham Henley and the hotel owners. They were deeply upset. Anne had seen no glow, but then she was well to its west.

Sean Knowles had been driving the Telstar, with his brother Patrick in the front passenger seat. His mother Faye, brother Wayne and their two dogs were in the back. Sean claimed that at around 4 a.m. (somewhere between Madura and Mundrabilla) they suddenly saw what they later told police was like an 'egg in an eggcup' – a slightly slanted balloon shape with a white vaporous edge and a yellow mid-portion. This thing had moved in corkscrew fashion around the road

'Their vehicle began to shake violently on the road from side to side . . . at this time they were aware of a high-pitched whirring or hissing noise . . .'

ahead, quickly confirming that it was not a car or truck. It then moved to their side and Sean swerved, almost hitting the untraced oncoming caravan. The floating mass now homed in on that vehicle, apparently attracted to this new 'target'. The Knowleses' relief was, however, short-lived, for the phenomenon resettled directly on to their roof. It then subjected them to a nightmare few minutes during which many events took place that will be now be familiar to readers of this book.

According to the official police report: 'Their vehicle began to shake violently on the road from side to side . . . at this time they were aware of a high-pitched whirring or hissing noise . . . [they] stated that they felt disorientated and that they noticed that their voices had become slow and deep when they spoke. They were unable to say how long the object was on the roof of their car, but during the time it was there it appeared to lift the vehicle off the road and forced it back down heavily . . .'

At some point during this gravity anomaly – probably when the hold was released and the Ford smashed into the tarmac – one of the tyres burst. This caused Sean to drive off the road and hastily exchange it for the spare. The thing had now gone, although they hid in fear in the scrub for some minutes until they were sure it had finally disappeared. Then they drove off in haste, leaving the car jack and other items from the boot where they lay. It was presumably while this hasty wheel change was taking place that Anne drove past them, soon to be overtaken by the speeding family as they fled the scene of this encounter.

Many interesting points emerge from later interviews by Keith Basterfield, who met the family in Adelaide next day and was able to study and test drive the Ford. Of immediate note is the reference to their voices changing in pitch at the height of the experience. This curious feature has occurred in other cases too (see p. 59), and probably relates to the pressure changes in the atmosphere associated with this 'levitation' effect. It just might be connected with distortions of space and time which would affect not only gravity and light but, one would reasonably expect, the passage of sound waves too.

The two dogs in the car became frantic (animals often seem badly affected in these cases, possibly due to greater sensitivity to high frequency sound – see p. 57). Sean also believes he was disorientated as they 'floated' upwards. A strong electrical smell was noticed in the car – and also reported by those at the roadhouse half an hour later. When Patrick wound down a window when they were close to the thing he became was covered in fine black dust. He felt as if something was taking over his muscles and his brain was 'being sucked out' – again, symptoms reported in other time storm cases. Faye Knowles says this sensation was more like 'something was going *into* our heads'. At one stage, as they floated under the thing, Faye says she wound down her window and put her hand on the roof. A dark mist entered the car and provoked the most severe physiological effects. It left powder over the seats. Faye also reported that her hand touched something 'rubbery'. For some time afterwards (again noted by those at Mundrabilla) the rear of this hand was red. The tingling rash that appeared was very much like that experienced in Tibet (see p. 5).

The roadhouse witnesses at Mundrabilla were able to confirm that the car had four small 'dents' in the roof as if some downward pressure had been applied; also that the dust was everywhere. But the Knowleses were in no mood to stay to discuss the matter further. At dawn – just after 5 a.m. – they set off for the state border a few miles east. Shirley Lundon, owner of the roadhouse, reported the matter to the police, while the two truck drivers borrowed a car and retraced the route looking for evidence. They found the place where Anne had passed the Ford. The roadside showed clear signs of a car going off at speed and of people milling about using a jack, but there was no trace of the jack itself. This and other contents of the boot was missing and never found.

The Knowleses eventually stopped later that morning to report the matter at a place called Ceduna. The police took samples of the dust and within hours the car was vacuumed by researchers so that it could be subjected to a number of independent tests, including one at the AMDEL (Australian Mineral Development Lab). The dust was found to be no more than material from the surrounding area, with no abnormal structure. Why it formed a mist is less obvious. ○

We might surmise that strong energy fields attract fine dust particles from the surrounding area, just as witnesses report their hair standing on end during alleged electrostatic attraction. This would probably create a fine cloud of debris clinging to the EM field and produce the characteristic dark grey/black misty shape often reported in daylight (see, for instance, p.52). This material would, of course, have a mundane local origin and some of it could be deposited on to any car that passes through what is effectively an electrified dust storm. However, the rather more bizarre effects on gravity, the sense of unreality, altered consciousness and the odd perceptions of space and time that follow require a little more ingenuity to figure out.[5]

8
Jumps Through Space

So far we have read reports suggesting that time storms can appear as dark mists in daytime, perhaps due to attracted dust particles from the local environment. At night they may glow with the resulting electrical energy. This EM field can also alter the state of consciousness of a witness, in which condition hallucinations may occur. But we have also seen some evidence of changes to the properties of gravity. Now we must consider cases where apparently real spatial dislocations occur.

ATLANTIC ADVENTURE

This case was told to me first hand by an elderly sailor who was never able to come to terms with what had happened to him. It occurred in the Atlantic – scene of more than one time storm adventure in this book. Indeed, it may be that a few real cases plus more dubious tales about ships sunk in quite explicable ways could be the basis for the absurd claims about the Bermuda Triangle.

Atlantic Ocean (USA), 1928

According to Bill, in the autumn of 1928 he was working on a large tanker that regularly took cargo across the Atlantic. After a lengthy voyage they were off the coast of Florida, nearing Miami. At about 8 p.m. on this October evening, Bill decided to go to the library to do some reading, but when he got there he was surprised to find how still and empty this part of the ship was. There had been no transition: it had just got extremely quiet when he was entering the library. A little perturbed, Bill went out on deck to see if the engines had failed as they did not seem to be making any noise. Indeed, the vessel appeared becalmed. But to his astonishment the entire ship was deserted. There were, he told me, always a few of the crew in sight at any time of day, especially near the library.

Bill reports that it was like being inside a bottle, with not even the air appearing to move. No sounds such as one would expect, like the waves battering the sides of the hull, were in evidence. But the biggest shock of all came when he went to look over the side, thinking that he had missed an emergency that might have led to the lifeboats being launched.

He says: 'Things were not normal. There was a grey misty sheen around us. Everywhere I looked, the sea and sky blended into one wall of seamless grey. The monotony went on forever. I could see no horizon. Nothing was moving. It was exactly as if time stood still and I was no longer a part of the world.'

After staring at this for some moments, Bill sat down on a walkway amidships, which anybody would have to pass through if they came out on deck. In this way he hoped to meet someone and find out what on earth was happening. Then he heard a crewmate hurrying towards him, shouting loudly and calling for others to follow.

'Where have you been?' he was asked. Bill later learned that they feared he had fallen overboard. After his initial relief came the realisation that this whole episode made no sense. He looked across the water and all was normal. There was no wall of mist. He insisted that he had been on deck for so long that if people had been looking for him they could not possibly have missed him on a flat-deck ship where everything and everyone was in view from this spot. The crew dismissed Bill's tale, saying he must have fallen asleep and dreamed this event. They asked where he had been, because they had searched every inch of the boat. He had been missing over an hour.[1] ○

WOBURN SANDS

Another voyage through the outer limits began in innocent circumstances.

Hockliffe (UK), 1992

The Smiths were a Bedfordshire family who on 8 August 1992 were going on a shopping expedition. They were driving a few miles south of the mysterious relocation case near Bromham (see p. 22). The mother, father and two young daughters were near Hockliffe and amusing themselves by singing Beatles' songs. Suddenly a 'strange mood' overcame them. They 'went in on ourselves', as Mrs Smith termed it. The children stopped singing mid-note. From their account it is evident that the Oz Factor took hold, causing a quietness to fall over the car. They stopped laughing, and all traffic on the otherwise busy road disappeared.

Simultaneously with this peculiar state of mind, the car was suddenly surrounded by, or drove unseen into, a bank of mist. It was a thick, foggy area in which there was moisture – not unlike a rain storm, but extremely localised. Visibility plummeted. The next thing the Smiths knew they were no longer in the mist, all sounds had returned and there was traffic once more. But they were not where they had been. After a few moments' disorientation they realised that they were in Woburn Sands, about eight miles from the spot where they had first encountered the mist. 'We just seemed to be there,' Mr Smith reported.

Although none of them was paying much attention to the clock, they felt a sense of timelessness that took some time to clear. Thoroughly bemused, the family drove into Milton Keynes. It was here that they began to notice the severe after-effects of the encounter. The children, very subdued and not their normal selves, took several hours to cast off the strange, sullen feeling. The parents were even more severely affected, with shooting pains and red rashes on their hands that took a day or so to fade. They reported a 'tingling' sensation, accompanied by a sense of muscle pain that bordered on paralysis. This may well be the effect of nerve ends regenerating. (see p. 46).

That idea is further emphasised by another feature that the Smiths recalled. Their body co-ordination was badly disrupted for about two hours afterwards. Mrs Smith had a struggle to open the car door, as she kept missing the handle in a way that left her embarrassed. Her husband fumbled with a petrol pump and was for a time unable to fill the car, a task he had done hundreds of times.

As Mr Smith well described it, 'We were out of synch with reality.' Indeed, so strange was this 'frequency shift' from normal reality that they actually entertained the bizarre idea that perhaps they had crashed in the mist and were wandering the world as phantoms.

It even drove them to go and visit Mrs Smith's mother later that morning and pose what must be the strangest question any parent has ever faced: 'Mum – are we dead?' But by then reality was already re-establishing its hold.[2] ○

COMPARISONS

This weird case is well supported by other events that the Smiths could not have known about.

Wirral (UK), 1967

Keith Daniel from Cheshire was a schoolboy in November 1967. As he was walking to a friend's house one afternoon, he was surrounded by very localised fog, accompanied by a high-pitched rushing noise that seemed to be falling on to him like a bomb from the sky. He threw himself to the ground and it vanished. Then he ran into his friend's house to tell the tale, only to feel foolish because nobody else had heard the sound or seen any fog. It may or may not be relevant that Birkenhead, where this event occurred, had been heavily bombed from the air twenty-five years earlier.

On 29 June 1971, now an eighteen-year-old, Keith was with a friend, trying to hitch a lift at 3 a.m. on a road that passes through Delamere Forest near Chester. Suddenly, an electric blue glow appeared ahead. As Keith says, 'It danced down the road – its movements extremely slow and erratic.' In a daze he began to walk towards it whilst his companion fled. There was then a jump in reality and Keith, feeling oddly calm, noticed he was walking *out* of the forest. He adds that there was a very peculiar after-effect: he was left physically and psychologically disorientated for an hour or two, with his body co-ordination out of synch. ○

During this state his senses were 'out of line' and not experiencing the world properly. Indeed, he was viewing ordinary things in extraordinary ways and hallucinating, rather as he expected to do if under the influence of drugs, perceiving things he knew were not there. The effects gradually subsided.[3]

Oxford (USA), 1975

Two other young men, Americans twenty-one-year-old David Stephens and an eighteen-year-old friend, were also in a wooded area – by a lake near Oxford, Maine – when they had similar problems at 3 a.m. on 27 October 1975. They set off in their car to find the source of a strange noise, then found the vehicle suddenly enveloped by a coloured glow. There was the by now familiar blink in reality, and they were instantly relocated about a mile away with the car pointing in the opposite direction. Neither of them had any idea how they had got to that place, but they were surrounded by a strange grey fog and found that something had prevented the engine from starting.

It was now dawn and the two men felt light-headed, with sore eyes. They were so utterly disorientated that it was difficult to stand up and their jaws would not allow them to form words properly, nor could their hands hold objects. It was as if they were babies again, having to learn how to cope with their bodies. This is exactly the effect described in various other cases, as already noted.

> . . . they were instantly relocated about a mile away with the car pointing in the opposite direction. Neither of them had any idea how they had got to that place . . .

For several hours these two men were in a strange state of consciousness, during which they kept hallucinating – for example, seeing snow falling indoors. They also saw what they thought was a spaceship but which was almost certainly the moon. Their senses simply perceived reality in bizarre ways.[4] ○

We might wonder if visual distortions and optical illusions are simple psychological reactions to the stresses of the trauma being faced or forced upon witnesses by the sensory malfunctions that seem to affect their bodies after immersion within the associated energy field. Is this why what are really time storms often seem to be mistaken for alien contacts or paranormal events?

Longmont (USA), 1980

Social psychologist Dr Richard Sigismonde told me how, on 19 November 1980, two of his friends, Mary and Michael, were driving through Longmont, Colorado, USA when a blue glow enveloped their car accompanied by a noise like rushing air. The car radio was filled with static and the headlights rapidly failed. Then the car was sucked up off the road and they were floating, gravity-free, for an unknown length of time. They were surrounded by a glowing mist and a smell like electric arcing. The next thing they knew they were further down the road (they do not even recall falling back on to it) and it was an hour later.

Mary, who was pregnant, developed a red rash on her abdomen within hours and was rushed to hospital suffering from what was assumed to be some kind of infection. Although she was very ill for a few days, the child was born safely, though prematurely. Possibly the most interesting part of the story – and something that Dr Sigismonde had never come across before, but we now have – was reported by Michael about the aftermath. He drove into the forecourt of a gas station to regain his composure, but found that he could hardly walk when he got out of the car. His balance was disturbed, his body co-ordination was no longer normal and he felt disorientated and 'not all there'. Indeed, the filling station attendant eyed him suspiciously, thinking he was drunk. Michael adds that he felt huge embarrassment at not being able to open or even judge correctly his passage through the garage door – he kept bumping into the doorframe as he attempted, without success, to get his hands and legs to work.[5] ○

The fact that these stories are all consistent despite coming from independent witnesses implies that these people are describing real after-effects from an encounter with a time storm. But how can an electrified mist transport people from one place to another, seemingly without the passage of any journey time?

9
Trips Through Time

GRADUALLY YOU HAVE SEEN THE EVIDENCE ACCUMULATE, MUCH AS I HAVE done over many years of research. The familiarity becomes startling, and, like me, you may now be able to predict what a witness is about to tell you. Consistency of evidence is precisely what science rightly requires of strange new phenomena, and these cases clearly provide it.

Of course, some witnesses will misperceive what they see and one or two are sure to be making up a story. This is a fact of modern life with any strange phenomena. I have tried to include cases with direct follow-up, which makes it difficult to accept the hoax or misperception theory as a complete resolution. Countless independent sources are telling much the same thing, with little chance that they know minor details of a time storm. That seems important.

This is not the world of ghosts and aliens where strong global folk wisdom exists. This is a virtually unrecognised anomaly. It is at least scientifically arguable that this consistent evidence reflects a fundamental reality. That is the premise from which I will continue, dismissing speculation about aliens or the supernatural and seeking to resolve these cases in terms of real – if perhaps extraordinary – physics.

The time storm has many quite modest properties, and we might well be willing to accept much of this as a reasonable extension to known science. But we must consider the simplest solution to a problem because it is often the most likely to be correct. Hoax and misperception should always be our first option in any consideration of these cases. I simply believe that they do not adequately explain the sum of all the data, and that it is worth contemplating other possibilities.

SCIENTIFIC LOGIC

Science progresses both by gradual *evolution* (one researcher building on the work of others) and by sudden *revolution* (rapid insight in which facts that have always been true are appreciated for the first time). The sun shone for millions of years before we knew the nuclear physics that makes it do so. Natural phenomena like fireball meteors whizzed through the air throughout recorded history and were deified as signs and portents, or even given a pseudo-scientific misinterpretation (for instance, they were once believed to be rocks thrown into the air by lightning strikes). In the end we learned the truth and now know that they are debris from distant parts of the cosmos striking the earth's atmosphere. Yet for much of our history that truth would have been regarded as supernatural nonsense.

So, whilst the evidence that forms today's supernatural is often misleading or wrong, there is no overwhelming reason why some data cannot mask real science. Indeed, the lessons of history suggest that it will do. There are always new things to be learned about the universe, and we probably have the best chance to see them in action within wonders and mysteries that are trivialised as 'paranormal'.

It is the task of science to weed out the nonsense and to define precisely what anything new that remains may tell us about the order of the universe. But many scientists have lost touch with that quest, understandably fleeing the wilder shores of paranormal sensationalism. Unfortunately, for all the nonsense they rightly avoid, some truths are missed as well.

Here strength of data, the improbability of wide-scale deception and the clear signs of real science shout to me that the time storm has a good chance of being established as real. Something is causing it to happen, and we shall only find out what that something is by studying it rigorously.

Such caveats were necessary to introduce one final set of time storm cases – of the type from which the name is most readily defined. For these simply extend what has gone before. They slip easily into the sequence of events and appear only as more incredible examples. Yet these incidents *are* storms in the fabric of time. They are cases that question everything that we think we know about temporal physics.

They appear to be evidence that time can be circumvented.

SALEN FOREST

We now return to Dawn, the witness whose story opened this book.

Isle of Mull (UK), 1987

This second event took place thirty-four years after that Himalayan episode, on 8 October 1981. At the time she was touring Scotland with a Christian Aid group and driving through the Salen Forest on the Isle of Mull. With her were Dwight and Geraldine, two American colleagues. Dwight had driven the car off the ferry and, after a couple of hours exploring Tobermory, the island's main town, they were enjoying the heather-covered moors on what was a beautiful autumn day. He had slowed right down to take some photographs when a mist appeared from nowhere and attached itself to the car.

Dawn, of course, knew what was happening. It was not an exact re-run of the events in Tibet, but notably similar. Dwight and his wife instinctively ducked below the windshield, fearing it would shatter, for there was a heavy pressure pushing down on them and a vibrating sensation that made the car feel as if it were moving sideways and upwards. The fog was now so thick that it was completely blocking the front view. All Dawn could see ahead was blackness, although there were swirls – undefined forms – moving within; 'a blurred silver shape' is how they were described. There was a sense of a vortex surrounding them, and she tried to shout but is not sure that anyone heard. Then the mist disappeared and all was normal again.

Or so they thought. They got out of the car in a shocked state to discover that the car boot was open (it had been locked) and its contents were lying on the road (another recurrent theme in these cases). Baffled, they decided to abandon their sightseeing trip. Within a couple of hours, Dwight and Geraldine were in denial. They said that an animal must have got into the car and they had dreamed the rest, but declined to talk further. ○

However, for me the deeper I probed into the story the more intriguing it became.

It was not clear if the car had moved during this experience. One part of the moors looked much like another to three strangers, and all they know for sure is they were still on Mull. The passage of time was also not consciously observed. But subjectively it only seemed to last moments. When they drove off and decided to return to the mainland they had not been aware of any temporal anomaly. But there was one.

'You know, that is very, very strange,' Dawn told me. She had only just recognised the problem when I quizzed her about the timings. 'We left on the ferry very early. It was just after noon when we saw the thing. But when it had gone, the sun had moved well across the sky. Is that important?'

I soon realised that it was. She added: 'When we got back into town [only a few minutes' drive] the shops were shutting. The afternoon just disappeared. Where did it go to?'

I also learned that during the incident the Oz Factor was in force. The witnesses had commented on how the road was oddly devoid of noise and traffic. It had not been like this before or afterwards, despite the fact that they were on a small island. Indeed, Dwight had said, 'That's the one good thing. Nobody else saw it.' This aided his ability to deny the events. In fact, he went off on his own to be 'alone with his thoughts' – something apparently well out of character and suggestive of the altered state of consciousness often noted.

Other anticipated effects of the energy field were also noticed. After the mist had gone it took the three of them several attempts to get the nearly new, otherwise faultlessly performing hire car to start. Dawn was wearing a wind-up wristwatch. This worked normally, but the two Americans had quartz digital watches powered by an electrical source, which were both found to be stopped shortly after the incident. Dwight and Geraldine had to call at a jeweller on the mainland and both needed a new power cell. There was an electric clock in the car. On arrival back in Tobermory they noticed it too had stopped, and it never worked again during the period of their hire. When they handed back the car at the end of their holiday they felt guilty about not mentioning the fault, but noted, 'How could we have explained what had happened to it?'

So once again we have an encounter with a time storm complete with the regular energy field effects and a force that seemed to move these three people and their car forward about four or five hours through time. One has to wonder if a passer-by might have seen the car surrounded by a grey mist, and then, when this had cleared, no car at all.

LOST IN TIME

Whilst a little different from the time storm cases so far, the following two reports have obvious comparisons. My friend and colleague Gloria Dixon, who enlisted the help of local paramedic Paul Ascough, considers this first one to be of great importance. Unfortunately, she reports, it was taken on by a UFO group and considered to be some form of alien contact. As a result it became very confused by unnecessary hypnotic recall. But the basic details are telling.

The witnesses were two couples who lived in West Yorkshire, a large area which in order to help preserve their privacy I shall not refine further.

Contrary to expectation, most people are not desperate to 'star' in the tabloids or reveal all on a TV chat show. The stranger the events, the more they want to protect their reputation. As a culture we sensationalise and even regard as 'disturbed' anyone with such a tale. If you have a responsible position to protect, anonymity can be a wise precaution.

Calder Valley (UK), 1995

On 15 July 1995 these four people were having a barbecue in the garden when the atmosphere began to 'feel strange'. It seems to have been a heaviness, with an electric charge as you might feel at the onset of a storm. They also began to note distortions to the flow of time – as if events were being compressed in their flow. In addition, objects were suddenly moving on their own from place to place – a glass moving from a table to the floor, for example. Also there was a strange state of consciousness (the Oz Factor) with its sense of isolation and the disappearance of all normal sounds.

At this point, subsequent recall of what happened breaks down. All the witnesses have struggled to piece together a correct sequence of events and remember only snatches. They do agree that a dark grey mass appeared and that a mist or fog seemed to envelop the garden. They also recall a beam of light. But beyond that it was just 'suddenly' dark – as if many hours had passed in an instant. Indeed, they all kept checking every time source they could find to assure themselves that it really was now hours after it should have been.

Once indoors, physical effects took hold. The two women fell into a deep sleep on the floor. One man was violently ill, and when his wife awoke she too felt nauseous. Over the next few days they all felt extremely tired, with muscle pains and tingling sensations, and two of them developed a strange red rash.

This was pretty much all their conscious recall. One witness said of the extraordinary effects on the flow time, 'It was like a video tape cut up and stuck together out of order.'[1] O

REALITY BLINKS

An important aside in this last case is the reference to how objects moved, as if reality instantly altered. It seemed that the environment changed in just one minor detail that was starkly noticeable because of this sudden 'jump'. There is a similarity here to the many accounts in which a witness 'awakes' in another place with a 'discontinuity' in memory providing no recall of the transition.

Other witnesses have likened it to shifting into a parallel earth where everything is basically the same but small things have changed. If there are co-existent realities, each one different only slightly from others, what would we experience if we moved 'sideways' from one track to another? Is it reasonable to surmise that the witness may perceive this shift in the form of reality blinks – just as are described here?

Two friends first alerted me to the reality blink idea by reporting an event that happened to them on a visit to the Kyle of Lochalsh in Scotland. They were standing eating fish and chips next to a car park when one turned to the other, eyes gaping, and said, 'Did you see that?' Both had. An empty car right in front of them had suddenly moved a few yards sideways. Peter said: 'We sort of paused mid-chip and shrugged. But whilst we both saw it, cars do not, of course, move sideways [it was not on a slope]. So it was a case of "Oh!" and on to the next chip.'

I have always wondered if in that instant they both 'jumped reality tracks' and saw the world shift into a slightly different version from the one that they had previously inhabited. Maybe we all make switches like this on a regular basis, but so slight that we do not notice minor changes except as occasional anomalies such as this. Speculation – certainly. But this incident *did* occur and reality blinks are apparently common, as we have seen in other cases. Something must explain them.

THE MEDWAY 'HELICOPTER'

Medway (UK), 1980

Edith Sage is a mother of three from the Medway area of Kent. On 4 August 1980, a warm, sunny afternoon, she was walking to the local corner shop to get some peas, annoyed at having forgotten them during an earlier shopping trip. Then, at 4.50 p.m., as she was walking down a small alley, 'Out of the corner of my eye something in the sky made me jump. It was like a smoke ring going round and round, with sort of sparks coming out of the edge of it.'

So far this sounds like a classic case of an electrified mist, as seen in many other time storms. But behind the smoke Edith saw what looked like a futuristic helicopter start to appear. It was basic-ally a large transparent bubble with military green and tan markings, like camouflage. Inside the bubble were two human beings wearing 'jump suits'. They were definitely just normal people. Mrs Sage stared at this scene as she walked towards the shops, then noticed a strange state that we recognise once again as the Oz Factor. 'Everything was muted. It was as if I was hearing things from inside something.'

Apart from this effect, and even after the 'helicopter' arrived, a 'peculiar mist' clung to the picket fence between herself and the object. It smelt sickly and she went dizzy. What happened next may or may not be a real experience. It was visionary in nature and involved dream-like events. It may simply be an hallucination triggered by the time storm energy fields. She heard the two men inside the helicopter talking 'inside my head' and saying, 'You said it would be all right,' 'I know, I know' and 'It's all right, she thinks we are army.' In other words this was an impossibly overheard yet oddly rational conversa-tion that conveys the impression of Mrs Sage having accidentally stumbled across some sort of experiment to whose success her pres-ence was considered a threat.

In a 'daze' Edith reports how she walked down the alley, leaving the 'helicopter' still there, bought her peas, had a conversation with a woman in the shop about a wedding and went on with the day as if the incident had never taken place. Indeed, as the hours passed she quickly forgot all about it. ◯

The episode simply vanished from Mrs Sage's mind as a dream would do, rather like Dwight and Geraldine on the Isle of Mull dismissing their encounter after they went into full denial.

Is this a psychological response? Can the mind not cope with what is seemingly impossible and so chooses to bury the memory? Or is it a natural consequence of switching reality tracks? Does our conscious mind bed down within the new reality framework into which we are thrust and seek to forget the switch? Is any vestige of that recall an accident rather than the normal way of things? Perhaps.

For the next few weeks Edith had great difficulty sleeping. She also began to notice impossible permanent changes to the alley. These acted as a hook that gradually brought the story of the mist back to recall. These changes are, Mrs Sage admitted, impossible, but she is adamant that this location had altered from how it was before the smoky mist was seen. They were minor changes – like a step narrowing, or a house having a path where none existed before. A tree also suddenly appeared where the smoke ring had been. Like Edith said, she knew where the ring was, knew now where this tree was, but 'if the tree had been there beforehand I could not have seen what I did. It would have blocked my view of the smoke.'

Somewhere within this bizarre tale may lie important truths. When Edith told all this to me soon afterwards I was flummoxed. I had not yet traced other time storm cases with which to compare it. But now I can see how much of this tale slots together. What she saw that day *was* a time storm – with its mist, electric field, smell and physiological effects. It affected her state of consciousness and may have induced visions.

But above all we have these reality blinks that Mrs Sage reported. The world at this location (and nowhere else) allegedly changed in minor but obvious ways in the immediate wake of the incident – just as household objects moved during the incident in West Yorkshire; just as the car in Scotland shifted its location in a moment; just as the scenery around a vehicle that encounters a time storm may no longer be the same as it was before. For here, bear in mind, what the witness regards as a physical jump of a few hundred yards from one place on a road to another might not be that at all. What if small details of their surroundings have altered because they have 'jumped reality tracks', thanks to the time storm? If they have now entered a slightly different reality where the environment is not exactly the same as before, would the witness realise this is what has happened – or assume that they have moved to another location on the road?

And might these 'jumps' from one reality track to another be an explanation for claims by various witnesses about them being 'out of phase' in the aftermath of a time storm experience (see p. 74). Is this the result of having to re-anchor themselves into a new reality framework?[2]

PARALLEL LIVES

Somerset (UK), 1974

According to Somerset man Peter Williamson, on 28 July 1974 – another sunny day, again with a barbecue in the garden – he too switched reality tracks. Once again (as on p. 83) the early proceedings were interrupted by a heavy electrical storm. The Williamsons' dog was seen to be cowering under a tree, unexpectedly spooked – perhaps by the strange atmosphere. Peter went to rescue the animal and take it back indoors. But as he went towards it, there was a huge flash, and when it was over Peter had vanished.

The police were called, Peter's wife Mary was put under sedation, and the children were sent to stay with friends. Despite a massive search there was no sign of the missing man. It was argued that a lightning strike nearby had disorientated the guests, caused them to miss what had happened and giving Peter traumatic amnesia. He must have wandered off in the confusion.

Then – at 8 a.m. three days later – Peter was found unconscious in nearby shrubbery with one foot in a pond. It was as if he had arrived there out of nowhere. There was no sign of how he had got into the locked garden (the gardener who found him had the only key). Peter spent several days in hospital suffering from shock, but had no recall of what had taken place. Then the dreams began and gradually grew more lucid. With time Peter began to suspect that they were more than his imagination. In the dreams he found himself standing in an unfamiliar garden, soaking wet. He began to wander the roads, dazed and confused; he was found and eventually taken to a hospital. Here he spent some time undergoing tests. He was able to recall the names of a doctor, a sister and various nurses, and the ward name. None was familiar to him in 'real life'. The dreams were long and mundane – one reason he came to suspect their reality.

The Williamsons' dog was seen to be cowering under a tree, unexpectedly spooked – perhaps by the strange atmosphere. Peter went to rescue the animal and take it back indoors. But as he went towards it there was a huge flash, and when it was over Peter had vanished.

From time to time the hospital had 'shimmered' around him in a sort of haze, and furniture appeared in places where there had been none. Then the ward would return to normal. This sounds like a reality blink. Another very telling comment by Peter about his dream (or memory) was that, when in the hospital and he heard his own voice spoken, it sounded very odd – as if it were echoing 'in slow motion'.

As Peter's condition improved, he had been allowed out for a walk around the grounds of the unfamiliar-looking hospital. Going down a

What form would a real time machine take? Probably not the most famous of all – Dr Who's police box 'The Tardis'! Physicists have defined the needs of a true life time machine and one of these is the requirement that it should be able to fly like an aircraft or helicopter (see p. 234).
© BBC

Mankind has always been fascinated by the idea of time travel. Even before modern physics established that it was not, in fact, impossible, science fiction writers often wove imaginative stories around the idea. H.G. Wells' *The Time Machine* was not the first of its genre, but was possibly the most influential (see p. 213).
© FORTEAN PICTURE LIBRARY

Photographs of ghosts are widespread. Often, as in this one taken in a church in Arundel, Sussex, in 1940, nothing was seen when the shutter was depressed, but a strange image appeared on the developed photograph
(see p.178).
© MARY EVANS PICTURE LIBRARY

Sometimes these 'ghost' photographs show images not from the past, but perhaps from the future. This picture taken on Burgh Marsh in Cumbria in 1964 seems to show a floating futuristically-garbed figure that was not visible to the photographer. He did, however, describe strange atmospheric effects, akin to those reported during time storm cases, that occurred when he attempted to photograph his young daughter
(see p.175).
© JIM TEMPLETON

lane outside, Peter began to get a sense of familiarity. Then there was no further recall until he awoke by the pond.

Researcher Colin Parsons stayed with the family for three days. The hospital was traced. It was a nearby cottage infirmary and did have a ward with the correct name and a doctor and sister as Peter reported. The doctor did not recognise Peter and the hospital records showed that he had never stayed there. It was suggested that Peter must have invented this dream in his mind from fragments of information in his subconscious (perhaps a conversation once heard about the hospital). ○

During this electrical storm did Peter shift into a parallel reality – one that was on a 'closely aligned' track? If so, does it suggest that we may return to our original reality? Of course, what if many Peters in many similar realities disappeared that night and the one that returned to 'our' reality was not the one who left from here? Maybe in some other reality track there is a man who returned to his family but seemed somehow slightly different.[3]

The world is full of stories about people who suddenly disappear, never to be seen again, or of strangers who arrive from nowhere without the ability to explain who they are or where they come from. Is it possible that in such cases we are seeing the result of a sudden switch in realities? It is a chilling thought.[4]

THE EMPTY CAR

I could discuss many further cases of alleged anomalies induced by a time storm, but will confine myself to two from South America. They involve major time dislocations rather than the few hours involved in the majority of episodes. It is interesting that in these extreme examples (like that from

Chile on p. 26) the period of time allegedly involved is often three to five days. This is the apparent maximum.

Linhares (Brazil), 1981

On 20 April 1981, Jorge Ramos, a representative for a chemical company, left his home in Linhares, Brazil, at 6 p.m. to drive the few miles to a meeting. He never arrived. When his wife Noemia reported his disappearance to the police that night she feared foul play, for he was normally scrupulous about reporting his movements. Next day the police began to investigate, and before long made a disturbing discovery. The Volkswagen car driven by Ramos was found on a side road just off the BR101, only a few miles outside Linhares. The key was still in the ignition. All his papers were intact. His samples and files for the meeting were lying there undisturbed. It was as if he had been abducted from the car, but there was no sign of a struggle.

The car was taken to police headquarters and subjected to forensic tests. There was no clue as to what had happened to Ramos – not until five days after his disappearance, when Noemia received a frantic call from her husband. Ramos said that he had been driving to the appointment when suddenly he saw a white glow heading towards him. Before he could react it had enveloped the car. He felt a sense of pressure on him, making it hard to move, and pains in his muscles. Then he found himself in a dreamy, floating state, and the next instant he was 'coming to' with his body still sore and disorientated. The car was gone. He was standing by an unfamiliar road, but was relieved to find all his money and personal possessions intact. He had no idea how he had got to where he was, but had to buy some medication to try to relieve the pains that were creating tingling sensations in his body.

Upon arrival at the pharmacy, he discovered for the first time the startling truth about his relocation. Ramos learned that not only was it no longer the evening of 20 April (it was in fact the 25th) but that he was nowhere near either his car or his home. In fact, he was in the town of Gioania – some six hundred miles from where his car was discovered by the police.[5] ○

A DISLOCATED MAN

The second Brazilian case also involves a salesman, named Onilson Patero.

Itajobi – Catanduva (Brazil), 1973

On 22 May 1973 he had been to Itajobi to deliver some accounts and was returning home to Catanduva. It was 3 a.m. and heavy rain was falling as he drove the last few miles. He was listening to the radio, but it became blocked by increasing static that eventually swamped the transmission. At the same time Patero noticed that his car was suffering electrical failure and his engine was losing power. He began to cruise slowly to a halt.

As this occurred, a blue glow swallowed the car and, fearing a truck was heading for him and might hit him since he was scarcely visible without lights, Patero used the momentum of the Chevrolet to edge off the side of the road. He had instinctively thrown one hand up to cover his eyes from the blinding glare. But no traffic did pass. There was now just stillness and silence. Patero scrambled out and saw that the vehicle was still surrounded by this blue glow. What was more, there was a heavy, suffocating pressure from above and his body began to feel terribly hot. He noticed what seems to have been a 'vortex tube' from the sky covering the car and tried to run away, but his legs were paralysed and he was struggling to breathe. His skin was now scalding hot.

Just before he collapsed into unconsciousness, Patero saw that the car looked very strange. It was as if its molecular structure was altering and he could see the background through it. It was virtually disappearing before his eyes. This may have been one of the hallucinations that seem to happen when the time storm really begins to affect one's consciousness.

Some time later, around dawn two passers-by found the Chevrolet at the roadside, with its lights full on but its contents, including a briefcase and notes, scattered on the ground outside. Patero too was lying on the ground, totally unresponsive. They concluded he must have had a car crash and been killed, and rushed to find a phone to call the police. When highway patrol officer Clovis Queiroz arrived at the scene he too thought Patero was dead. But suddenly he stirred, then screamed. Thinking that the man was suffering from shock, the police officer secured the area and drove Patero to the Padre Albino Hospital, where he was kept under observation for the next twelve hours by Dr Elias Chediak.

Meanwhile, the police investigation of the 'accident' found no sign of a crash or a robbery. The papers scattered about the highway contained many cheques, but nothing was missing. There was no reason to contradict the seemingly absurd tale that Patero was telling them about the glow that attacked his car and made it go transparent. Major physiological effects followed. Spots like bruises appeared on his abdomen, causing him to be re-admitted to the hospital a few days later. All that Dr Chediak could do was confirm that in his opinion the witness was coherent and there were 'no symptoms of mental debility'. The marks on the abdomen were not identified but resembled burns.

All of this is an intriguing encounter with a time storm. But it did not end here. For this was just the first of two experiences that Patero was to allege. On 26 April 1974, Patero went from Catanduva to Julio de Mesquita, a short trip that should not have required an overnight stay. He promised his family he would come home that night but did not. In fact, when he was about to cross a bridge at Guaranta another huge glow swallowed up his car and 'instantly' he found himself wandering around a plantation in daylight, completely disorientated and unsure as to how he had got there.

Patero's car was found by the police on the bridge at Guaranta. A search was mounted, but the missing man was not seen again until Cesar Menelli, a plantation farmer, saw Patero sitting dazed and soaking wet in a spot on a hillside that is very difficult to access by foot. Patero asked where he was. He also should have asked *when* he was. For it was now five days later than his last recall – an event that to him was just 'moments before'. He was near Colatina, over five hundred miles from where his car had been abandoned. Despite two days of grilling by police in Colatina, Patero would not change his story.[6] ◯

Certainly discussion of reality blinks, jumping between parallel reality tracks and the time travel consequences of such events has to be termed speculation. But these cases do suggest a pattern. Whatever the truth, we have a global collection of data, usually misreported as alien kidnaps (without any serious justification). When looked at, as here, we see a remarkable array of clues that just keep on recurring and make sense in terms of the physics of EM energy fields. They allege dislocations in time and space, and even changes to the framework of reality. We need to ask what could account for these widespread and extraordinary claims.

Now we must try to find out.

PART TWO

•

UNDERSTANDING THE NATURE OF TIME

Scientific Perspectives

10
Tick Tock Time

I HOPE THE FIRST PART OF THIS BOOK HAS ESTABLISHED THE BASIC PROBLEM. There are cases from around the world that seem to be describing a phenomenon of nature. This 'time storm' appears able to distort gravity, to move things through space and possibly even allow travel through time. If we are to understand whether such a thing is possible, we need to investigate what science knows about the nature of time itself. You will see that – perhaps surprisingly – this brings us full circle.

But first, stop reading for a moment and listen to the world. Think about what you can hear. Perhaps there is a rhythmic beat of music from a distant radio set. Maybe outside a workman is using a pneumatic drill. Or can you hear the ebb and flow of water on sand? Then again, if you listen carefully, the faint tick-tock of a clock may appear – a sound often present, but which your conscious mind filters out. Let it sneak past your auditory defences.

These things have one feature in common – time. They have a resonance or a regular pattern that reinforces our assumptions about the way the universe works. That intuitive awareness of life is that time flows steadily, inexorably, from past into future. It moves through a succession of moments that we refer to as 'now'. Its patterns are the score to the music of life and are an integral part of our reality.

There can surely be no doubt that time exists. Everything we experience seems to say that it does. But there is a big question mark over that statement of the obvious. What we see and experience as reality science now suspects could simply be an illusion. It is a persistent one, born out of the building blocks of the cosmos. But it may be that time has no true existence at all.[1]

That is a frightening thought from which to begin our look at temporal physics: to think that everything we find familiar in our surroundings is insubstantial, like the transient images of a dream world in which days can rush past in seconds and moments can go on for ever.

> *Time, as you can see, has never been as simple as we might like to think. It is a fluid thing that adapts according to our state of consciousness.*

Which is the true time – the thirty minutes spent waiting for a bus that seem to drag so slowly, or the half-hour of pleasure when talking with a loved one you have not met in ages? Which is more real – the endless summer holidays of childhood where everything is new and exciting, or the two-week break between hours of working drudgery that is over before it appears to have begun?

Time, as you can see, has never been as simple as we might like to think. It is a fluid thing that adapts according to our state of consciousness. It seems to have very different rates of progress, not the 'velocity' of one second per second. It can speed up, slow down, stretch out or even stop as a result of subtle influence like biological mechanisms.

THE HUNT FOR NOW

The tenuous nature of time is easy to recognise. Just ask yourself how long 'now' lasts. You know that there are moments which have happened (the past) and others yet to happen (the future), and that in between the two is supposed to be a very short instant that we call 'now'. But how long is that instant? Is it a trillionth of a second? In fact any length – no matter how fantastically small?

The purpose of the term 'now' is to bridge the gap between past and future. But that presupposes there is a gap to bridge. Indeed any gap, no matter how small, would require a finite period to cross – just as when you cross the shortest bridge it takes time to walk from one side to the other. But if 'now' actually takes time in order to happen, then what part of it is in the future and what part of it is in the past during this passage? And is any part of 'now' ever really 'now'?

Before you give yourself a headache trying to work this out, just content yourself with realising that great minds from philosophers to physicists have wrestled with these dilemmas for thousands of years. Nobody is sure if there even *is* an answer.[2]

Perhaps this is simply a false premise, because we don't yet have the science to measure anything as small as a 'now'. Perhaps this paradox of the basic unit of time requiring time to happen proves that there is no steady passage of 'nows'. Or perhaps the way that 'now' is a timeless boundary between past and future says something more profound.

For if past just melts into future and there is no length or duration between the two, then what is the distinction between past and future? Indeed, is there any distinction? Or does one smoothly flow into the other and are both simply words we use to describe different parts of a simultaneous whole? Is our language of time a convenience to accord with the illusion of past and future that we perceive?

Right away our common-sense view of time moving steadily forward is in trouble. Nor is this the end of the problem. What is a deceptively simple phenomenon descends into chaos when looked at more carefully.

A BRIEF HISTORY OF PHYSICS

Science has always depended upon two things – observation and intuition. From the days when the human race first learned to communicate we have looked at the world, sought order behind it and pondered the rules that might cause this order to occur. That is what science is all about.

Early speculations about time depended very much upon the cyclical nature of many things. The tide came in, went out, and came back in again. Plants grew, matured, withered, died, and the following spring new ones appeared. The belief in reincarnation – that we return to earth in a new body after death – is central to many religions. It almost certainly evolved in the human psyche because it is in accordance with the 'way of things' that these perceptions of nature seem to imply.[3]

However, taking things at face value collapsed when Renaissance scholars such as Galileo established that the sun did not rotate around the earth, as it appears to do. In fact, the earth is in orbit around a giant furnace in the sky. The seeds of 'heresy' took several early scientists to their deaths at the hands of the Roman Catholic Church. It took the science of physical astronomy to provide direct observation of space and the keys to the truth. For now people could see what they could not see before – the motions of the planets and even the moons of large planets revolving defiantly *not* around the earth.

Our forebears' false belief about the earth being the centre of God's universe was grounded in their limited ability to make observations, imprisoned as they were on the surface of this planet with apparently tiny objects in the vast universe beyond. Once we were able to boost our perception with telescopes and other instruments, we could see what was real and build order from observation to create new theory.

Between 1660 and 1900 huge strides were made. Isaac Newton, in a brilliant flash of insight (a thought experiment after seeing an apple fall from a tree), realised that all things in the universe are falling too, under the influence of gravity – big things attracting smaller things, like the earth with the apple. From this he could show by mathematics how the moon was attracted to the earth and the earth to the far more massive sun; and how, because they were in motion, and because vast distances were involved, the earth did not actually fall into the sun, but all were dancing in a tightly locked 'gravity waltz' throughout the aeons.

Despite all this progress, the principle of observation leading to speculation and confirmation ruled and time's role remained unchallenged. Newton believed it was fundamental to the universe that all things flowed like a river into the future. Nothing in his laws of motion, or in the deeper understanding that followed, called into question this perception. Indeed, some of his laws just would not work without it.[4]

One of these is the concept of thermodynamics. Observation tells us that a hot object next to a cold object will transfer heat outwards. That's why we can be 'burned' from touching a hot stove or from touching a cold freezer. It does not matter which way the rapid energy transfer goes (from the stove to us or from us to the freezer), it still affects our fragile body tissue. This is easy to understand once you realise that heat is energy and that something with lots of energy seeks equilibrium with something that has less – rather like a rich philanthropist choosing to share his bounty with the poor.

With more complex awareness we learned that all energetic things degenerate across time by 'feeding' lesser energetic systems. Along with this diminishing comes greater tendency towards chaos. This is a one-way street. A robot charged with energy can rampage around a pot factory and wreck the place before its batteries run low. What could not happen was a power-exhausted robot being put into a wrecked factory and gathering energy from nowhere, re-creating order by returning all the pots as if new.

This balance of energy and its one-way progress is called entropy and it defines reality. Time is vital and moves as we perceive it to do in a singular direction. Things live, they wear out and they die. The energy they lose may in other ways trigger new life (like flesh becoming fertiliser that begets new plants), but in the overall scheme of things, the birth, life and death of the universe seem confirmed as real.[5]

Then, in the early twentieth century, the day of reckoning dawned.

THE THEORY OF RELATIVITY

Two revolutions during the twentieth century destroyed two thousand years of delusion that we knew the basic truths about life. The first of these was the theory of relativity, and again it took a genius and a thought experiment to see it. German physicist Albert Einstein worked out the concept that would shock the world whilst daydreaming as an office clerk in Switzerland in the early 1900s. He did so by contemplating what you would see if you chased a beam of light at very fast speed.

Imagine racing a speeding train on a road that runs parallel to the track. If your car is not moving and the train flashes past at 125 mph, it seems to go by you in a blur. But as you drive after it, its speed relative to you reduces. As you reach 100 mph it is now only moving away from you fairly slowly. If your car (and the traffic laws) permit a speed of 125 mph, you can match that of the train. What happens now? Relative to you, the train seems not to be moving any more. If you open your window and a passenger in a carriage on the train does so too, you can clearly see each other and exchange words. Yet anyone standing in a lay-by on the roadside sipping a cup of tea as your car and the train rush past would be able to see very little amidst the confusion of sound and light that whizzes along at what seems a great velocity.

That, very simply, is what relativity is all about. Except that Einstein went well beyond these everyday experiences to the sorts of speeds only achievable by electromagnetic energy fields such as light, which travels over ten million miles in a minute as opposed to the two miles covered by the speeding car and train in the example above. But then Einstein realised – and went on to to prove, using mathematics devised by a man called Lorenz – that at these amazingly high velocities the train would no longer appear to stand still.

You could not, in effect, make a light ray stop dead in its tracks. If you could, extraordinary things would happen: by stopping light you would be pretty much stopping time, because we experience everything by virtue of the information reaching our senses. So if no new information can reach us because it appears to stand still, from our point of view no new events are happening.

Einstein knew this was absurd. As such he assumed, then proved, that the speed of light will always be the same no matter where you are located. Light can never stand still. Nor can any EM radiation field. In fact, it never slows down – it just travels very, very fast all of the time. Unfortunately, once he took this assumption forward and started to unravel its implications, far from successfully removing the awkward improbability that you can stop time by moving very fast, he found he had introduced many incredible new consequences. Indeed, the original alternative might even have been preferable!

A STARSHIP ENTERPRISE

The fact that light, like all EM radiation, moves very fast but at a none the less finite speed, has been known since 1675 when Ole Roemer measured the movements of Jupiter's distant moons through an early telescope and unexpected time lags appeared. Einstein's theories of relativity (published in two parts – the simple version in 1905 and a more complex version in 1916) established the mathematical ground rules.[6]

A hundred years ago tests of relativity were difficult, if not impossible, but today we can make very, very small things inside particle accelerators (see p. 107) travel at close to the speed of light. Every single test run like this has proven Einstein right. Relativity, despite the logical absurdities that follow from its equations, has been verified beyond any room for doubt.

Here is an easy way to see one problem that relativity creates for our concept of time. Imagine it is twelve noon on a day in some future year when space travel has become commonplace. At that moment the *Mars*

Voyager leaves Mars for earth and the *Starship Explorer* sets off from Mars base heading towards the nearest star system (Proxima Centauri). Owing to advances in science, both are travelling at a large fraction of the speed of light (although not at the speed of light itself, as only energy fields without mass can go at such a velocity – not spaceships or people).

Now let us imagine that at 12.01 p.m., a minute after both craft leave on their journeys, a mad scientist blows up the moon. Logic tells us that the event occurs one minute into the flight of *both* spacecraft. But logic is not vindicated in this situation, as Einstein showed.

What needs to be remembered is that the *Mars Voyager* is heading very fast *towards* earth (and its moon), whereas the *Starship Explorer* is travelling at a similar speed *away* from both. Since the speed of light is constant, the light revealing the moon's destruction will reach the *Mars Voyager* well before it gets to the *Starship Explorer* (seconds, or minutes, perhaps even hours, depending on the speeds of the spacecraft involved).

Why? Because the Mars vessel is heading towards the light rushing at it from the moon, closing the gap and giving it less relative distance to travel. The light heading for the *Starship Explorer* has to catch it up as it races away from our solar system, giving it a longer relative distance to travel. Since the speed of light stays the same, it takes less time to travel a shorter distance and the *Mars Voyager* sees the light – and so experiences the event of the moon's destruction – well before the *Starship Explorer* can.

If the *Mars Voyager* sees the explosion at, say, 12.02 p.m. (on its clocks) and the *Starship Explorer* only at, say, 1.02 p.m. – over an hour later into its flight – at what time does the moon actually blow up? Is it 12.01, 12.02 or 1.02? In fact it is all three, because there is no right or wrong answer here. Time is relative to where you are, how fast you are travelling and whether you are moving towards or away from any situation.

EXPERIENCING THE FUTURE

Although this may seem suspiciously like an artificial situation, it isn't. Such space journeys will occur one day. And the same effect is relevant now. If we send a rocket to Mars, even at 'modest' speeds (twenty-five times as fast as Concorde *is* modest, relative to the speed of light), there are problems. News of any fault takes time to reach NASA at the speed of light, and by the time an immediate reply is sent, it may already be too late to do anything about it. The further we travel, the worse this effect becomes.

Even travelling by jet aircraft involves relativity effects. This can be proven by taking two identical clocks, setting them to start simulatneously at twelve noon and flying one in Concorde one way round the earth and a second in a similar jet going in the opposite direction. Because the earth itself is moving very fast around the sun, this simulates an experiment like the one involving the two oppositely moving spaceships. The speeds involved here are only hundreds of miles per hour (a tiny fraction of the speed of light), so the time difference that is introduced is in the order of a small part of one second. But it is not zero.

The result is predictable, for such experiments can now be carried out with ultra-accurate atomic clocks. They prove that events do not happen everywhere at the same moment. *When* they happen depends on where you are and how fast you are travelling. It is not impossible for an event that happens tomorrow, as far as one person is concerned, to have actually happened yesterday, relative to somebody else.

In fact, we all experience this effect without knowing it. Look up tonight at a star. Watch it twinkle. Then realise that this star is a sun so far away that the light you are seeing may have left on its journey to your eye two hundred years ago. The star you look at might have exploded (in our time frame) during World War I, but you must leave a message to your great-great-grandchildren about it because they will be the ones who might 'see' that event happen. Even if it 'really' occurred ninety years ago, we will not observe it on earth until the twenty-second century. So much for the obvious flow of time!

Bizarre consequences emerge. Think back to the two spaceships. Suppose it was possible (although we don't know how) for the *Mars Voyager* to send an 'instant' message to the *Starship Explorer* when it sees the moon explode. If it does so (at 12.02), the captain of the *Starship Explorer* could announce to a stunned crew: 'In fifty-nine minutes and ten seconds, if you look through this screen focused back on earth the moon is going to explode.' The captain will, in effect, have seen the future before it happens. This is because in one sense it already has happened – just not in the frame of reference relative to the *Starship Explorer*.

Whilst there is cheating here (it assumes a way of sending a message faster than the speed of light), it is instructive. As a thought experiment, even if never achievable, it shows that the laws of relativity prove that a perception of an event does not only follow *after* the event has happened. Cause and effect, long regarded as invariable, are not a real property of the universe. Here the captain of the *Starship Explorer* received the effect (awareness of the moon exploding) before the cause (the event itself).

Logically, before relativity we might have argued that we can never see today what will not happen until tomorrow. How can you get drunk *before* you consume two bottles of wine? Otherwise, what if you smash the bottles and so never drink them? In that case you won't actually get drunk, so how could you have seen yourself drunk in the first place? This paradox seems to prove that cause must trigger effects and never the other way around, and thus infers that the consequences of relativity are flawed, if not impossible.

But as we have just seen, this indefatigable logic is incorrect. You *can* experience an event that has not yet happened, in the sense that in another relative frame of reference it has. So for a person to experience the future might not be absurd. In fact relativity, far from precluding time travel, in some ways almost makes it a certainty. This conclusion, despite being

proven by experiment, has terrified physicists
ever since, but nobody has found a way to
escape what it means.[7]

*. . . relativity, far
from precluding time
travel, in some ways
almost makes it a
certainty.*

TIME DILATION

Unhappily, the havoc wreaked by relativity allows a further odd effect.
This is as a result of something that Einstein called time dilation.

The Einstein/Lorenz equations calculate how a series of physical properties alter as speeds increase. Whilst the speed of light is constant, not
much else is. As anything goes faster its mass increases, its length decreases
and the passage of time reduces. These are in some senses actual events.
If you fly on Concorde, you will grow (by a few fractions of a second)
younger – rather you will age less rapidly – than someone who stays at
home. You will also – relatively speaking – grow heavier and shrink in
size. Such effects will return to normal when you go back to the same
relative frame of reference as everyone else, but the shorter period of time
you experienced will be permanently noticeable. You will literally have
aged a little less.

These effects are only very slight until you approach the speed of light,
and no method of travel can yet convey passengers this fast. But we can
make sub-atomic particles do so, and in this way measure their 'lifetimes'.
Time dilation has been proven to make particles age a lot more slowly at
very fast speeds.

At the CERN particle accelerator in Switzerland, tiny particles called
muons have been made to travel at 99.4 per cent of the speed of light.
Relativity predicts that for them time should pass much more slowly. And
it does. Although they normally decay (break apart) in a two-millionth of
a second, they live thirty times as long – exactly as predicted – when
made to move at this large fraction of the speed of light.

If human beings in a spaceship had been similarly speeded up, the effects would have been equally dramatic and far more remarkable. If they flew on a trip away from earth for just one week, leaving Cape Canaveral on 1 January, at the end of that week the astronauts' calendar would read 8 January. But not for the technicians back at Canaveral. For them, the date would be some time in August!

Travel even faster, and the effects become much more pronounced. If you take a trip to the Proxima Centauri star system at close to the speed of light, it is going to take you maybe ten years of your time to get there and back (that is because, even at light speed, all the stars are very far away). Ten years might seem like a big chunk out of your life, but it is as nothing in comparison to what you would find when you got back home. Whole centuries might well have passed. Everyone you ever knew would be dead.

The maths shows that at close to light speed mass grows towards becoming infinite, length contracts towards becoming zero, and time 'slows' towards a total halt. Nothing can be of infinite mass (you would need infinite energy to move it – and there is only finite energy in the universe). Indeed, nothing can have zero length (because if it has no length, how can it exist?). So this implies that it is impossible for material objects ever to fly at the speed of light. A spaceship moving at 99.999 per cent of the speed of light would have to keep adding more and more energy to move faster and faster until at some point it would need access to every energy source in the universe and would still not have reached the speed of light.

These increases in mass and decreases in size are not physical events. You, the astronaut, would not literally shrink to an atom-sized lump weighing trillions of tons. In so far as the starship is concerned, all would seem perfectly normal. But the world outside this spaceship would change in its dimension in a relative way. This change would make it appear to you as if the length of your journey had shrunk – meaning that less time would be needed to travel its full length. Hence a faster passage of time would occur, even though you would not notice time moving any more swiftly on your journey.

However, what is worth noting is that whilst changes to length or mass are mathematical abstractions, the reduction in the passage of time would look real. You and everyone else would actually be noticeably 'out of phase' upon your return. You would have lived less time than anybody who did not go with you – only seconds or minutes if speeds were modest, but potentially even a short hop in a starship could see you move centuries into the future.[8]

TIMELESS ENERGY FIELDS

So time travel is an apparent reality, thanks to relativity. If you could design a spaceship that could move at close to the speed of light, you could set off from earth and then come back in a parabolic arc. To you this may be a very brief journey from take-off to landing. But moving at speeds very near that of light, many years could pass in a blink back on earth. So, in a ten-minute jaunt like this, you could visit the year 2100 and see what it was like. There is no trickery involved. You *would* time travel.

There is a problem, however. Unlike what you see in science fiction movies, you would have purchased a one-way ticket. Relatively allows travel into the future. It does not tell you how to get back.

Unlike what you see in science fiction movies, you would have purchased a one-way ticket. Relatively allows travel into the future. It does not tell you how to get back.

Again, these bizarre time travel possibilities have been proven by experiments with sub-atomic particles. We have sent these into the future by accelerating them to enormous speeds. But there is something rather curious about what is going on here. We saw that the massive changes imposed on both length and mass are subjective – not literal changes to your size – but the effect on time appears real. So why is time different? The answer could be that it is not. Just as our shrinking in size during a very fast journey is a mathematical construct, so may it only *seem* as if we have travelled through time. We will have only truly done so if time itself has a linear form on a path from past to future – and relativity suggests that things may not be like this.

We can grasp a little of the head-twisting confusion posed by this problem if we appreciate that whilst relativity shows that nothing can travel at the speed of light, all EM radiation (such as light) clearly does. This happens because these fields are not material objects, but an energy wave form. As such, and according to Einstein, they do not violate the rules. However, what they do as a consequence is still very disconcerting. They have infinite mass and energy and no size whatsoever. And time does not exist for them. This almost makes energy fields appear God-like, being in some respects the timeless, spaceless reality that underpins everything. Nearly all physicists quickly brush that unnerving thought aside.[9]

This may appear of little relevance to the real world since energy fields are not material things, although they do affect the real world. Indeed, electromagnetic energy fields fuel reality. And there is increasing speculation by scientists that consciousness – the thing that turns inanimate objects into the mysterious life force that nobody yet comprehends – may itself be some sort of unrecognised energy field.

If so, perhaps this confirms mystical ideas that our consciousness must exist in a timeless, spaceless realm and only our material bodies are locked into the permanent illusion that time flows in a linear way. Maybe it is all just a question of relative perceptions as suggested to us by Einstein.

As you will see later in this book, there is a significant paradox between the time-rooted reality that we believe to be 'real' and the timelessness that so-called paranormal events indicate. One possible reason why such a gulf exists is that the true nature of time suggested by relativity theory differs from our mundane perception. Another could be that consciousness *is* a timeless energy field rooted in a linear, material world.

In fact, return now to our thought experiment in which the captain of the *Mars Voyager* wants to inform the *Starship Explorer* that the moon has just exploded. This concept of a timeless energy field (our consciousness) may be the key to how knowledge of that event can by-pass the speed of light. For if mind is a timeless energy field, it can literally be everywhere (and 'everywhen') at once.

QUANTUM PHYSICS

Relativity deals mostly with very big things, such as enormous speeds and long journeys through space. But it has serious implications for the everyday nature of reality, especially time.

The other major revolution that took place in science during the twentieth century is called quantum physics and deals with the world of the very small. It is even more disturbing than the theory of relativity in regard to our comprehension of time.

Even since the age of the Greek philosophers, the theory that matter could be divided into small, invisible parts (atoms) has been mooted. But the idea fell into disrepute for centuries because it could never be proven that all visible objects were composed of matter too small to be seen. Indeed, only during the nineteenth century did scientific instruments become sophisticated enough to reveal observations that suggested that this ancient view might be correct. Atomic science went on to change the world – for good and evil.

However, at first it did seem as if this theory was wrong. Observation had discredited it.

Since the early nineteenth century it had been known that light, like all radiating energy fields, had the form of waves. An English physicist called Thomas Young demonstrated this by cutting two thin slits in a piece of card and shining a beam of light through them. If light had the form of tiny invisible particles, as long-held theory suggested, these unseen 'bullets' would pass through the slits. But, of course, some would go through one slit, some through the other, and then strike a screen behind to 'build up' two patches of light. The light patches would vary in intensity according to the number of 'bullets' that passed through each slit. So you would see two diffuse patches of light – one behind each slit. Indeed, you do see just one fuzzy patch like this if there is only one slit for the light to pass through.

But, as Young showed conclusively, you do *not* see this expected effect with two slits. Instead you get a long band of light and shade. He demonstrated that this band came from peaks and troughs in a wave – the peaks where there was maximum intensity, the troughs where there was minimum. His two-slit experiment thus established that light (and by inference all EM energy forms) had to be in the form of radiating waves.[10]

Unfortunately, some decades later German physicist Max Planck proved exactly the opposite!

WAVICLES

Planck established that light did indeed come in the form of tiny packets of energy analogous to invisible bullets. He called these packets 'quanta' (from the Greek word meaning 'amount' or 'quantity'), and in 1905 the young Einstein entered this exciting new field and established the rules of what became known as 'quantum mechanics'. Indeed, Einstein won a Nobel prize not for his theory of relativity but for his rapidly vindicated solutions to quantum theory.

These quantum particles are better known by their individual name

– light quanta being called 'photons.' Non-scientists may recognise this term from the imaginary weapon aboard the USS *Enterprise* in TV's *Star Trek*. The 'photon torpedo' is basically, therefore, a big flashlight!

Taking this quantum theory as a starting point, Rutherford and Geiger, two scientists working at Manchester University in 1909, found a way to split the atom into small particles of this tiny size. Their success showed that atomic theory was sound. But, of course, what their experiment also did was release huge amounts of energy in the process (the forces that got 'tamed' to create the atomic bomb and are now used to fuel power stations). This energy is an outpouring of the wave energy (radiation) from the particles within atoms.

These undesirable side-effects were unknown to scientists at the time, and many pioneer physicists and chemists suffered from radiation exposure – Marie Curie paid with her life for such work. Eventually, the complex reactions that occur inside the atom as chains of rippling energy are set in motion were understood. Even now, Rutherford's colleague is best known for the measuring device named after him that records the radiating energy emitted by atomic processes.

Deep within the atom, the basic building blocks of matter are particles, as Planck and Einstein showed. Or they are wave energy, as Young's experiment demonstrated and as the radiating fields coming from atomic reactions inferred? It was almost as if light and other EM fields could be particles or waves, either or neither, according to circumstance. Indeed, the term 'wavicles' was coined and used for a time to paper over the cracks left by a lack of understanding in quantum theory.

TIMELESS REALITY

In 1923, the French physicist Louis de Broglie established a mathematical link that helped resolve the dual nature of all EM fields and led to a whole new field of physics. It would soon leave many scientists gasping with incredulity, and even the pioneers, such as Einstein and Planck, struggling to accept the consequences of their theory.

In essence matter was found to comprise a flux – a myriad of energy fields whose complex interactions created what to our eyes often appear as particles. Large mass objects have small energy wavelengths, small mass objects have larger wavelengths. This is why we tend to see the material world as particles (because the energy wavelengths are normally too small to be noticed), and yet sub-atomic reality appears wave-like (because the wavelengths here are large enough to be more significant).[11]

Nevertheless, this discovery proved that at a fundamental level all reality was immaterial and not rock-solid. The hard, logical universe that behaved like ping-pong balls bouncing off a bat was in truth a sea of invisible radiating energy in the form of waves. In an almost spooky sense something clearly tangible (the real world) was being created out of what was a close approximation to nothing (the seething flux of radiating energy that exists within the heart of all matter).

Think back to relativity theory, and you will see one of the problems that this realisation brings. Material objects are governed by finite laws, such as the speed of light and the inability to have zero dimensions. Radiating energy fields are not so governed. Indeed, EM waves appear to be timeless and spaceless.

Once again, through the dawning awareness of quantum theory, a very unpalatable truth has apparently emerged. Although we see a solid, time-bound universe, it is a deception created out of 'true' reality. That reality – at the heart of all things – is more properly immaterial, timeless and spaceless.[12]

We have already argued that our perception of the world is a convincing illusion and that true reality is timeless. This extraordinary concept gains support from the laws of quantum physics.

That news was a nightmare for science. It led to assertions from some quarters that the theory must simply be wrong (but, like relativity, it has been vindicated beyond any reasonable doubt through experiments with sub-atomic particles). Other scientists fell into stunned silence or stubborny refused to accept the inevitable. Even Einstein eventually tried (and failed) to prove his own work wrong.

THE UNCERTAINTY PRINCIPLE

In 1927 a great irony in physics occurred when Professor George Thompson won the Nobel prize for proving wave theory. His father had earlier won the same prize for demonstrating that particle theory was true. Neither of them was wrong. Particle theory applied under the right circumstances (more massive matter). Wave theory dominated at a deeper level (where mass was extremely small).

The way in which reality could vary according to how you view it has a neat symmetry with relativity physics. And it was not the only connection. In relativity, the important perspective is always that of the observer. If you are in a spaceship moving close to the speed of light, what you see would differ markedly from what an observer outside would see. To them it is *you* that is altered and their world stays the same. Whilst time would flow differently within each frame of reference, the experience of time – both to you in your spaceship and to the person watching you flash by – remains subjectively identical.

So it is, perhaps, with quantum physics. We may be experiencing the illusion of time because it suits our frame of reference. Ultimately, it all depends upon perspective. The person who *perceives* is the one who establishes the type of reality that he or she experiences. This idea is worrying, but seems an almost inescapable consequence of quantum physics.

To see anything requires photons of light sent to activate our senses. But something has to cause these photons to be emitted. This means, in effect, knocking on the quantum door with a beam of energy and getting the photons to respond. If we do not knock on the door, the photons stay hidden. So in order to see anything, or indeed to experience reality, we have to do something that actually helps force that reality into being. We change what *can* be witnessed by the very act of seeking to observe it.

Ludicrous as this concept seems, it is established. Seeing is not so much the cause of believing as believing is, in fact, of seeing. One of the first to set this bizarre prospect into mathematical rules was the German physicist Werner Heisenberg. In 1926 he defined the rules of quantum reality. Later he formulated his 'uncertainty principle'.[13]

This principle states that to measure the momentum of a particle you have to disturb its location. To measure its location requires you to change its momentum. You can never precisely define one without altering the other. The same is true with the properties of energy and time. Measure one accurately and you must change the other. As a result you can never know energy *and* time together to any precise degree. Some uncertainty is inevitable within the fabric of reality.

This does not just mean that our experiments will always have a built-in margin of error. It says something more disturbing. Within the universe everything becomes just a set of possibilities. You can only state the mathematical likelihood of an event occurring. You can never be absolutely certain that it *will*. All reality at a quantum level comprises interacting energy fields that are timeless and spaceless. But these interactions are actually governed by the laws of chance. You can say something *may* happen. You can define how likely it is that it *will*. But you can never say for certain that it is actually *going* to occur.

Einstein hated this idea so much that he derided it with the sneering comment: 'God does not play dice with the world.' Sadly, his optimism that Heisenberg's theory would be found wanting has evaporated with increasing experimental research.

Einstein was wrong. Heisenberg was right. God does play a mean game of dice.

CREATING REALITY

There is an easy way to envisage what goes on within the heart of all matter. Imagine you have a helicopter and can fly above a new housing estate in which the planners have thoughtfully provided a central park. To get from one side of the estate to the other, walkers must traverse this field, but no pathway has been provided. They must just make their own way from one gate to the other.

If you take a flight above this field before the estate opens you will see grass below undisturbed by passing feet. But if you take another trip in a few weeks' time, after several hundred people have trekked across, you will notice changes. The more people tramp from gate to gate, the more these changes will become visible. From high above, what will you see? Probably the first traces of a central swathe where most people have chosen to walk. They have taken the easy route from gate to gate, following the most direct line, and the effect of many people doing that has left a visible trail.

But swoop your helicopter down a little so that it hovers just above the park. Now you may see faint lines left by others that have taken more individual routes, perhaps when walking their dogs. They have chosen to use less direct paths and have left only vague marks because there are relatively few such diversionary wanderings.

Now, as you hover, when the next person comes to the gate how can you predict the route he will use to cross to the other side? You cannot do it. You do not know if this person is a botanist and will head off to the far corner to inspect a clump of flowers before making for the other gate. Or perhaps he is rushing home for lunch and will make a bee-line straight ahead. All you can say is that it is more likely he will do the latter than the former. You can also map out a probable line he will follow to get from gate to gate. But it's unlikely he will follow it exactly, and he may opt for a path across the park that is utterly different from the one you define.

This is how reality emerges from the random flux of energy fields deep within the heart of all matter. We can never say for sure that one quantum will behave in a specific way, but we can make a reasonable probability estimate as to what it will do. The chances are high that we will be close to correct. But the quantum could behave wildly and unexpectedly, and no exact prediction is possible.

The reason why we see not a highly unpredictable universe but a seemingly predictable one amidst this chaos is a result of the vast numbers that are involved. Yes, a single quantum might behave oddly, but most will not; and as there are trillions of such events occurring each second, the overall balance is predictable to a high degree of assurance. But that degree is never 100 per cent.

In our analogy, you could return to that field in your helicopter in a year's time. Although you would know that a few people would surely have taken the long walk from gate to gate by all sorts of rambling routes, you also know that the vast majority will not have done so. The visible effect on the grass can thus be accurately foreseen. You *can* predict that you will find a trail down the middle leading from gate to gate.

QUANTUM LEAPING

The model of atomic structure gradually defined by quantum mechanics is a strange one. But again, it has been established by experiment.

Deep within all matter there is a vast array of particles, including ones with charge (like electrons), others without (like neutrons), some that are virtually ghost-like and can pass through matter almost undetected (like neutrinos) and a host of oddities even deeper within the framework of sub-atomic structure (like quarks). Many of these are so short-lived that a thousand generations are born and die during the course of one scientist's coffee break. If such particles had conscious awareness, then time in our reality would seem to be virtually standing still. The entire lifetime of a muon is merely a fraction of a second to us. Pondering this difference between realities gives further insight into the basic futility of seeing time as a simple process.

The deeper into the atom one probes, the less particle-like do things appear and the more the wave properties come to the fore. At the heart, we may surmise, is pure timeless energy. But we cannot yet penetrate that far, and given the limitations of our material instruments maybe never will.

The constant ballet of motion that creates reality comes in the form of what are called quantum leaps. From this you might imagine one particle frog hopping about inside the atom in some easily definable manner, but again this is not what happens.

In fact, all particles are in constant flux, jumping randomly from one energy state to another. These leaps are unpredictable. They may go from higher to lower or lower to higher intensities. They do not follow any pattern. There is no sense of rhythm. In fact, here within these trillions of vibrating energy fields, where we might expect to discover the basis of time, there is instead chaotic timelessness.

ORDER OUT OF CHAOS

We can get a sense of how reality emerges by imagining thousands of black starlings high in the sky. They appear as tiny dots wheeling and moving like a living cloud. Yet each bird behaves individually, and as we watch our eyes detect patterns – probably just random clumps of birds that form a dark patch here or there. We are seeing order in chaos and imposing a pattern by way of our own conscious observation. Indeed, more than one such flock of birds has been misreported as an alien spaceship because someone's imagination has seen patterns that are not there.

This effect also happens in atoms and molecules. Prevailing forces bind them together in some loose array. In truth there are trillions of particles and vast numbers of random quantum leaps that create the occasional illusion of pattern. Several things manufacture reality out of this. Firstly, chance clumping within a vast sway of events. Also statistical probability decrees that some things are far more likely to occur than others. And – but to an unknown degree – there is an effect of our own conscious observation that allows a pattern to emerge from confusion.[14]

When a particle makes a quantum leap within the heart of an atom, it does not simply jump from one energy state to another. If a photon hits an electron, the energy release can trigger the start of a quantum leap. The electron sends out a burst of energy waves that reflect all possible leaps it might make. These 'probability waves' in essence test out the various states into which the quantum could possibly enter – like a general sending a thousand scouts in every direction to decide the best way to advance. After trying all these states simultaneously, it plumps for one and leaps. Once in this new state, it remains there until the next quantum leap is triggered, for instance by a collision with another particle, perhaps milliseconds later. In this way there is a constant hum within the atom as gigantic numbers of probability waves flash around and interact in a timeless void, and quanta leap from one state to another, and so on incessantly.

This mad world of leaping particles, ghostly sub-particles, statistical probabilities and inter-acting energy fields, all in a state of null time, is the loom from which reality is woven.

This mad world of leaping particles, ghostly sub-particles, statistical probabilities and interacting energy fields, all in a state of null time, is the loom from which reality is woven. What we experience emerges from a maelstrom of changes occurring in a constant blur that turns statistical probabilities into actual manifestation, and that we then observe and describe as reality.

As you can see, reality is not the hard-edged phenomenon we assume it to be. Indeed, it is far more like a dream than the mechanical workshop envisaged by Isaac Newton. Newton was not *wrong*. His theories still work well for the large-scale world in which matter waves and statistics are less obvious – the world that we routinely experience. It is just that quantum physics and relativity are more right, being how we define the subtle inner and very deep workings of the universe.

There are, of course, sure to be new discoveries in physics – possibly even new revolutions. But these will not disprove what we have learned about time during the past hundred years. Uneasy as the crown may fit, what we see – a timeless, shifting, ghost-filled energy wave tapestry – is at the heart of the universe.

11
Real Time

JUST HOW DOES REALITY EMERGE FROM SUB-ATOMIC TIMELESSNESS? THE problem has generated more argument than possibly any other phenomenon during recent years, and there are still huge differences of opinion. But mostly it comes down to one debate. The answer that seems true (consciousness causes reality to appear) is too much like mysticism for most scientists, who desire all things to be more amenable to experimental proof. So they desperately seek another way that makes more sense. Unfortunately, it also has to explain what we experience.

THE COPENHAGEN INTERPRETATION

The 'Copenhagen Interpretation' of quantum mechanics was one of the first attempts to define how reality 'condensed' from a sea of statistical wave forms. A group of physicists – some from this Danish city – met, actually in Brussels, and struggled to find an answer. Their conclusion, in effect, was that they did not really know why quantum theory worked, but it did – so let's get on with it.

The spectre of the observer being the architect of reality appears in most arguments. Heisenberg noted that the probability wave patterns he defined must surround everything. The waves do grow less strong with distance, but like all energy fields never die away completely (the gravity from a far distant sun, for instance, has an infinitesimal but still real effect upon us). This suggests something awesome. Everything in the universe can be said to interact with everything else – and whilst bigger and closer bodies affect each other far more, tiny and distant bodies are still part of the complete equation.

Few scientists like this sort of supernatural imagery, although it still appears today in different forms, such as in the Gaia theory. This is popular with New Age logic and argues that the earth (and even the universe) is some sort of collective entity where no part can act without having some consequence on the rest. Often misconstrued as meaning that the earth is 'a living thing', what it really says is that the earth is an interacting system, which according to quantum physics is in some sense true.

Physics rails against the idea that reality does not come into being unless we let it. Even so, when the Danish physicist Niels Bohr first studied the levels from which quantum leaps occur, he concluded that '[no] elementary phenomenon is a phenomenon until it is a registered phenomenon.' This means virtually the same as the old Eastern proverb questioning the nature of reality, which asks 'When a tree falls in a forest and nobody is around, does it make a sound?' New physics says the tree is silent unless somebody hears it!

Bohr is far from alone. Many physicists have decided that the Copenhagen dismissal of things as a 'statistical picture' did not go far enough. Massachusetts Institute of Technology physicist, Eugene Wigner, was even willing to argue that 'consciousness collapses the wave function' – what we see is what *becomes* real.

THE ROLE OF CONSCIOUSNESS

Physicist David Bohm noted that in quantum physics probability waves try out all possible realities, then opt for one state to make the appropriate leap. Much the same thing, he said, seems to happen with evolution.[1]

Life progresses by way of mutation, which consists of a wide range of variations on the initial genetic combination. Many mutations are not successful. Occasionally one occurs that conveys real advantage (such as a bigger muscle ratio, longer plant stems or great visual acuity). This chance mutation has a higher statistical chance of survival and so may occur again, eventually nudging the life form down that particular path. Progress and change seem to happen in a co-ordinated manner to a grand plan, but are really the outcome of various options being tried out and either kept or discarded.

From a completely different perspective, this may be true with human consciousness. Studies of both dreams and fantasies have revealed to psychologists a probable purpose for both. These inner visions test out new situations in which we might one day find ourselves. In effect, they rehearse the possible consequences for our mind. So we set ourselves up in a position of winning the lottery, being shipwrecked on a remote island or any number of other scenarios both likely and unlikely. The mind tries these out and gauges our response.[2]

Parallels appear with quantum leaping. Possibly this is a mechanism that the universe has found to operate successfully, and so it is applied in all sorts of unexpected places.

It may also be another reason to take seriously the idea that consciousness is the means by which probability is transformed into actuality. If indeed the same basic rules apply to both sub-atomic particles and the human mind, these two seemingly unrelated phenomena could be intimately connected through their modus operandi.

SCHRÖDINGER'S CAT

Physicist Stephen Hawking has said that when Schrödinger's cat gets a mention he feels like reaching for a gun. Einstein, too, was horrified by the thought experiment that this quantum physicist once dreamed up. It is likely, however, that Schrödinger actually meant the experiment to appear so absurd that it disproved the very concept that it may actually prove!

In simple (and updated) terms, a cat is placed inside a box next to a phial of deadly nerve gas. An electronic trigger is tied to the outcome of a single quantum leap within an atom. If the (unpredictable) leap occurs one way, the trigger releases the gas and the cat immediately dies. If it occurs the other way, the phial remains sealed and the fortunate puss survives.

All this seems simple enough. We might assume there is a calculable chance (50/50) that in any given time the appropriate jump will occur, or not occur, and the cat will live, or die. All you need do is open up the box and discover the fate of this poor test subject (hence this being a *thought* experiment!).

The problem comes when you match that perfectly reasonable assumption with the truth as dictated by quantum theory. For the wave function that determines which particular leap occurs only collapses when something *causes* it to do so. If you sit there with no information about what goes on inside the box, the laws of physics seem to imply something crazy: the cat is both alive and dead, because both options result from the probablity waves in motion. These do not crystallise into an actual event until an observer measures the result. Open the door and the cat *will* be alive or dead, depending upon the quantum leap that has occurred. But the life or death of the animal will be very much a consequence of your opening the door (or switching on a video camera to take a look inside – indeed, any act of measurement). Ludicrous as it seems, something has to collapse the wave function and – in the absence of any better option – that something appears to be the person who makes the observation.

The difficulty, of course, is this: how can we envisage a cat being both dead and alive as it awaits an outside observer making a move to determine its fate? Worse still, imagine that the trigger is electronically linked to a second phial of nerve gas inside the room where the experimenter sits pondering the moment to check on the cat. If the experiment produces the result in which the gas in the box is released and the cat dies, it simultaneously releases the gas into the room where the experimenter too instantly dies.

Now we have a real problem. Must we envisage the experimenter being both alive and dead in some limbo waiting to make an observation on the state of the cat? And if he opens the door and the cat is dead, would not the experimenter already be dead because the second gas phial was broken when the cat's fate was sealed? But if the experimenter was dead because the cat was already dead, then who opens the door to collapse the probability wave and kill them both? Or are we to assume that at the moment the scientist opens the door the wave function collapses? If so, does he at that instant kill the cat, does the cat kill him, or are they locked in some bizarre quantum suicide pact?

Some scientists feel there just has to be a flaw in this argument somewhere, because the deeper you get embroiled in thinking it through, the more ludicrous the whole thing becomes. They suggest that we are overlooking what Bohm calls a 'hidden variable'. Something else, as yet unknown, actualises reality from these statistical probabilities, but common sense decrees that it is not consciousness. However, so far no credible alternative has been successfully demonstrated.

CATACLYSMS

As you can imagine, Einstein was utterly unimpressed. He said, with an obvious dig: 'I cannot imagine that a mouse could drastically change the universe by merely looking at it.' But it took until 1957 for someone to come up with a way that might allow consciousness to collapse the wave function without provoking the sort of insanity otherwise inferred.

Physicist Hugh Everett suggested that rather than the poor cat (or scientist) existing in limbo until someone observes the outcome of any quantum leap and brings a specific reality into being, *all* possible options occur simultaneously. In effect, this quantum event creates two separate realities (one with a live cat, one in which it is dead). All that an observer's consciousness does is to experience one or the other.

In this version, the scientist does not kill or rescue the cat. Two realities are formed, and the observer merely experiences one of these without making any difference to the state of the cat.

But if you develop this argument further its neat solution becomes strained. For a start, billions of probability waves will be involved in even the smallest situation. Are we to imagine that the universe is literally splitting into unthinkably large numbers of parallel realities every single moment? If so, by now, given the long history of the universe, the number of realities out there would be staggering – although such a concept is perhaps no harder to accept than a universe that may otherwise be infinite.

Another worrying consequence, if Everett is right, is that literally any possibility must occur somewhere. If a person dies at midnight tonight, there will be universes in which circumstances conspire so that this person does not die. Indeed, universes must exist in which the secret of eternal life is discovered and so that person never dies. By that definition, every person that ever lived must still live on in versions of the universe. Moreover, none of us will ever die, since some realities must involve our eternal existence.

Whilst on the one hand you might perceive this as exciting news – almost mathematical proof of life after death – it also has a suspicious feel of being just as absurd as Schrödinger's cat. If so, it seems likely to be wrong. It is, after all, merely a theory.

Opinion on this radical concept is divided. Some physicists, like Stephen Hawking, have liked its essence because it seems to remove consciousness from the 'creation of reality' and sees the universe boil down to statistics and mathematics (no doubt a physicist's view of heaven). Others, such as Paul Davies, have commented wryly that it is 'cheap on assumptions, expensive on universes'.

In 1974 Evan Walker devised a moderation in which the various universes set in train were not real, but virtual, and consciousness was constantly creating an individual 'true' reality by cutting a path through a chain of potential wave functions. But how do we define what is real and what is virtual?

A QUANTUM MIRAGE

There is evidence for virtual worlds, and it emerged in February 2000 from physicist Don Eigler and his team at the IBM lab in San José, California. Using a special instrument called an STM (scanning tunnelling microscope), it is possible to draw a contour map of objects as small as single atoms. This work uses an incredibly fine needle (one atom thick at the tip) and applies a voltage to it. When the STM is held near a conducting object, such as metal, electrons flow across the gap and the readings create a map.

This device was used in San José in 1990 in an amusing experiment aimed at physically moving just thirty-five atoms to spell out the letters IBM on a thin surface of nickel. But the practical advantages, for which the team was then and is still searching, are immense. They include building incredibly small machines out of atoms (called nano-technology) which may allow massive computing power to be packed into tiny spaces.

In the course of this STM work there was an unexpected event: what they call a 'quantum mirage' was produced. In effect, their scanning and manipulation of atom-sized objects produced a ghostly reflection of the energy fields that are electrons in one single atom. This mirage was projected into a different location where the real atom never was. The real atom was visible as expected, but its mirage (a third less intense) was in a statistically predictable point nearby as a phantom reflection.

The scientists found that this was not a mathematical abstract. The ghost atom was in many ways really there. The best analogy offered is of the image of the sun created when you project it through a pinhole on to a card. This image is an accurate representation of the sun formed by actual photons from that planet. It even has physically real properties (for instance, its heat can cause a fire). Viewing the reflection will allow you to observe changes on the sun itself, such as watching sun spots cross the surface.

Quantum physicists are now debating how to allow the 'quantum mirage' of an atom to interact with a real atom which they can introduce. The signs are that the mirage is real enough to let that happen. The result would be a molecule not connected in any physical way but bonded in a unique fashion that is 'half real and half ghost', as physicist Hari Manoharan calls it.[3]

Such cutting-edge research shows that by talking about multiple realities and virtual worlds we are not debating abstract things. These seemingly bizarre states are in many senses actually out there.

Think of the universe as like a vast ocean with trillions of waves – the interacting probabilities of sub-atomic reality. Every person with consciousness is like a vessel sailing this ocean. As our mind cuts across a wave, it causes this virtual reality to collapse into an actual reality, leaving many other unrealised waves all around. The sequence of collapsing waves caused by sailing through this virtual ocean manifests to that person as reality (perhaps begging the question: do we each create our own, perhaps utterly different, version of the universe?). The apparent sequence created by this motion might be perceived by us as the 'flow' of time. Does this explain why we experience a linear existence from past to future when the 'true' reality (that vast ocean of probability waves all around us) has no fundamental time at all?

PARADOXICAL PROOF

Sure that 'God does not play dice' and that consciousness cannot collapse the wave function, Einstein got together with two other physicists and created a devastating new thought experiment that he believed would prove this impossible. The so-called Einstein–Podolsky–Rosen (EPR) paradox seemed to show that tenets held dear by physics, such as the unreachable limit of the speed of light, would have to be violated if this experiment worked. Since these had been proven inviolate, the experiment could not work. But if the experiment did not work, something was wrong with quantum theory because it suggested that it should work.

The EPR paradox was set out in 1935 and involved taking two linked sub-atomic particles and sending them off in opposite directions. According to theory, if you changed a property of one, the other particle would change in compensation. The change would not be subjected to the speed of light but would happen immediately. This image of two particles communicating so fast that they broke unalterable laws of the cosmos seemed impossible. So something had to be wrong with our understanding of quantum physics.

Imagine two twins born on 1 January 2000 in London. They are separated at birth and are raised in different environments. On 1 January 2021 twin A celebrates a birthday in a London slum, whilst twin B comes of age in a luxury waterfront apartment in Sydney. Now consider pushing twin A off a wall and breaking his leg (merely as a thought experiment!). What happens to twin B at that same moment?

Logic (and Einstein) say nothing does. Whilst genetic factors could predispose both twins to develop similar diseases, for instance, nobody can be genetically conditioned to get pushed off a wall. So if twin A suffers this fate, it is absurd to think the same thing will happen in Sydney.

Similarly, with the EPR experiment, if one particle develops a wobble you might think the twin particle could do so too because they were both 'programmed' to have a wobble. But if you do something to one particle to change its properties, the now distant twin particle surely cannot be affected.

TWINCHRONICITIES

In fact, there are some real-life cases that are oddly relevant here. Known as 'twinchronicities' (a blend of 'twin' and 'synchroricity' – see Chapter 12), they may be a consequence of some as yet unrecognised 'hidden variable' within reality. For instance, in April 1997 AA patrolman John Spur went to the aid of Mark Fagence, who was stranded at the Keele service station on the M6 motorway in Staffordshire. Shortly after getting him to his home seventy miles away in Warwickshire, Spur was stunned to see the same man flag him down. In fact, it was not the same man but Mark's identical twin Guy, whose car had also broken down that day.[4]

It is tempting to see strange forces at work here, but the odds of such an event happening sooner or later are not great. We never hear of the many cases where twins don't have breakdowns on the same day – only of the occasional fluke, which as a consequence seems to take on a much greater significance than it deserves.

However, there are cases more like the EPR paradox. For example, on 22 June 1997 a Welsh holidaymaker named Gareth Griffiths was undertaking a parachute jump over Florida with his instructor, Michael Costello. There was a problem with the linked chutes and the men plummeted to earth from five thousand feet, but Costello managed to position himself to take the brunt of the impact during the free fall. The heroic instructor died as he crashed into an orange grove, but his companion survived. Gareth's twin David was five thousand miles away in Wales. But at the exact moment when Gareth was plunging towards what he thought was certain death, David woke in bed with a start, looked up and felt a strong sensation that left him positive that his brother was in terrible trouble.[5]

Such incidents happen sufficiently often to suggest that coincidence is no answer. In another case, reported from Scotland in 1963, one twin was studied in hospital for problems centring on a 'bug' she claimed must be burrowing inside her left ear. A psychiatric diagnosis was reached because no medical cause for her pain could be detected. At the same time, her twin brother was in that hospital having tests on the same ear – his problem turned out to be a fatal brain tumour. The two twins had been separated for years and had no idea both were living in the Dundee area, let alone that they had gone to the same hospital with identical symptoms. But a bug burrowing into one's ear is not a bad symbol for a tumour.[6]

EXPERIMENTAL PROOF

Physicists, of course, tend not to read – or certainly to take seriously – allegedly paranormal happenings like these, even though some, like those cited, are well documented. So to many physicists the EPR paradox offers all the guidance needed to know that communication across distance beyond the speed of light is just not possible.

In 1964, as practical science began to catch up on theory, a way was suggested to perform the EPR experiment using a particle accelerator and by changing the spin of one particle. In this way it would be possible to see what happened to the particle's 'twin' that had gone off on its own after both had been formed in a collision. Einstein had gone to his grave nine years earlier, certain that his paradox would one day be vindicated in the laboratory. Now it was crunch time. The experiment was eventually conducted in 1974 by two physicists in California, and the result was exactly in accordance with quantum mechanics. Change the spin of particle A and the spin of particle B changed to match. They did behave as if 'telepathically' linked across vast distances. Einstein was wrong.

In 1983 Alain Aspect at the University of Paris took the experiment even further. More sophisticated equipment now made it possible to prove not only that the two particles appeared to be linked in some unexplained way, but that if a message was being sent it was travelling beyond the speed of light. It was as if they were literally one particle, however physically far apart they were.

Indeed, physicist John Bell has argued from this data a widely praised mathematical proof that has shaken science once again. It suggests that since quantum physics is now undeniably true, either the speed of light is not constant (as all evidence says it is) or the principle of 'local causes' must be wrong. This is an equally cherished concept and argues that only interactive systems within local space can be closely connected. In truth this boils down to two equally frightening conclusions – the apparent reality of either faster-than-light travel or telepathic-style contact between particles across vast distances.

A series of further experiments has not made things any more comfortable. In one test at Rochester University in New York, two sub-atomic events occurring in the same place but at different times were also found to be 'magically' linked, just as had been two events in different places at the same time.

So when we talk about the basis of sub-atomic reality involving events that are both timeless and spaceless, evidence is mounting from hard experiment – not just theory – that this is literally true.

MIND CONTROL

The dreaded realisation that consciousness may indeed collapse the wave function and somehow create reality was further enhanced by an experiment in 1989 at Boulder, Colorado. Here the 'observer effect' was actually tested by sealing highly charged particles inside a magnetic bottle that prevented their escape. Their responses could then be observed by firing a laser through this EM field and viewing the result.

What happened was again exactly what quantum mechanics says should happen. The degree to which the particles made quantum leaps depended upon the extent to which someone used a laser to observe them making these changes. Seeing *did* alter the experiment and changed reality. How or why is far from clear, but that it happened was undeniable.

What this experiment also vindicated was that subjective time (see p. 98) might have a true basis. As we grow older, time seems to fly past more quickly. The old expression 'A watched kettle never boils' refers to the way events subjectively happen more rapidly if you don't pay attention to them. We have assumed this to be a psychological phenomenon – that time moves more swiftly if you have distractions than if you focus your mind on just one thing. But quantum physics seems to have discovered that there is a literal truth here too.

The passage of time, as measured by the number of quantum leaps taking place in the Boulder experiment, did indeed move more rapidly if you did not observe what was going on. And the more that you decided to watch (the greater the number of observations of the experiment that you made), the slower the passage of time that unfolded – if you measure this effect by way of the quantum leaps.

So we seem to have uncovered not only a world in which events are linked by unknown forces across a timeless, spaceless universe, or one in which consciousness somehow makes reality emerge from within a sea of interacting probabilities, but also a universe in which the rate of flow of time can be made to change simply through our conscious acts. We can make time slow down and speed up!

SHIFTING REALITIES

We have reached a view of time by way of modern science that should have left you bemused. It also baffles most scientists. Of course, it is possible that we are missing something fundamental, that one day a new Einstein will define the key that will make sense out of all of this. What such a theory will not do is to change the nature of the experimental evidence. It might help us to understand it better, but it will not prove our basic ideas wrong. Yet science continues to seek ways in which we can comprehend these surreal phenomena, because they defy much of the world as we are used to seeing it.

Recent attempts by physicists include that of Jack Sarfatti, who has tried to define how faster-than-light communication between particles (or radiating waveforms) might even allow some sort of sub-space information transfer across time.[7] David Bohm sees a 'wholeness' to the universe (an 'enfolded order', as he calls it) that must exist at the deepest level of reality. In this new realm, our concept of local space and of separated events will prove to be misperceptions of parts of one connected system.[8] And then there is John Wheeler, who has extended the concept of the many worlds interpretation for quantum events into a vision of multiple universes. This overcomes the problem of how one particle 'knows' when another particle changes its spin during EPR experiments by arguing that – since *all* the possibilities really occur – there is no direct causal link behind the apparent changes that we see.[9]

Hard evidence has laid the ghost of Einstein's protestations, and multiple realities are gaining a new foothold. Some now see this concept as perhaps the best way to define what may be going on. Of course, it also casts up eerie images, such as that of our consciousness shifting universes from time to time as we saw with 'reality blinks' (see p. 84).

This is just one area where science can benefit by input from unusual phenomena. During the past century, science has been dragged kicking and screaming into wild places. At the same time it has largely fled from the horrors of the paranormal. But we need not share the scientists' reticence in considering such alleged happenings like those odd events in the Himalayan foothills described in the Introduction. As you may now appreciate, seemingly amazing and illogical phenomena are less absurd when seen in the context of the new physics and its experimental evidence. This is the journey we shall now take to investigate a range of anomalous events concerning time and discover how scientific theory may help understand them. I ask you only to bear two things in mind.

Firstly, I cannot prove to you that all of these events *really* happened. It is my opinion that most of them did in some sense or another. Whilst the word 'alleged' should properly be applied as a caveat to them all, it should not be used as an excuse for dismissing them. My twenty-five years' experience in this field tells me that strange phenomena like these do occur, and with a consistency that demands resolution. My first-hand research into many of these cases tells me they need to be taken seriously.

Secondly, whatever problems of strangeness or credibility some of these reports may cause, they are no more incredible than what physics accepts about the nature of time or reality. It is my opinion that these cases offer vital missing clues that most physicists do not realise are out there. They form the unseen hard evidence from real-world experience that we can marry with theoretical physics and use to gain deeper insights into the meaning of time. Even if that prospect proves over-optimistic, or we pay too much attention to the occasional tale which deserves a simpler explanation (an inevitable risk when sailing uncharted waters), the price is still worth paying. Some of these events are genuine anomalies and pose serious questions about the nature of time and space. And the need to understand these things is the domain of scientists because they have the knowledge to provide the answers.

But as scientists, in the main, decline to come to view this mountain, then I am bringing the mountain to them instead.

12
Synchronicity

COINCIDENCES HAPPEN. EVERYONE KNOWS THAT. BUT WHAT DOES THIS statement really mean?

In the autumn of 1999, my mother, who did the Lottery with the same numbers every week and had done so for four years, was getting frustrated at never winning anything. Then, when we were in a shop paying a weekly bill, the assistant smiled and said, 'That will be £7.77 – must be your lucky number.' We gave it no more than a passing thought, but when we returned to the car we discovered that parked in the disabled bay beside us was a vehicle with a licence plate that included the numbers 777. Mildly intrigued, we were about to drive away when I noticed the mileage indicator on our own vehicle. The final three numbers read 777.

My mother took little further persuasion to play the number seven in all Lottery options that weekend. Seven came up twice, allowing her to win a modest sum. I did work out the mathematics here. There are not huge statistics involved (odds of several hundred to one). But were they meaningful statistics?

Many people play the Lottery and win because they match the random numbers despite odds of millions to one. So an individual win is not significant, and the same rules apply as are in force inside the atom. When you have so many quantum leaps taking place, any one is sure to happen sooner or later, somewhere or other. You only notice it if it proves important to you.

Yet here, what effect is had on this equation by the appearance of the number 7? It cropped up in three differing circumstances within minutes and was unquestionably what made my mother select the winning combination that week. So does it turn a coincidence into something more?

This is a much harder question to define and it brings to light a phenomenon above and beyond coincidence, known as 'synchronicity', that literally means events that occur together in time. Another common term for it is 'meaningful coincidence'.

A CONNECTING PRINCIPLE

At the very least, the addition of these other factors that motivated the choice of correct Lottery numbers compound the statistics enough to make this coincidence greater than it might otherwise have been. But in truth the difference between coincidence and synchronicity can be simply stated. A coincidence is a random set of chance events that may seem strange but in mathematical terms is a fluke. A synchronicity is a random set of chance events that cross the artificial horizon – what we might call the 'boggle threshold' – and imply that hidden rules may be at work to engineer such a grouping.

Although this whole idea sounds like mysticism, it is physics. Remember that all reality is a maelstrom of energy fields that transform into the real world via human consciousness; and that within these energy fields and quantum states are statistical events that happen one way, not another, and so define the universe that we perceive. It is therefore not particularly absurd to suspect that meaningful coincidence is more than chance. It could be visible surf on the ocean of probability.

Perhaps it is a consequence of how the chaos of the sub-atomic universe (particles, wave forms and energy fields) becomes the apparently ordered world of people, cars and Lottery tickets. Synchronicity could be a means of discovering clues about the 'phase difference' between the way physical reality emerges from mere probability and mathematics. Indeed, meaningful coincidence could be tangible evidence for that threshold between the very small and the very large. It could even hold the house keys to reality.

Fifty years ago the idea of synchronicity as a connecting principle between two realities was defined by a unique joint research effort. This involved the noted Swiss psychologist Carl Jung, who had defined the mind's collective unconscious, and Wolfgang Pauli, a Nobel prize-winning quantum physicist. They brought together their individual insights from seemingly opposite directions and saw precisely how the interaction of these apparently separate occurrences may well generate what we regard as a coincidence.[1]

THE TRANSPSYCHIC REALM

The collaboration of these men took the form of two long essays, eventually published as a book, that approached the question of how reality comes into being.

Jung believed that at a deep level all conscious entities were linked by archetypal images, which he called the collective unconscious. Indeed, for him this was the basis of mythology and inspired the real world that we experience. His ideas (in a traditional sense) are still widely accepted, but most psychologists prefer to forget his forays into 'non-science'. Yet Jung regarded these as essential to his argument. He believed that the collective unconscious explained ESP, the alleged ability to detect information in the mind by way of extra-sensory perception (to Jung it was mental resonance at this level) and precognition, the claimed capacity to see images of events in the mind before they occur (brought about because time and space disappear in this hidden realm). Indeed, one of his last works was a still useful book about the then new fad of UFOs, in which he discussed how collective symbols in the human psyche figured strongly in the data.[2]

Pauli felt that the mind was somehow responsible for 'collapsing the wave function' and creating the physical reality that we see. He went further and considered that our mind at this deep level had actual responsibility for the creation of physical laws. In a very real sense the universe that we lived in was of the form that it takes because we *made* it that way through our subconscious manipulation of quantum reality.

These two ideas naturally came together to define a realm, which Jung termed the 'transpsychic', where this maternity wing of the cosmos is based. It was from here, both argued, that so-called psychic events emerge. It was in here that synchronicity made the ground rules, just like relativity or quantum mechanics do in other areas. Synchronicity was, in effect, the law that governed how reality came about.

Jung termed it an 'acausal connecting principle', to infer that it linked occurrences into apparent coincidences without the direct space–time restraints we expect. Such limitations do not apply where sub-atomic physics and mind converge.

THE EMOTIVE KEY

Another important discovery that these two great scientists offered is one that was to take forty years to be proven by experiment. It concerned the importance of emotion.

Jung and Pauli believed that emotion oiled the wheels of synchronicity. In the transpsychic realm, an emotive event was much more likely to provoke a synchronous reality (that is, a corresponding real event). Stories about meaningful coincidences would suggest that this is true because they frequently involve deeply emotional matters. The mother–child bond, a loved one, death, victory, success, depression – all seem to be somehow involved in the events that generate synchronicity.

However, apparently trivial things, too, can form the basis of a coincidence – such as a car number plate or the figures on a shopping bill. But apparent triviality can sometimes be an illusion. What seems insignificant may lead to an emotionally important state of mind, such as the one we may have when winning the Lottery. So what seems emotionless may not be so within the transpsychic realm.

Jung also found that the event manipulated was often your own future emotional state. In other words, in a premonition or through a synchronicity you did not actually *see* the future or *create* an event. Instead, you almost communed across time with your own mental reaction brought about by the event when it happened. Often that state of mind would be linked with a real-world incident, of course, so it might incorrectly seem that you are triggering an actual event when you were in fact reading your own mind.

Research into ESP and precognition supports this idea, and it may mean that a coincidence can act as a bridge between your present and future states of mind. In our time-rooted concept of reality, where past turns into future by a steady progression, this seems impossible. However, in the transpsychic realm, Jung felt there is no fundamental time for it to be considered 'out of'.

It is now widely accepted by psychic researchers that within reported phenomena such as ESP, precognition and even UFO close encounters there is a 'prone' personality. Studies of witnesses using standard psychology tests have revealed that such people tend to be of above average intelligence, visually creative, with an unusual level of memory retention, the ability to shuffle images in the mind and with a high degree of emotive response.[3]

This matches the predictions of Jung and Pauli for the kind of people best able to access the transpsychic. Yet this image of a 'prone personality' that has a regular sequence of strange experiences is not theory but has been derived by empirical research. It is an image that often goes against the desires of some paranormal theorists who are more keen to prove that aliens are really out there, not that there is a special kind of person who might see them as a recurrent phenomenon of *inner* space.

HOMING OBJECTS

One of the areas that first generated interest in synchronicity is homing objects. It was in the 1920s that the American journalist Charles Fort collected such odd stories, like the one about the wedding ring lost in the sea that turned up years later when the couple in question ordered a meal at a restaurant and found the ring inside a fish that must have once swallowed it.[4]

Here, it was as if some manipulation of reality arranged for the couple to be in the right place at the right time and order the only fish that would reunite them with their ring. Indeed, events like this have happened often enough for it to be regarded as a phenomenon in need of a solution rather than an isolated story for which a silly theory has been invented.

Wilhelm von Scholz collected similar examples at about the same time and cited to Jung one case in which a woman lost a roll of film containing emotionally significant photographs and then two years later, in a city miles away, bought a new (and therefore undeveloped) film. When it was processed, by some fluke it was found to be superimposed on her long-lost missing photographs – presumably because the two had been mixed up in a laboratory 'accident'. Here the argument would be that this was no accident. Events were arranged to ensure that the owner was reunited with her pictures.

In 1997 a baby falcon escaped from a conservation sanctuary in Kent when the owner, Eddie Hare, tripped and she flew loose. All seemed lost when the bird did not return. But three weeks later she was found in a hedge near Great Harwood in Lancashire, over three hundred miles away. The man who found her, Peter Wall, called Hare on the number he found on the bird's leg ring. Amazingly, Wall had just arranged to visit the stately home in Kent where the bird was housed, despite having no connection with the place or with Eddie, and so he was able to take the bird with him and return it to its owner. Here you can get a sense of the emotional and motivational factors that may organise reality so that the right people are in the right places at the right times to bring about a synchronicity.[5]

TAXI SYNCHRONICITY

I believe synchronicities happen to everybody – perhaps often. We just tend not to pay much attention to their workings, even if they subtly direct our lives. I have collected them for many years, and encourage you to do the same if you dispute the findings of this chapter.

Edinburgh (UK)

Here is a strange story told me by the Jenkins family from Leicestershire, who during the 1980s went to Edinburgh to visit their daughter who had moved up there. On the spur of the moment, Mr Jenkins decided to try to find an old friend from his RAF days called McKirdy. They had known each other in the town of Wadinatrun in Egypt, but had lost contact since the end of World War II. All he knew was that McKirdy had lived in Edinburgh many years before, but whether he still lived there forty years later – or was even still alive – he had no idea.

> *I believe synchronicities happen to everybody – perhaps often. We just tend not to pay much attention to their workings, even if they subtly direct our lives.*

There was one person named McKirdy with the correct initial in the phone book, but just as he was about to dial, Mr Jenkins chickened out from calling what might be a total stranger. Instead, the family decided to go on a scheduled coach trip to see the sights. However, they then discovered that the trip had been cancelled because there had been too few bookings that day.

The family searched for a phone box from which to call their daughter, and having found one by a taxi rank, Mrs Jenkins dialled whilst her husband wandered about 'aimlessly' on the pavement. Then a taxi arrived to discharge a fare – so close that Mr Jenkins could read the name on the driver's licence displayed on the side of the cab. It was his long-lost friend. ○

Although on the face of it this is a random set of events, it is worth considering how many choices made by the family (especially Mr Jenkins) brought it about. Had they chosen to do anything else but visit the bus station that day, they would not have met McKirdy. Had they booked any of the trips that were not cancelled they would, of course, have not been there either. Had they not chanced to find a phone by the taxi rank rather than one of several others nearby, they would not have met Mr McKirdy. Had Mr Jenkins, instead of his wife, made the call to his daughter, his chance meeting would not have occurred either. Had he not walked in exactly the right 'aimless' path to place him close to the taxi at the moment it drew up, again none of this would have happened.

Here you get a real sense of many random events – those junctions between realities created at each decision point within Wheeler's vision of parallel universes. These junction points must all be 'tripped' the right way in order for a synchronicity to happen. It is easy to envisage some part of Mr Jenkins' subconscious being aware of the bigger picture and at this timeless level creating a domino effect within quantum reality to engineer this chain of events.

I suspect that these sorts of events could be extremely common, but that 99 per cent of them go unrecognised by the people to whom they occur.

COSMIC JOKER IN THE PACK

If indeed we manipulate (or at least guide along) reality at some timeless level then it will work, as Jung suggests, rather as does the creation of our dreams and fantasies. This is not through the same sort of logical thinking that we use normally. Studies of dream states show that our unconscious mind frequently uses symbols and even puns to convey an effective message. Psychologist Ann Faraday has noted many of these in her surveys of collected dreams, and one of these from a dream of my own (decoded by a psychology test with a psychiatrist afterwards) illustrates the point.

I dreamed of escaping a flood on a grand piano. The psychiatrist revealed that this was a symbolic pun, based on simple word association, that my mind had conjured up whilst dreaming. 'You needed a ship to escape on,' he told me. 'The first shipping line your mind thought of was P & O, and your dream set this into wonderful imagery by creating a "piano" for you to sail on.'

This leads to the prospect of the so-called cosmic joker that may engineer reality through quirky events that are brought into being. Fort supported this idea, although he had no concept of quantum physics that would give it any objective basis. Amazingly, today we can see that the cosmic joker would probably be a predictable consequence of merging synchronicity with psychology.

Merseyside (UK), 1982

A case we can see this effect at work was reported to me by Merseyside man Bill Williams. In 1982 he was in desperate need of a particular kind of hammer for an urgent household chore. Search as he might, no local store had one. Feeling annoyed and fed up, on the way home he wandered into a back alley and got lost. Then there was a crash. Looking around, he saw that a hammer of the exact type he needed had literally fallen out of the sky. He looked up at a row of windows from where it seems certain the tool must have fallen. There was nobody in sight, possibly because whoever dropped it had realised that they had nearly hit a passer-by and so had rapidly vacated the scene. Bill picked up the hammer and said a silent thank you. ○

> **Then there was a crash. Looking around, he saw that a hammer of the exact type he needed had literally fallen out of the sky.**

Aside from the humorous idea of a cosmic force sending a hammer falling from the sky, we can see again how a seemingly fantastic chance event may involve simple motivational choices. Here they could cause Bill to wander into the right spot, causing a person with a hammer to appear at a window and fumble at just the right moment. When we perceive this coincidence as a set of splitting reality choices that engineer one version of reality, it is less bizarre than it may at first appear.

My own version of the cosmic joker experience happened in north-west England, where I then lived. That day I was working on an election night special of the weekly programme to which I contributed for independent radio in Liverpool. As part of my regular investigations into strange phenomena, I had already just discussed the idea of objects that fall out of the sky (not hammers, but showers of frogs, fishes and seeds). Science speculates that whirlwinds can suck these up in one place and deposit them miles away. They are an amusing scientific mystery that has been widely recorded.[6]

Two days after my falling objects segment was transmitted, I was back at the studio to make the election special, concerning odd things that had befallen hapless politicians. I went upstairs to check out my mail and found one letter from a listener. He had posted it to me two days before, and asked me in passing to tell Phil Easton, one of the DJs, that 'Skidrack' had written and was now on the 'Kipper Express'. I had not got a clue what he was talking about.

As I always did my weekly show in the morning and Phil Easton worked later in the day, I rarely saw him. That Thursday he was presenting the midnight election results special, so there was no real chance of my encountering him mid-morning. But just as I was getting ready to leave, in he walked, having come in on impulse as he passed nearby. I told him about the letter and he translated. 'Skidrack' was one of his fans, a motorcycle enthusiast, and that week he had gone on the 'Kipper Express' – the Liverpool to Isle of Man ferry – to watch the hugely popular TT races.

Only then did all of this fall eerily into place. On Tuesday, I had presented my programme on fish falling from the sky. Because my boyfriend, too, was a motorcycle fan he had gone to the Isle of Man to watch the races. On my own for a while, I had gone out to the cinema and emerged to find a thunderstorm closing in. I decided to run for the bus rather than walk home but stepped on something slimy, unseen in the gloom, and skidded several feet before crashing to the ground. Fortunately, only my pride was hurt – I noticed that the cause of my downfall had been a single kipper discarded on the pavement. Perhaps a bird had dropped it, I concluded, or a van delivering to some shops.

Thirty-six hours later I read the letter that had already been posted to me when I had this minor accident. It linked the Isle of Man races (the reason for my being out that night) with both skidding and kippers (the twin and very unusual sources of my accident). I had in my own way ridden the 'Kipper Express', and somehow realities had collided in this bizarre and coincidental fashion.

No doubt the cosmic joker found it all most amusing.

USING SYNCHRONICITY

It is fairly clear that if I had not been 'on alert' for synchronicity, I would probably not have paid any attention to incidents like the one just described. But I find that the more you look, the more you find synchronicities unfolding around you. I am sure this is true for everyone. However, I realise that if these synchronicities are occurring constantly and they reflect the undercurrent in which consciousness might shape reality into patterns, perhaps we should pay closer attention to them.

Once, for example, I heard rumours that Brian Ford, the DJ with whom I worked each week, might be leaving the station. I knew his departure would probably deal a fatal blow to my own radio slot. So I spoke to our producer, Wally Scott, who said it was not true so far as he knew.

In fact, Brian did soon leave for a new job, and as a consequence my radio slots came to an end. Despite Wally's (then honest) statement that Brian was not leaving, reality may have tried to give me a gentle kick and get me prepared. As I left the studio after my conversation with Wally, I walked straight into a newspaper placard in the street – no doubt because I was not looking where I was going! The placard was telling a story about a local car factory dispute, but the headline read, with delightful irony, 'Ford's boss denies rumours'.

Quite the most amazing example of synchronicity I have experienced involves synchronicity itself. It again ties in with my work at Radio City in Liverpool, and I think there is a reason for his. Researchers studying precognition have discovered that when you get involved with exciting events they tend to stimulate an increase in strange phenomena, possibly because new experiences entering your senses activate many neurone pathways in the brain and these require a larger number of probability links to be tested out. This plethora of quantum activity could make synchronicity statistically more likely. The period I spent working for this radio station was exciting for a young writer and my neurones were no doubt on fire.

The incident in question occurred in May 1983, when I chose to announce on my show that 'Next week I will look at synchronicity.' My producer Wally Scott was concerned about my use of this odd word, which he had never heard, and asked if I could refer to it as something else. He said that the station's audience was mostly 'teenage, record-buying people' who would 'not know a word like synchronicity'. We debated this for some time, but I promised to explain all in my tease – a short promotion for next week's show that would be used as an advert during the coming week's transmissions.

As I planned this tease, life at home suddenly got very dramatic. A major robbery occurred nearby and the thieves chose to dump their getaway car right outside my front door. This was a mistake, because directly opposite lived a detective. So after getting home I spent some time helping the police with their enquiries about when I first noticed the car, and so forth.

My tease on synchronicity written, I was about to leave home and take the bus into Liverpool to record the item when the phone rang. The caller had first rung the radio astronomy science centre at Jodrell Bank, and, as they often did, they had passed her on to me. The story concerned what they termed a 'star falling from the sky' which had been seen in the early hours of the previous night.

Notes taken on the case, I left for the studios. When I arrived, I learned that two youths had died the previous night in an unexplained tragedy. They had hastily discarded their bikes, fled on to a railway track and been struck by a freight train.

As I scoured the news wire reports in the studio, my suspicions grew. The 'star fall' just reported to me had occurred in exactly the same part of Merseyside at the same time in the middle of the previous night. I guessed the object was a bright meteor, but I could imagine how two youths might have left their bikes and set off to investigate, possibly not realising they were crossing a railway line on which trains operated even at 4 a.m.

But should I tell the police? They were baffled by the tragedy, yet I had promised confidentiality to the witness who had called me. I went to the studio where Brian Ford was hosting his daily programme, and between records sought his advice. There was a large glass window allowing visitors who entered the reception area to watch the DJ 'live' in action in the soundproofed studio; the DJ could also see out. As I asked Brian if I should tell the police, into the reception area marched two uniformed coppers! They had come to the building on an unrelated matter. But as you can imagine, I said to Brian, 'I think I have my answer.'

So I set off for home determined to broach the subject with the detective who lived opposite. On the bus through the Mersey Tunnel, I was mulling this over as I idly flicked through a free newspaper picked up in the city centre. My jaw dropped as I read the news that a predicted hit album was shortly due for release. Its title was to be *Synchronicity* and the artistes were The Police.

I told the detective my story. Later he reported that whilst they would probably never solve the boys' deaths, my explanation was perfectly credible. Perhaps I had helped put the record straight and prevent these youths from being suspected of any wrongdoing, as some people were unfairly speculating.

The *Synchronicity* album appeared soon after I told the CID my story and was a massive global hit. Within days of my being told by Wally Scott that a teenage, record-buying audience would never understand the word 'synchronicity', they were all singing it! The number one single taken from the album, written by Sting and also called 'Synchronicity', discussed Jung's 'acausal connecting principle' using those very words. In one seemingly nonsensical line – to my total astonishment – Sting had written 'A *star fall, a phone call, it joins all – synchronicity.*'

13
Future Imperfect

STORIES OF SYNCHRONICITY MUST SEEM VERY ODD IF YOU HAVE NEVER GIVEN much thought to time. But they lead to an even greater source of discomfort. Often such cases act like portents of the future, as if somehow you are given a private insight into coming events that it would be invaluable to know in advance.

This concept of seeing the future – or precognition – is one of the oldest reported phenomena. It was recorded by Greek scholars and you can find it in the works of Shakespeare and Dickens. It is certainly not a product of the space age, where anything supernatural is considered fair game for tabloid speculation.

Of course, the fact that millions of people throughout the ages have *apparently* seen a future event does not mean that they really *did* glimpse tomorrow. The sheer number of incidents is staggering and obviously something must lie behind them, but we cannot merely assume that this is a massive problem with our concept of time. Most scientists will reasonably suggest that these are chance 'hits' amidst millions of unfulfilled prophecies. It seems impossible to calculate how many 'visions of the future' we should expect to happen purely at random through mundane coincidence, but the seemingly large number of claims of precognition may be beyond that level.

AN INSTINCTIVE RESPONSE

A friend of mine was driving on the M62 motorway near Warrington, Cheshire, when for no apparent reason she swerved her car straight into the fast lane. She did not look before making this switch. If a car had been coming up behind her they would have crashed, but fortunately there was no other vehicle there. Seconds later the truck that had been dead ahead of her shed its load, which crashed onto the motorway, bouncing like a bomb across the carriageway precisely where she would have been if she had not moved out of the way.

Here, it seems, we are drawn to the assumption that a precognition – or gut reaction – saved this woman's life. But need that be so? For example, when a truck is carrying a loose load there may well be perceptible changes in its behaviour. It may wobble slightly, for instance. We may not consciously notice this change, but it is possible that our subconscious mind could be aware and produce an instinctive response. However, would making a dangerous swerve be an *appropriate* instinctive response?

A similar incident was told by the kitchen staff of Winston Churchill, Britain's wartime prime minister. One night during the period when Britain stood alone against a Nazi-dominated Europe, Churchill was hosting a dinner at 10 Downing Street in London. A German bombing was under way, as on many nights during 1941. It was customary practice to 'tough it out' and not appear to be responding to the pressure of the blitz, designed to force the UK into submission. Churchill, as leader, would never show any sign of fear and run for the air raid shelter, determined as he was to demonstrate his (and Britain's) stoicism. All his staff knew that they, too, must see the night through regardless of the consequences.

But on this particular night Churchill went into the kitchens, telling his staff to leave and to head straight for the shelter. They were dumbfounded and took some persuading, especially when it became clear that the prime minister himself intended to continue hosting the dinner. But

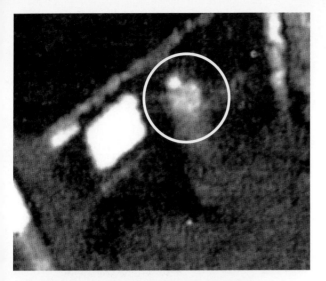

Three stills grabbed from the security camera footage, from a factory in Florida in 1996, show what may be a time storm in action. The man (circled) by the factory gate is swallowed up by a growing patch of light that is coming from above and seemingly accompanied by electrical interference. When the glow vanished the factory worker had disappeared. He reappeared just under two hours later, physically sick and disorientated, as the light beam recurred. The video remains contentious and has been studied by experts with the UFO group MUFON as a possible alien abduction. However, it has many of the features of a time storm (see p.187).

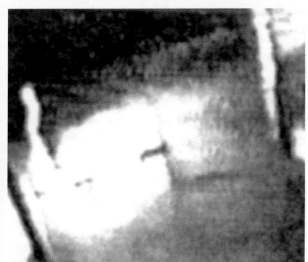

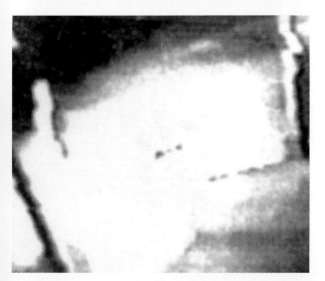

The front page headlines that greeted the strange lights seen in Rendlesham Forest, Suffolk (1980) close to the site of radar energy research plant. To the media this was a UFO – and by inference an alien contact. But was it perhaps something more down to earth? (see p. 231).

An artist's reconstruction of the strange case in Livingston, Scotland, in 1979, when a forester encountered a misty sphere and suffered major physiological effects during the close confrontation that followed (see p. 218). © ROY SANDBACH

go they did – luckily for them – because minutes later a stray bomb fell several hundred yards away, causing severe damage. Churchill and his guests were shaken, but not in an area that was badly hit. However, the kitchens were nearly demolished.

In another case, from Tacoma, in Washington state, USA, a woman backed away from the window by which she was doing the washing up after seeing 'blood' whilst her husband mowed the lawn. Had she reacted consciously she would have banged on the window to warn her husband, as he was the obvious focus for this sense of danger. But luckily she acted quite differently. The mower hit a large stone, tossing it right through the window and sending shards of glass all over the area where seconds earlier the woman had been standing.[1]

Cases like this seem to be a low-level precognition when only a feeling is sensed. Indeed, such presentiments are far more common than a stark vision of the future in a dream. This

> *The mower hit a large stone, tossing it right through the window and sending shards of glass all over the area where seconds earlier the woman had been standing.*

suggests that if there is some ability to see ahead of time, it is happening at a subconscious level, probably in what Jung termed the transpsychic realm. It also suggests that this subconscious insight may often stimulate behaviour even when people have no conscious realisation of why they are acting as they do. This matches well what we found about synchronicity and how it triggers switching reality tracks at a quantum level.

Most of these cases involve apparent awareness only seconds ahead of an event. In fact, such a short time lag – when nothing other than an instinctive response *can* follow – is almost the norm. Research into the patterns of precognition has shown that there is a mathematical relationship between the number of cases and the time between precognition and its apparent fulfilment. The greater the gap, the less the number of cases. In very few cases, in fact, is there a period of more than a few days between precognition and event. The average time lag is between several minutes and a few hours.

A typical case was reported to me by actress Shirley Stelfox. It was one of several in which she was involved along with her late husband, Don Henderson. One night Don came home and asked: 'Did you hear about Torvill and Dean?' The celebrated ice dance duo were then household names. Don reported that as he drove home alone that night he had heard on the car radio that they had won a big championship and scored an amazing six out of six from every judge.

Shirley knew there was a championship in progress, but said she did not think it was yet time for the final. So they put on the TV news and heard that Torvill and Dean had won a heat, but while they had been awarded excellent marks, they were not at the level that would cause the presenter to use the phrase that Don recalled: 'unprecedented in world skating.' Something of an argument ensued: Don said he knew what he had heard, but the facts seemed to prove he could not have done.

Come the final, three days later, the couple tuned in to watch and, not to their surprise (Don had experienced other precognitions), Torvill and Dean *did* indeed win with the perfect score of six out of six from every judge. What was more, the excited TV presenter used the precise words that Don and Shirley had been arguing over for seventy-two hours because Don insisted he had in some sense already heard them.[2]

NEURONE SENSITIVITY

Remember that, at a quantum level, energy or matter sends out probability waves to test future states. We know that the specific option selected may be a consequence of consciousness collapsing the various wave functions. Moreover, we have seen that the human mind (especially in states of reverie such as dreaming or fantasy) adopts a similar process of trying out future mind states by creating imaginative 'trial runs'. To this evolving picture we can add what we know about mind and brain.

There are ten thousand million neurones (brain cells) that interact across a vast forest of junctions via electrical impulses. These impulses are triggered by hormonal fluctuations within the body. Since electrical energy is being generated, the neurones create waves that are subject to normal quantum physics laws. Mind is therefore, in a very real sense, an energy field formed within the brain.[3]

When the neurones interact, they create a staggering number of possible connections and our near infinite range of emotions and experiences (in other words, mind). This is somewhat analogous to the many worlds theory of quantum physics, where a multitude of possible realities all exist and we only experience the one that we consider to be the real world. As you may recall, physicists such as Everett (p. 127) and Wheeler (p. 135) defined such many worlds as necessary to explain how quantum physics otherwise defines basic laws of nature.

Tests have shown that our neurones are sufficiently sensitive to react to one photon of light – that is, a single quantum event. It is therefore quite reasonable to argue that this vast network of brain cells and their emitted fields of energy are in tune with the various probability waves that are being tried out at the sub-atomic level. In simple terms, this means that the brain may be theoretically aware of all the possible future states that could occur within a single quantum event before a specific leap occurs. If so, it may even be capable of nudging that leap along one direction or another.

This would give us an explanation for the domino effect within synchronicity, where the mind somehow seems to set a train of events in motion, presumably by causing a long sequence of wave functions to collapse in a meaningful order. The outcome is an apparent flow to reality – or a coincidence.

However, there is another consequence we need to consider. The neurones should also be able to detect every possible future quantum state even before (in our frame of reference) one event, or a chain of events, becomes 'reality'. The energy field behind the human mind would, in effect, resonate with these many probability waves and 'detect' likely future mental states as they are being 'tested out'. Some of these would never happen, but some ultimately would become what we experience as reality.

Once we understand how both quantum physics and the human mind function, precognition becomes almost expected and certainly logical. If this model of mind is true, we would simply *have* to see the future, or at least many *possible* futures, because our mind is in tune with these through their probability waves. Indeed, we would all at some inner level constantly see possible future states within our minds.

DÉJÀ VU

We are all familiar with the sense of déjà vu where we seem certain that an event has already happened even though we can be sure that it never has. Psychologists have tried for years to understand what this common sensation means. Although vague and insubstantial, it is powerfully convincing when it strikes.

Perhaps we now have an answer to this riddle. In déjà vu the mind seems to get a sense of familiarity, but can never actually say what is about to happen. It comes across more as a feeling in some unreachable level of our mind rather than a consciously accessible preview of a real event.

What may be occurring is this. If our brain is constantly aware of the vast array of future possible transition states at a quantum level, there must be some deep core within our consciousness that registers them all before they actualise. Because we would be swamped with trillions of never-to-be-fulfilled virtual possibilities, and could never function properly if we were truly aware of them all, there has to be a mechanism that stops these things entering the conscious mind.

Indeed, psychologists have long argued that memory is not so much about remembering things but about forgetting them efficiently. This is because the brain needs to store information highly selectively and to learn how to dump the rest – billions of items of irrelevant data that would just get in the way.[4]

The danger of unwanted and normally suppressed information filtering through from the unconscious is shown in schizophrenia. Here, a physical breakdown allows the conscious mind to be overwhelmed, with devastating consequences. Possibly déjà vu results from a breakdown of a similar suppression process which normally keeps at bay vast numbers of unfulfilled quantum transitions.

During any complex operation, such as driving a car, we do many different things at an automatic level. If we stop and think about the decisions needed to make driving possible, we find ourselves performing poorly. We may even become incapable of driving because we are submerged by information. Imagine that effect multiplied a billion times and you can see the problem that would ensue if we were normally aware of these countless quantum fluctuations regarding a myriad possible futures.

If a breakdown occurs in this suppression process and some sense of possible future states gets through, I suspect it would appear as a vague familiarity such as we experience with déjà vu. We are actually sensing the distillation of billions of possible emotional responses to near future events. This creates the sense of overall familiarity, but not any awareness of a single coming event.

Indeed, déjà vu should perhaps be considered as a reverse form of nostalgia. This curious state of mind is a distilled and heady brew of all the emotional mental states connected to our recall of a specific time or event. Because some of these states are good and some are bad, the sense of nostalgia is a range of intertwined bitter-sweet emotions that tag our memories – a cocktail of many past emotional states that are normally buried deep within our subconscious. When we experience nostalgia, these memories are temporarily dredged up as a range of assorted moods.

Déjà vu may be a similar distillation of mind states and emotional responses that also escape by some accident of neurone transmission or hormonal stimulation. The only difference would be that, whereas feeling nostalgia causes us to replay past and actual experiences, re-creating the overall 'feel' of some past event, déjà vu does the same in connection with future and virtual experiences. We sense a cocktail of emotional impressions relating to probability waves testing out all near future possibilities.

STATES OF MIND

One of the first scientists to study precognition, over a hundred years ago, was Dr H. Saltmarsh. He saw right away that precognition occurs at the same deep level of perception where we now know that we sense probability waves – the place where nostalgia, déjà vu, awareness of quantum transitions and perhaps the actual decoding of reality takes place. He said of this: 'Precognitions occur only when the subject is in a state of dissociation – that is to say they are affairs of the subliminal or the subconscious mind.'[5]

This is a very important discovery. Precognitions tend to occur during altered states such as dreaming and reverie. When people drift into sleep, engage in automatic processes that free their minds to wander, or are engaged in relatively mindless pursuits that favour daydreaming, apparent visions of the future seem to be encouraged. If people are engaged in normal, conscious thinking or heavy mental exercise, the shutters are down and this information does not flow.

It cannot be unimportant that the states of mind which facilitate this phenomenon are the same ones that have been found to give our minds 'test runs' via daydreams, fantasies and dreaming. This has to be the link between mind states and precognition.[6]

Nor can it be irrelevant that psychological profiles of witnesses who frequently have visionary experiences suggest that these experiences happen to a specific type of person. They are visually creative, with unusual levels of memory retention and an apparent enhanced ability to enter altered states (a form of reverie). In other words, they are the very people who by their psychological nature have best access to those special states of consciousness in which these experiences seem to happen.

You and I might occasionally have one of these experiences when we chance to enter the correct mental state. But to have these experiences on a regular basis probably requires you to be prone to entering the inner realm where these phenomena are taking place.

DREAMING TRUE

Unsurprisingly, many precognitions occur during the dream state.

Surrey (UK)

Carol, from Surrey, reported a typical example: 'I went to bed as usual on Friday and woke up at 4 a.m. on Saturday with a very bad migraine. All I could think of was that I had to go to work because my cousin was meeting me there and there was no way I could contact her. Sitting up in bed with

> *'I got this vision, like a little television set . . . I saw this racing car crash and catch fire. There were two men in white overalls pulling this man out of the car . . . I felt awful.'*

a cold flannel on my head and my eyes shut I got this vision, like a little television set . . . I saw this racing car crash and catch fire. There were two men in white overalls pulling this man out of the car . . . I felt awful.'

In the terrible emotional state caused by the migraine and the power of this vision, Carol related the 'dream' to her cousin. Hours later the TV news carried a report of a terrible crash during a motor racing event in which driver Nikki Lauda had been badly burned. It was a duplicate of the event in Carol's vision. Incidentally, she had no interest in this particular sport.[7] O

Carol's case displays a number of features found in tens of thousands of similarly recorded episodes.[8] For example, it is common for these visions to occur after you have been asleep, then woken up and drifted back to sleep again. It is probable that the transition period between waking and sleeping is the key: it may provide access to these deeper unconscious levels, but retain sufficient conscious awareness to allow some memory to be stored. Most dream memories are not retained long-term.

Another clue could be the migraine: such attacks produce hormonal changes in the body and have been known to precipitate visions. They affect the firing of neurones within the brain, and people prone to such a problem might conceivably be 'conditioned' towards precognition when they happen. Again, a study of witnesses who report paranormal experiences found that they suffer from migraine at a level five times higher than that found in the rest of the population. So there would seem to be some connection.[9]

Also note how the image of the car crash was later seen on a TV screen. Precognition involves access to our own possible future mind states rather than direct visualisation of a coming event. As such, what matters is the eventual point when the witness discovers the news and experiences an emotional response to it. If that is a big story reported on TV it seems to increase the chances of that event being perceived ahead of time, because this TV watching in a sense offers the feedback that can provoke a major emotional response.

This helps explain why emotive and vividly traumatic events seem to produce the most examples of precognition. They would involve the largest number of probability waves tied to your own future mind state, even if they are not images of personal events. This is because you will have contact with (and a response to) news that is widely reported.

WHEN PROPHECY FAILS

A serious problem with precognition is illustrated by this next case.

Reno – Hawthorne (USA)

Don and Lynda Austin used to drive regularly between Reno and Hawthorne, Nevada along a flat road stretching for miles through the tumbleweed-strewn desert. Because of the dearth of traffic, no speed limit was in force. Any accidents were invariably fatal because the cars involved would be travelling at speeds of up to 100 mph.

Shortly before they were due to make one trip Don, dozing in his armchair, awoke with a start. He said he had just witnessed the two of them driving along a certain stretch of the road near railway tracks at their usual high speed, then unexpectedly meeting a line of cars, out of which a tan vehicle pulled right into their path. It was impossible to avoid a head-on collision. 'If we speed, we are going to be killed,' he insisted.

Next morning, they took more care than usual and, as they approached the relevant location, sure enough the described line of cars did appear. As they slowed right down to about 15 mph, a tan car *did* pull out right into their path. But Don had anticipated this and had driven off to the side of the road, ensuring that the speeding vehicle passed them safely only a few feet away. They could tell from the stunned look on the face of the other driver that he had not seen them until the very last minute, since he had apparently been concentrating on overtaking the line of cars. If the Austins had been in their expected position on the highway, at their normal speed, the tan car would have driven straight into them. ○

The side of the road was mostly just loose sand and the wheels could barely grip, even at a slow speed. The Austins are certain that if they had been travelling at even a 'safe' speed, they would have lost control and crashed into one of the roadside utility poles. And if they had been doing their usual 80 mph, it is unlikely that they would have survived. They feel Don's dream saved their lives and those of their three young children who were travelling with them – not to mention the driver of the tan car.[10]

You can see the problem here. Don dreamed of a future accident that did not happen – so he had a *failed* precognition. But, of course, all the other elements of the experience came true. There are in fact a large number of cases like this for which the term 'precognition' is not strictly correct because they fail in what a precognition is supposed to do – to see an actual future.[11]

Many sceptics use such cases to justify the implausibility of precognition. But, in fact, by the model of time that is being revealed here they are perfectly reasonable. If you remember, the mind senses multiple future probability waves. Since many of these will follow closely similar paths, the overall theme here – the line of vehicles, the reckless driver of the tan car and the fatal collision – will happen in most versions. Being repeated so often, this general theme will be the easiest to sense up front – just as in the many worlds theory of quantum physics most worlds that split off from decision points will be closely similar at first because as yet only relatively small changes will have occurred at branch points across short periods of time.

Of course, all versions of reality will diverge as time goes by. This may be one reason why precognition seems mostly to involve events that are not far ahead. These would have probability wave variations that are very similar to each other and so may be more accessible. They may also appear to us to be more real because there are many versions nearly alike. Sensing a probability wave that is far removed from present reality may appear like imagination because of its oddity whereas one close to current reality would seem credible enough to be accepted as potentially true. For a precognition to be considered as genuine foresight, it has to be considered possible. Only closely similar probability states would. If you perceived a dream in which you woke up tomorrow with two heads and a tail, you would rightly dismiss it as fantasy, but if you dreamed that you woke up with a hangover you might expect the worst!

So there will be future possible states in which the Nevada car accident is avoided. Indeed, arguably, the entire process of being made aware of a coming event through precognition may be said to operate for 'survival value' in the nature of evolution. If our future is fixed, it would serve little purpose to be aware of it. If reality can be honed and shaped by collapsing the right wave functions, then there is survival value in becoming aware.

. . . seeing the terrible outcome of some future event ahead of itself has acted, as a more ordinary nightmare may do, to warn of the consequences of certain possible acts . . .

We might therefore argue here that seeing the terrible outcome of some future event ahead of itself has acted, as a more ordinary nightmare may do, to warn of the consequences of certain possible acts – regarding occurrences you can stop from happening. Alarm bells start ringing, making the conscious mind take note and allowing the alert individual to collapse future probability waves along a more favourable path.

Unfortunately, there are doubtless many cases where the warning signs are not heeded and the worst case scenario actually happens. But both outcomes are in a real sense precognition.

QUANTUM FEELERS

The problem with the human mind is that it is not a computer. Whilst we can argue the way that precognition should operate in an ideal world, this is a mechanical process never duplicated in reality. Humans are too complex to write up as a sequence of equations.

Psychiatrist Dr Ninian Marshall blended physics and mind science to suggest that 'quantum feelers' might detect the period ahead during which an event could be foreseen. If reality splits into many versions that increasingly diverge, some 'worlds' will eventually evolve very differently from each other. However, over the course of the next few minutes or hours most versions would stay fairly similar.[12]

We have also seen that emotion is one key to precognition. A mother is far more likely to sense danger to her child than she is to sense a threat to a total stranger. Other problems are caused by the way our minds operate, using symbols to clothe images. In one case a person described seeing a mass of red and cream buses and a plane crashing nearby. They 'knew' from the identity of the buses (a personal interest) the location of the town where the plane would crash. The buses had no part in the actual crash (which did occur), but were presumably used as a symbol by the dreamer's own mind to speedily impress where the event was going to happen. A different person may well have visualised something else to represent that same town. So any attempt to understand this precognition would have failed without decoding which parts were symbolic and which were more literal.

Again, the fact that we see our own future mind states (not the actual events) can cause difficulty. In one of my dreams I saw a paper factory on fire. Within twenty-four hours this event happened, but in reality I made the mistake of *thinking* there was a fire when it was just a furnace reflecting off low cloud. I had an apparent precognition of my own mental error, not of a real fire – fortunately for the factory workers.

Unfortunately, all these factors have to be taken into account when seeking to unravel an apparent precognition. This makes it easy to guess wrong, but hard to know what a precognition is trying to tell us.

TIME LOOPS

One type of precognition brings us full circle and poses very difficult questions about how we must conceive of time. These are what I call time loops.

A simple case was told me by Simon from London. In 1980, he was visiting a doctor who was taking a record of his dreams. Simon related a very odd one he had had the night before, about a long white scar appearing on his arm, and asked the doctor why he thought he would have such a dream.

The doctor replied, 'A long white scar – you mean like this?' and rolled up his sleeve to reveal the precise mark on his own arm.

Superficially this case seems simple to understand. Simon had a dream in which he saw the revelation of the scar made to him the next day by the doctor. The problem is that this doctor only revealed the scar *because* of the dream that Simon had described to him. In other words, time went in a loop, because the cause (the reporting of this dream) actually followed the effect (the dream itself), rather than the way round that we are accustomed to contemplating by all our traditional thinking about time.

Of course, as you have seen, relativity physics casts doubt on the universal validity of cause and effect. To be honest, if cause and effect fail as a physical law, it virtually means that time as a logical progression fails too. Time loops clearly challenge the validity of cause and effect.

Here is another example.

Yorkshire (UK)

Mrs Woodhead from Yorkshire told me how she dreamed of meeting a friend whom she had not seen in many years and with whom she had lost all contact. She shared the news with another friend, who next day visited her own mother in hospital. Through a series of chance events, this woman ended up meeting Mrs Woodhead's long-lost friend in the building. Recalling the dream, she was able to arrange the very reunion of which Mrs Woodhead had just dreamed. But that reunion only happened because of the dream that it *would* happen, then because it was reported to a third party, who seemingly 'collapsed' appropriate wave functions in order unconsciously to bring that fore-seen event to fruition. ○

I think cases of this sort have to make us question the illusion that is time. They imply that the order we see and the flow to time that we normally experience cease to have meaning at the level of quantum physics and relativity.

One last case neatly shows off the paradox.

Chesterfield (UK)

Michele from Chesterfield told me of a bizarre dream in which her boyfriend's best mate called as she was making a banana sandwich. He said that her boyfriend had fallen off his motorcycle. 'Oh, yes?' she said and burst out laughing. The dream seemed odd to her because of this totally anomalous reaction. She knew that in real life the phone message would cause her to be distressed and fearful for the safety of her boyfriend – certainly not to laugh.

Soon afterwards, she reported the dream to both her boyfriend and his mate in the pub. Then they all went home. A few hours later, as Michele was making a banana sandwich, the phone rang. It was her boyfriend's mate repeating the line she had earlier told him from her dream. Sure that the two young men had got together to pull her leg because of her description of the dream story, she reacted instinctively and burst out laughing. But her boyfriend's mate had forgotten the dream and the accident was real. Her boyfriend *had* come off his motorcycle and was hurt. O

Here we see very clearly how a time loop is utterly incompatible with normal views of time. Michele had a dream about her own future mental state. Note that she previewed her first contact with the news rather than saw a vision of her boyfriend crashing his bike – an event that she never witnessed in any form – exactly as the rules of precognition defined by this chapter would predict.

If the crash had featured on TV news it might have been different. Michele may then have 'seen' it and her dream might have visualised the actual accident instead. But here there was no such visual feedback to fuel the dream, which therefore previewed her emotional roller coaster when hearing the news by phone.

Of course, what the dream also did was preview her totally extraordinary emotional response to the news – an event that only happened as a consequence of her having had the dream in the first place. If she had no reason to suppose her boyfriend's mate was joking, she would not have laughed at being told of the crash. But she only *thought* he was joking because he had been told about the dream. So the dream

> If we probe, via the many strange phenomena of time, into the centre of reality itself, we suddenly discover that space, time, past, future, cause and effect are simply words.

contained an advance awareness of an emotional state of mind that directly resulted from the dream that foresaw the same emotional state . . . you get the mind-blowing picture!

Cause and effect is shown by cases like this to be a concept in deep trouble. It seems to be a principle we live by in general life because it often *appears* to work. But when you by-pass the illusion of time-bound reality it falls. If we probe, via the many strange phenomena of time into the centre of reality itself, we suddenly discover that space, time, past, future, cause and effect are simply words.

14
Time Slips

ONE OF THE ODDEST THINGS THAT I HAVE EVER EXPERIENCED HAS LITTLE TO do with time and nothing to do with the paranormal, but is undoubtedly instructive about both.

It occurred in June 1974 when I was undergoing extensive medical tests in Manchester. A nurse was taking a blood sample when she was called away urgently and asked me to hold the needle until she returned. I do not know for sure exactly what happened next – I can only describe it as a 'jump' in the flow of reality. One second what I have just described was taking place, the next I was staring at a very strange white-tiled image. I was utterly confused, as if I had been 'beamed out' from my seat in the medical unit to some totally alien environment.

I vividly recall the thought that flitted through my head when I became aware this was not an illusion. It was: 'So – all my life until this point was a dream. Now I have woken up to the real world.' It was an eerie sensation, a numbing shock to the system.

The effect lasted only an instant, after which my disorientation (which is what it actually was) was replaced by recognition. I had fallen on to the floor and was now staring up at the ceiling having (I later discovered) fainted for a few seconds. To me there had simply been no experience during the intervening moments. I had 'jumped' from sitting on a chair to the new reality of staring at the ceiling from the floor. Because to me it was one continuous experience without any passage of time, it created this bizarre impression of awakening into an alien realm.

Although there is nothing inexplicable about this fleeting experience, it has allowed me to empathise with some of the really bizarre time-related anomalies described to me. When witnesses say that their whole concept of reality shifted in an instant, I know what they are struggling to convey: to comprehend that the universe is utterly different from what they thought, but to have little hope of persuading others of that extraordinary revelation. One woman described it in these words: 'Imagine walking across the moors and seeing the *QE II* liner right in front of you. You know it cannot be there, but still know that it is. The world has changed for ever, but nobody could believe you.'

I can grasp something of her sense of helplessness.

A TIMELESS REALM

Cleveland (UK), 1986

In 1986 Mr West of Cleveland in the North of England had just undergone heart surgery. As he recovered in hospital, he struggled to get out of bed to go to the bathroom, and then found himself experiencing a reality shift during which he was no longer 'all there' in the world that he had known.

First, he felt a profound silence and stillness around him – the sensation known as the Oz Factor which we have met often. Mr West then describes the curious sense of *needing* to travel into the past and doing so. No longer was he looking at a man in a neighbouring bed appearing to call frantically for help. Instead he was taking in a completely different scene, clearly many years earlier.

In the unfolding images – watched as if he were inside an ongoing TV drama – he could see a woman giving birth, a doctor wearing a stove-pipe hat and many small details of the surroundings. Then he felt a tugging sensation, as if he was being weighed down by an invisible anchor, and was pulled back to bed. He could now see himself

– or his body at least – collapsed on the bed, with medical staff giving him emergency treatment to restart his heart. Mr West knew nothing further, simply 'blacking out' until much later when he regained consciousness in the hospital.[1] ○

An experience of this type is not rare – or at least many of its features are not. They can be interpreted in several ways. The most rational would be to assume that a heavily medicated (and physically distressed) man suffered a hallucination as a consequence of either the stress or the life-saving drugs that he was taking. However, some doctors who have collected reports of similar cases argue that the 'mind' temporarily detaches from the body and has what is known as an OOBE (out-of-body experience).

In this case, as in quite a few others, it extended into a NDE (near-death experience), where at a point of severe physical trauma and a crossroads between life and death, Mr West 'embraced eternity'. Often such cases produce remarkably consistent claims of trips to some after-life. Voyages through time are rare, but not unheard of.[2]

Interestingly, Mr West interpreted this neither as a hallucination nor as a trip to heaven. His perspective was that he perhaps entered a timeless realm beyond the physical and saw his own moment of 'birth' as the soul behind the child of this pregnant woman.

Since he was in a *timeless* realm the fact that the birth occurred 'long ago' is not the issue we assume it to be. Nor did it mean that this was a vision of a past life. If there is no flow to time, it is no less valid to say that he was experiencing a vision of where he might have gone *next* if he had died at that moment. For, if there is a continuance of our soul, life energy or spirit (as there may, or may not, be), and if the essence of reality is timeless, then we should not presume that any sequence of lives would occur chronologically. We may move to yesterday when we die!

HIGHWAY HYPNOSIS

Many time slips – in which people find themselves suddenly in another era – occur in situations of sensory isolation, for example when in bed at night or on a lonely road in a car. These are curiously like the patterns of the time storm in which the Oz Factor induces sensory deprivation.

Psychologists have long identified this state in car drivers who enter 'highway hypnosis' and shift levels of consciousness. It is a possible cause of unexplained accidents, surviving drivers having sometimes reported that they 'saw' turn-off roads and junctions that were later proved not to be there. They tried to follow them, running into other vehicles or crossing the central reservation in the process.[3]

> *Many time slips – in which people find themselves suddenly in another era – occur in situations of sensory isolation, for example when in bed at night or on a lonely road in a car.*

We might argue that in such cases the drivers have simply had a daydream or imagined things that do not exist. But note an interesting point. These drivers do not see pink elephants or aircraft taxiing along the roadway, but houses, turnings or passers-by. They see nothing outrageous or absurd, as within dreams and other hallucinations, but things that are perfectly consistent with the environment and credibly once part of the local landscape. That the drivers might visualise an actual scene from the past of this location whilst in an altered state of awareness is often one possible interpretation of this 'hallucination'.

A PATTERN OF IMAGERY

Surrey (UK), 1968

Mr P. Chase told researcher Joan Forman of an occasion when he was waiting for a bus in the Surrey countryside in 1968. Getting bored, he went for a stroll and found two thatched cottages with a sign on the wall dating them to 1837. He admired their beautiful gardens. Later, at work, Chase mentioned these to a local man and an argument ensued because the man said there were only two modern brick houses at this spot. Mr Chase refused to accept this and that evening took the same walk. There were no cottages, just the brick houses. Investigations by Mrs Forman established that thatched cottages had once stood on the site but had been demolished early in the twentieth century.[4] ◯

Note again here the long period of isolation that probably facilitated a daydream. But even if we accept, as seems most likely, that Mr Chase 'imagined' these cottages, how did he imagine buildings that were once really present and make modern ones vanish that were actually now there?

Mount Lowe (USA), 1974

A similar refusal to believe the obvious was reported by Bo Orsjo from Sweden, who moved to the US west coast in 1974. He took a hike alone up Mount Lowe, just outside Pasadena in California, and was impressed by the quaint green hotel he encountered halfway. He sat at its edge eating his packed lunch watching a maid sweeping up in the strange, shimmering 'misty' light.

The problem was that nobody believed him, because they insisted there was no such hotel up this mountain. In the end he returned with a friend, determined to show him, but they found only rubble. Research quickly disclosed that a millionaire called Lowe had once started to build a railway, but only got halfway up the mountain before his money ran out, and so built a magnificent hotel on a railroad to nowhere. Orsjo confirmed that the photographs show the same place he visited. Unfortunately, that was not possible because it burned down in 1937 and by the time of his mountain hike had long since crumbled into ruins. ○

Again, it seems, as in many other cases I could recite, the climber was alone, starved of mental input for hours and somehow lulled into that state of consciousness that seems to afford access to Jung's transpsychic realm. Once there, he spent some minutes living within a scene from at least forty years earlier.

ALTERED STATES

We have noticed along the way a number of pointers that suggest the nature of these time slip experiences. One is the Oz Factor; another is the 'timeless' moment that it induces.

In Joan Forman's excellent work collecting anecdotal time slip cases, she heard witnesses tell her about the Oz Factor, though they often did not realise what it was. On page 60 of her study, a Cornish woman describes how she 'passed over a threshold into a world of utter silence, surrounded by a sort of silvery light.' On page 69 there was 'an absence of noise . . . sometimes to the point of noticeable quietness.' On page 146, during a time slip, 'time seemed to be non-existent,' one man reported.[5]

It seems important that these descriptions surrounding time slips precisely match those in precognition and other strange visions that witnesses have been reporting for twenty years as the Oz Factor. And they also feature regularly in time storm cases described earlier in this book.[6]

Also of note are the cases in which witnesses refer to strange electrical effects, as if the atmosphere is charged with static electricity. Almost a century ago, the SPR (Society for Psychical Research) researched a story told by two well-to-do Englishwomen, who visited Versailles and apparently experienced the gardens as they were during the time of Marie Antoinette. They had noted a heavy electrical aura to the weather that day.

Is this electrical energy often noticed in the air the symptom of a time storm that triggers a time slip experience?[7] It even crops up in cases that might be time slip images from the future, for instance in a photograph of a futuristic floating man taken in May 1964 by fireman Jim Templeton on Burgh Marshes, Cumbria whilst filming his daughter on a picnic. Jim tells me that the weather on the marsh that day was unusually charged with electrical energy and nearby cows were clearly disturbed by it.[8]

I think these clues slot together rather too easily with the data from the first part of this book for us not to appreciate that they surely mean something about the phenomenon we are investigating.

VISIONS OF YESTERDAY

Although witnesses may believe that they actually slip into the past, it may be easier to view these 'trips' as powerful visions superimposed in a thoroughly convincing manner on to our normal perception of the world. Remember those drivers who see a turning off the road which is no longer really there? Such distorted perception can lead them to disaster because in truth they are still driving on *today's* highway.

If so, then any climber who saw a mountainside hotel that was not actually there, but who acted as if it was real, could step dangerously close to a cliff edge by not seeing the surroundings as they truly are. So we need to understand how such powerful illusions can happen and how they can take the place of present-day reality for more than just a few seconds. Hallucinations are rarely that persistently overpowering.

Liverpool (UK), 1966

In June 1996 Frank, a police officer, and his wife Carol were shopping in Liverpool city centre. After the couple had split up to go on separate errands, Frank was about to meet his wife near Central Station when he noticed that the area had suddenly become unusually still and quiet. The city centre bustle had been replaced by a cobbled street containing people dressed fifty years out of style.

He noticed that the area had suddenly become unusually still and quiet. The city centre bustle had been replaced by a cobbled street containing people dressed fifty years out of style.

Suddenly a horn blared and a box van drove past. Frank read the name on it, as well as that on a nearby store selling handbags, and took in various other details. Then the scene suddenly shifted back to normal, although a woman in the vicinity, looking disorientated, told Frank that she had experienced exactly the same time slip effect and was terrified by it.[9] ○

There really was a store of this name at the same spot fifty years ago. Moreover, when this incident was reported on local radio, several callers rang in to say they had noticed similar time shifting effects as they walked in this part of Bold Street. I have walked this location several times myself, but never experienced any unusual sensations, although an electrified railway runs beneath this spot. Does its energy field provide a clue?

I feel some unease about this story, as I have no first-hand evidence for it. But it does fit what I have found from other cases, so may be true. Yet surely these reports are visions. If Frank had physically time shifted, then countless people in 1996 would have seen him 'vanish' and reports from the past might be expected, alleging a mysterious 'futuristic' looking stranger who appeared out of nowhere.

One young woman has independently (and long before the above incident) told me of her own experiences in this part of Liverpool city centre. She recalls how on several occasions she became aware of other people walking around her in old-fashioned dress. They seemed to drift along and only she was aware of their presence. It took a while to realise that they were not actually there. But in this case there was only a partial 'time shift.' She remained aware of the modern day, seeing her contemporary surroundings and experienced the past superimposed. She knew it was a form of vision.

Interestingly, this teenager also told me how she was once out walking and saw an old-fashioned aircraft crash into the Dee estuary. Later checks revealed that no such accident had occurred that day, though an aircraft had fallen into the water during World War II, over twenty years before she was even born.

On another occasion she was alone in some fields when the scenery just shimmered and melted away to be replaced by an old house, in front of which were nurses and men in military uniforms. The witness was able to describe to me in great detail what she saw. Then the empty fields returned. She is adamant it was a powerful hallucination, but it overlaid the normal landscape to *seem* real. Such a house did once exist in the area, but was pulled down over fifty years before her birth.

In this case there was good evidence that the girl was powerfully gifted at creative visualisation. She was able to imagine vividly things which others might only see fleetingly in their mind's eye.[10] Possibly this is what happens with a time slip. Certain people can hallucinate, visualise (call it what you will) so strongly that it dominates reality and seems to *become* real.

Of course, vision or not, the problem is that in many of these cases people see a scene they do not know was once real. How can we say of these things that they are simply hallucinations?

GHOST RIDERS IN THE SKY

Folklorist Dr David Clarke has for several years been collecting stories not unlike that reported from the Dee estuary. But these concern a repeated vision of a ghost plane so consistently described and seemingly real that many witnesses refuse to believe they have seen anything other than a genuine aircraft crossing the skies. Unfortunately, air traffic control and the lack of radar evidence usually confirm that the plane they saw last flew half a century before!

The incidents centre around the Longdendale area of Derbyshire. In 1943 Lancaster bombers used the reservoirs here to practise low-level runs, notably with the famous bouncing bombs used in the Dam Buster raids on the Ruhr. Old pilots may never die and their planes may still keep flying. There have been numerous sightings near Ladybower and Derwent Dam of what seem to be Lancasters flying low over the water in complete silence. These have occurred both at night and in the daytime. Checks have always revealed that the very few surviving aircraft of this type were nowhere near Derbyshire that day.[11]

Hope (UK), 1995

Tony Ingle, walking his dog at Hope, reported a typical case in April 1995 when he saw a plane (a Dakota in this case) suddenly appear forty feet over his head. The propellers were going round, but despite the terrifying proximity of the large plane, it made no noise before seeming to 'crash' over a ridge. He told Dr Clarke, 'Everything was silent. You could hear a pin drop . . . it was terrible, a very eerie sensation.' Again, note the Oz Factor effect. ○

The location of every single one of the few Dakota aircraft in the UK that day was traced. None was airborne. But a USAF Dakota did crash near Hope in July 1945. Indeed, the desolate moors have claimed many aircraft because mist can rapidly obscure the dangerous terrain of the High Peak.

Sightings are so frequent that the local mountain rescue teams are called out several times a year and always investigate in case a real plane has gone down. These teams know the 'ghost plane' stories well enough to accept that something strange is going on – that something is considered by some of the locals to be a time slip silently re-running the last fateful moments of these wartime heroes.

DISTANT ECHOES

Can events truly replay like some real-world video projection?

Baltimore (USA), 1947

Arthur Foore of Baltimore, Maryland, describes a strange night in the spring of 1947 that he has never been able to forget. He had been out dancing and at 2.30 a.m. returned by taxi to his apartment, where he lived alone protected by heavy security locks. After bounding up the steps, eager to get to bed, he double locked the door, threw his clothes off and collapsed on to the bed. Yet within seconds of doing so and switching off the light he apparently came home again!

That is to say, Foore heard someone bound up the steps two at a time, just as he had done minutes earlier, unlock the door, double lock it, then enter the room. Listening in mounting shock, Foore felt the bed depress and witnessed a complete re-run of himself taking off his clothes and then climbing in. He felt something press against his body and it all got too much. He turned on the light, but silence had returned and he was alone. As Foore reports, he only stayed put because of his certainty that he was experiencing an action replay of his own arrival. 'If I did not think the person was myself, I would have made a new door!'[12] ○

Yet this is not a unique story. Roy Sandbach and I interviewed Nina Smith, who lived in an isolated cottage in Yorkshire's Calder Valley (see also case on p. 83). She was especially concerned about the 'electricity drains' in this old building. The power company could not explain how her house seemed to 'suck' energy from the air. Electrical equipment such as her washing machine would overload and even explode, and light bulbs rarely lasted long.

We noted large quartz crystals in the stone from which the house was built and in the surrounding landscape. When put under pressure, such crystals are used to emit electrical sparks, and can operate watch batteries and lighters. Research at the US Bureau of Mines in Colorado and experiments by UK geologists have indicated that in nature these effects can be magnified. In large rocks, great pressure can be exerted by the terrain and put the quartz under strain, which can produce sufficient power to create a strong localised energy field.[13]

> *The power company could not explain how her house seemed to 'suck' energy from the air. Electrical equipment such as her washing machine would overload and even explode, and light bulbs rarely lasted long.*

Several things can produce such pressure. One is a fault line, another the weight of a body of water such as that found in reservoirs or estuaries. We have already seen cases from the Dee estuary, the Mersey estuary around Daresbury and Moore, and the reservoirs in Longdendale. A fault line runs right beneath Nina Smith's house.

Research in Canada by Dr Michael Persinger, a specialist in the effects of electromagnetic radiation on the brain, has discovered that such generated energy fields stimulate the neurones. In his lab, people who have been subjected to similar artificially created energy fields describe a sense of isolation, detachment, dreaminess and visionary experiences – just what witnesses to these anomalies claim.[14]

Atmospheric energy can be triggered by these geological processes. These terrestrial forces can produce changes in brain chemistry perceived as odd physiological sensations. Because the parts of the brain best able to commune with timeless reality are stimulated here, we might expect time anomalies to follow. People who are visually creative and see things vividly may well consider as real what others regard as hallucinations.

All of the clues seem to be in place. Put them together and we may have a way to explain time slips. But equally, perhaps, an event could be 'recorded' by these energy fields and potentially visible to everyone.

Pictures seen on a TV screen are no more than decoded electrical signals. Emotive events can apparently cause the strongest energy fields at a quantum level, and these fields can be detected by some part of our mind. From this we might reasonably deduce that electrical fields generated by natural forces might be open to modulation just as TV signals are. If so, they could retain an emotional 'energy track' of a powerful past event, such as a crashing aircraft. Indeed, one day we may be able to build a device to decode such recordings. If so, it suggests that the world's first time machine may prove to be a VCR!

London (UK), 1995

A curious story that might offer clues about this bizarre possibility was reported by Alex Brattell from East London. He lived in an apartment in a converted Victorian warehouse and had a security camera which screened a narrow view of any visitor standing at the door, complete with backdrop of the warehouses behind. The camera was removed for servicing, but after it was put back visitors were shown on the monitor against a background of terraced houses that were not there.

The servicing company could only suggest that a previous image, possibly from a location where the monitor had formerly been used, had 'burned' on to the screen to create this ghost image. O

Of course – what else *does* make sense? That the repairs to the camera somehow allowed it temporarily to act as a time machine? So far as can be discovered, no such houses ever existed in this location. Alex himself wonders if this may be an image of an alternative reality, in which the present version of this world contains this street scene built instead of the warehouses.[15]

There are other cases suggesting electronic recording of out-of-time events.

Oldham (UK), 1991

One of the most remarkable is the tape made by the security camera at the Butterflies nightclub in Oldham in October 1991. After an alarm was tripped one night, the police brought the owner to the scene. No robbery had taken place, but at the precise time the alarm was triggered the camera had recorded a white form, seemingly a man, but not actually in the deserted building. The camera showed him walking along a corridor, then passing straight through a wall. ○

Whatever this image really is (and ideas about tape or camera 'burn-in' of old recorded images were again considered here), it seems to fit the pattern. Whilst the image had no mass and was not real in the sense that solid matter proved no obstacle, it had energy and could trip the alarm and modulate a camera signal.[16]

Even stranger were reports that I received from three separate sources. The witnesses told me they had seen a brief image over-ride their normal TV channel. The picture went to static, then showed an undefined image for a few seconds, while a voice seemed to explain that this was a test transmission as part of a scientific experiment from the future. There seemed no purpose to the images (nothing was promoted), and nobody ever saw this phenomenon more than once. All the cases occurred in 1991. This experience is not dissimilar to the plot of the movie *Frequency* (2000), but that fiction came years after these real cases.

I tried to establish evidence of an aborted TV advertising campaign or a hacker who had mischievously tapped into normal broadcasts – as has happened. But I found none, and the latter idea seems unlikely as the reports came from places as far apart as South Wales and Lancashire, where totally different transmitting stations are involved.

Quantum physicist Dr Gregory Benford writes credible fiction about future possibilities in science. In his novel *Timescape* he argues that the first serious experiments in time travel will one day involve the sending back through time of electronic signals using the principles of quantum mechanics. They will not involve a time machine. Even as he was writing an imaginative story about interference on computer screens detected by scientists in the 1960s but caused by physics experiments in the twenty-first century, similar events were actually being reported on British TV screens!

Fluke, hoax or aborted TV advertising campaign, it could be. But it is by no means improbable that, if some way to send images through time is discovered (as it may well be in the near future), it will involve energy fields that could be modulated and detected by equipment such as TV sets and VCRs.

FUTURE TIME SLIPS

Most time slips involve images from the past. But if time is not a linear flow, then future time slips ought to be possible. Of course, one problem is that time slips in which the past recurs are usually obvious, whereas how would we know if a scene was from the future? Take the terraced houses seen on the East London camera. We imagine them from the past, so if there were no houses in this location we consider a parallel reality. But what if in fifty years' time someone builds a row of terraced houses in this very spot? Then this image seen in 1995 could actually be from the future. We probably just would not assume such an origin.

Joan Forman recorded a case from Londoner C. H. D'Alessio in 1975. He recalls walking along a tree-lined street near his home and entering a detached, dreamy state. A sudden silence enveloped the area and D'Alessio could see that the road and the houses along it were made out of a shiny silver material that seemed synthetic. Road vehicles were floating past him as if riding on beams of energy. He believed this was a future scene.

Futuristic road traffic is one thing, but what if air traffic from the future is seen? Witnesses today would be most unlikely to assume they have seen an aircraft from the future. Their experience would almost certainly be hijacked by UFOlogists as another example of an alien spaceship.

> *In a famous time slip vision, Harry Martindale reported the bizarre sight of a number of Roman legionnaires marching through a cellar as he worked. They then marched right out through a far wall.*

There may be many future time slips sitting in the files unrecognised because they are woefully misinterpreted.

In a famous time slip vision, a York man, Harry Martindale, reported the bizarre sight of a number of Roman legionnaires marching through a cellar as he worked. They then marched right out through a far wall. This was presumably some kind of image being replayed, but the key was the way in which the soldiers' feet were not visible but hidden beneath the cellar floor. It was as if these images were marching on the old road surface as it was long ago. This, of course, would be below the current ground level, now built up over the centuries by roads and house floors.

Nor is this unusual. The figure captured on the video camera in Oldham seems to walk through a door not there today. So in 1991 it may *seem* to us to walk through a wall, but if it is a video replay that would not defy logic. And the futuristic man filmed on Burgh Marsh (assuming this photograph to be genuine as the witness insists) seems to float *above* ground level. We might anticipate this as a person walking on a floor in

The crop circle in the field at Preston Brook, Daresbury, Cheshire not far from a particle physics research plant. This shot was taken moments before a car driving up the hill (centre right), moving right–left across the field of view was 'tugged' mysteriously across the road towards the circle. It then rammed the author's parents' car with horrendous consequences. Their car is just visible beside the gate (centre right) seconds before the impact that followed (see p. 210). © JENNY RANDLES

Nikola Tesla was one of the first scientists to demonstrate that massive atmospheric electrical energy can create unexpected side effects on both people and the environment. Such effects appear to be occurring during time storms. In this modern recreation of one of his experiments an enormous 'Tesla Coil' is generating high frequency energy bursts within the laboratory. © SCIENCE PHOTO LIBRARY

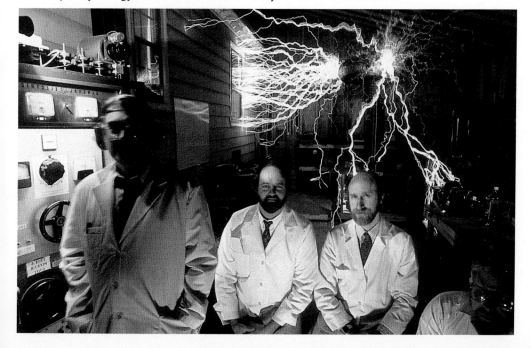

Psychoanalyst Carl Jung was a pioneer in relating modern scientific research, such as quantum physics, to internal imagery within the mind. He conceived of the collective unconscious, the importance of mental images and visual creativity and (with quantum physicist Wolfgang Pauli) defined the idea of synchronicity as a connecting principle between two realities (see p. 139).
© HULTON GETTY

Brilliant physicist, Professor Stephen Hawking, has considered the implications of time travel within the known laws of cosmology. Whilst unhappy with some of the apparent implications and aware that restrictions might be found, he also recognises that the possibility of real life time travel may be inferred by our current knowledge of the universe (see p. 124). © UPPA

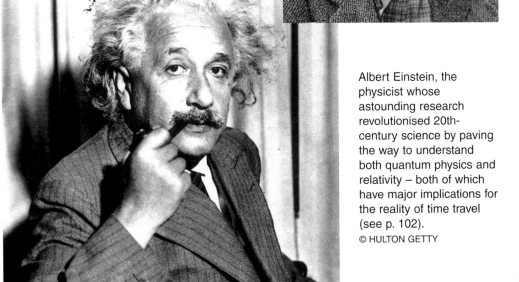

Albert Einstein, the physicist whose astounding research revolutionised 20th-century science by paving the way to understand both quantum physics and relativity – both of which have major implications for the reality of time travel (see p. 102).
© HULTON GETTY

a yet unconstructed building at a spot where today there is only a field. Or consider a car moving on a road that will be resurfaced several times as the ages move forward – would all these not in our terms seem to float above ground level?

LAPSES IN THINKING

Can we establish any evidence that people do *literally* travel through time, and not just in some dream state? This is where the curious phenomenon of the time lapse comes into its own.

Time lapses are remarkably common. I have investigated perhaps fifty claims reported to me from the UK, and thousands are on record worldwide. Here is a typical recent example.

Glassboro (USA), 1999

Evelyn reports how she and her husband went shopping in Glassboro, New Jersey a few days before Christmas 1999. They arrived at the open-all-hours Shoprite store at 5.30 p.m. and collected some groceries into a trolley, ending up with ice cream – deliberately purchased last to prevent it from melting before they got home. There was no discontinuity of recall, but as Evelyn put the ice cream on the counter to pay for it, the contents ran all over the place because they had melted.

The item was replaced and they went outside to drive the short distance home. It was very cold, so they did not dawdle apart from briefly stopping to talk in the car park. When they got home with their shopping they were stunned to discover that it was 11 p.m. – five hours later than it should have been, at least according to their recall of a trip that had lasted barely an hour.

So baffled were this couple that they checked every way they could to discover what had happened. They confirmed the time on all their clocks and watches. They even asked Shoprite to go over their security video tapes. Nothing odd was found. They had arrived at the shop at 5.30 p.m. and left it five hours later, despite having no understanding of how they could have lost so much time doing a quick grocery run.[17] ○

This incident found its way to the UFO community. You might wonder why. There is nothing within the story to suggest the presence of aliens, but time lapses are like gold dust to UFO hunters. They perceive this missing time as a period during which the witness has been inside a flying saucer, and methods such as regression hypnosis are often employed to try to prove this theory. They do this by inducing an altered state through hypnosis to stimulate the memory of the missing period. However, hypnotic regression just as often leads to fantasy, making it next to useless when exploring a phenomenon like an alien visit.

To my knowledge that has not happened at Glassboro, and this story remains as just a gap in memory. Personally, I suspect the frantic efforts often made to establish an alien contact in these circumstances are dangerous and misleading. Adopting dubious methods to retrieve 'memory' can confuse and complicate.

With hypnosis there is no way we could be certain that any recall is a genuine account of what happened during the missing time. But all too often what we know for sure is that the raw report as described above is transformed into an exercise in speculation that becomes promoted as if it is proven. From here all manner of theories about aliens performing medical examinations swamp the only facts that are established. Here those facts are the apparently missing time. Hypnotic recall of an alien abduction might seem to help unravel the truth in such cases, but if (as must be very possible) there were no aliens, then it has simply led us away from any proper understanding of an intriguing temporal anomaly.[18]

I believe we should avoid doubtful methods that seek to link this experience with a phenomenon for which there is often no justification except guesswork and expectation.

MISSING IN ACTION

Time lapses feature heavily in the time storm, as already seen, for instance, on p. 83. It is my belief that using these experiences as a springboard from which to seek out mythical alien kidnaps has been a gigantic mistake that has led UFOlogists astray and deterred scientific commentators from appreciating the true importance of these common anomalies. Once you are willing to avoid assumptions about the nature of these events, you can begin to seek out what they really mean.

To conclude this chapter I want to feature another extraordinary case being studied in the USA as an alien contact, though this is merely a presumption. It was never reported in this context and has no direct suggestion of extraterrestrial presence. Viewed as it really is – perhaps physical evidence for a time lapse – it is far more interesting.

Florida (USA), 1996

In 1996 a video tape and covering report were submitted anonymously to a US TV station. The case has since been deeply researched by several people experienced in this field, including psychiatrist John Carpenter, physical scientist Ted Phillips, criminologist Dr William Schneid and computer analysis expert Dan Ahrens, mostly working with the group MUFON (Mutual UFO Network). They are all agreed that this was not a hoax, but a genuine and baffling recording submitted by people who felt their credibility would suffer if they were publicly associated with such an odd set of events.

We do know that the events occurred at a small factory in Florida. It was 11.16 p.m. and the security guard was monitoring four linked cameras viewed on a split screen in his office. These showed various vulnerable locations, such as the back gate and front entrance to the factory. The tape itself shows all camera feeds together as a worker walks towards the rear gate through a loading bay and appears to look at something. Then a fuzzy white glow arrives and covers the area where he stands, and simultaneously some electromagnetic interference briefly affects the picture. The glow is present for a couple of seconds. When it has gone the cameras are all working normally but the man has disappeared.

A frame-by-frame analysis shows this worker's near-instant disappearance, swallowed up by the glow. Study of the shadows, burn-in effects of the glow on the camera lens and so on all support the reality of these images. The security guard reports that he went to search for the man, but he could not be located. Then, one hour fifty minutes later, at 1.06 a.m., the cameras record his return.

Again this is very sudden. All the factory lights go out, a similar fuzzy glow appears and within a fraction of a second the man is seen within this light as the glow rapidly fades. He is in distress and on all fours. Moments later he lurches forward and is violently sick.

The security guard, seeing the worker staggering about in this disorientated way, went out to help him. The stunned man could recall nothing of his ordeal: he had a two-hour gap in his memory. In total shock he went home and reported next day that he was too sick to work. He never returned to the factory.[19] ○

This case is very consistent with the global pattern that time storm cases reveal – including the misty light, the electromagnetic field, total disorientation, physical nausea and missing time. But never before have these reputedly been captured in action like this. Of course, under the circumstances we ought to remain cautious pending more information. But, I can see no reason why time storms could not be filmed if they are real. So this case just may be the kind of hard evidence we must seek out for the reality of time travel.

15
Travels Through Time

EVEN IF YOU HAVE FOLLOWED MY ARGUMENT AND AGREE THAT I HAVE ONLY sought to push back the frontiers of known science, not to reinvent them completely, you may be starting to get twitchy. The very idea of travelling through time seems absurd.

Perhaps research will prove that time travel in any practical sense is prevented by as yet undefined scientific laws. But once again we have evidence to review that may cause us to question that expectation. Yes, there is a leap of imagination required. But it is not one that is beyond credibility.

Indeed, it strikes me that considering time travel may offer a satisfying way in which to look at what is otherwise puzzling evidence. Remember that journeys through time do not have to become possible tomorrow, or even soon, for us to find contemporary evidence. We can try to establish now if it will *ever* become a reality. By its very nature, even if perfected hundreds of years from now when people will presumably know far more than we do at present, travel through time may leave its mark in our world today. Put even more simply, if there is no evidence of time travellers in our past or current history, it is likely to mean that time travel is impossible – because if it *is* possible people from some future age ought to be already visiting us!

If you do not like the direction in which this book is now heading, you are welcome to dispute any of my inferences. However, whilst my interpretation of these events is open to debate, the cases themselves are generally speaking not. Something caused these baffling things to happen, and if what I suggest is anathema to your view of science you still need a better alternative.

A FOGGY DAY IN LONDON TOWN

A very strange story was reported by Keith Field about the day that his life was saved in mysterious circumstances.

Camberwell (UK), 1963

It was January 1963, a foggy day in Camberwell, London, and he was a seven-year-old playing in the streets with his friends. They had discovered a box of fireworks left over from the November bonfire night celebrations and were watching rockets explode. Then they set up a line of sparklers and attempted to put them out with a hail of snowballs gathered up from the icy pavements.

Oblivious to what was going on, Keith realised too late that he was standing in the middle of the road and a car was heading straight for him. The driver had not seen the child because of the fog, but was now bound to hit him as he was only feet away. As Keith says, the moment he understood what was about to happen 'time slowed'. The car seemed to reduce to a crawl, like a film winding down, and then virtually stop. At the same instant, he felt a peculiar sensation in the air around him as if a crackling energy field had appeared. A bluish haze drifted in to fill the gap between Keith and the now static oncoming vehicle and totally enveloped it.

Whilst this extraordinary phenomenon was taking place, Keith reports something with which we have become very familiar – the Oz Factor. 'There was not the slightest sound,' he notes. But as soon as the blue cloud covered the car, sounds of his friends screaming and the traffic blaring returned as did the flow of time. The car horn was sounding a long, continuous note. The car itself had stopped in its tracks as if it had hit an invisible brick wall.

A passer-by rushed to the vehicle and found the driver slumped over the steering wheel. Several people, looking from house windows, had been alerted by the fireworks. When the police arrived, these observers told them that the car had stopped suddenly, without skidding. A detective later visited Keith's family to ask a few questions. The officer said that the car driver was dead, presumably from a heart attack. The car's speedometer was stuck at just over 40 mph, as if frozen into place. ○

Some force, as if aware of the impending disaster, had intervened. But who would know that this random tragedy was going to happen and so be ready to act? Perhaps someone to whom the accident was now history.[1]

A VISIT FROM THE FUTURE?

Although in Keith's story the link with time travel is circumstantial, another case seems more clearly to involve visitors from the future.

Pennines (UK), 1942

Bernard, from the North of England, reported his experience to me. A happily married man, he trained as a nurse and rose to a prominent position in that profession. This is why he asked me to protect his identity, because he feared that his credibility and employment prospects could suffer. He admitted that he had talked in confidence to several psychologists at work, hoping that they could find some explanation for what had happened. None could offer an obvious resolution. You will see why.

During World War II, Bernard, then a young boy, had befriended a girl called Angela Shine who had been evacuated from Surrey. One summer day in 1942, they walked up a hill east of Manchester, as they often did, in an area where a firing range usually allowed them to look for spent bullets. Two things happened suddenly: there was an overwhelming air of calmness and quiet that descended over the hills (the Oz Factor again) and a strange sensation of drifting off and losing consciousness.

The two youngsters sat down by a tree and drank in the strange calm in a state that Bernard described as some sort of 'reverie'. However, what happened next was no mundane vision or apparition. Frankly, it is hard to say what it was as neither Bernard nor Angela could explain.

They became aware of voices. As the two of them sat up to watch, they could see that two men were now standing over them, discussing the children as if not expecting to be heard. 'Here they are,' one man said. The other man was holding something in his hand and kept looking at it, reading off a string of numbers as if from an unseen dial. A conversation followed in which the two men discussed concepts that made little sense to Bernard, but he could get the gist of it. They were talking about time as if it were a landscape to be navigated. Occasionally they would pause and say something in admiration, such as, 'They are beautiful children, aren't they?'

The two men were certainly human and had a handsome appearance. They wore unusual synthetic-looking, bright suits – very out of place in the wartime austerity of Britain. At the time neither child assumed them to be time travellers. All sorts of ideas, such as angels, came to them but were dismissed.

Bernard recalls that a lengthy discussion followed and the two men started talking *to* the children. They described events that would happen in their lives, and seemed to be reading from a script of Bernard and Angela's future as if to these visitors it had already happened. Then they warned the youngsters to say nothing. It was a 'secret'. When Bernard asked who these strangers were and where they came from, one of the two smiled, looked at the summer sky and replied, 'From a long way away.'

Then the two men told the children they needed to sleep. Bernard recalls a light glowing brightly above their heads, but he is not sure what it was. There was a feeling of warmth and then they lost all awareness until they awoke shortly afterwards. Their memories of the experience were patchy and they spoke little of it, content to head off home for tea.

Near the foot of the hill they met a farmer who asked who they were. When they told him, he said they should hurry home. There they were greeted by worried relatives. Although the children believed that they had been away for just two hours, they had been missing for more than a day. Nobody believed they had been on the hill looking for bullets, as the area had been thoroughly searched and the two of them had simply not been seen (oddly reminiscent of the sailor on the Atlantic tanker ship: see p. 71).

Bernard and Angela spoke little of their experience, wanting to fulfil their promise to the strangers. They realised that they had shared a 'dream', but, more importantly, both had an unexplained mark on their arm (in the area Bernard now recognises as the brachial artery). This small puncture mark was enough to convince them that this event – whatever it was – really did happen. ○

DESTINY

If Bernard and Angela really did encounter time travellers from the future, this meeting seems innocuous. What purpose did it serve? Of course, it need not have served any. Perhaps it was merely a chance encounter with a future time traveller on an exploratory flight from who knows when.

Rodney (USA), 1968

In 1968 Sharon Cooper from Rodney, Michigan, was the mother of a two-year-old. She had left him sound asleep in bed and was sitting on the porch talking to some friends while she waited for her husband to come home from night shift at the factory. Suddenly, the neighbours all saw a glow on the road in front – it just 'materialised'. The women puzzled over it as a car approached fast. The vehicle seemed to weave about, as if a drunk driver were at the wheel. But as if seeing the light (now on a collision course), it swerved off to the other side of the road and moved away, still seemingly out of control. After taking their gaze off the fast-disappearing car, the women looked back, but the tree-sized glow had gone.

> *. . . to Sharon's horror her son was in the middle of the road. He had slipped out of the bedroom, [gone] round the back of the house and on to the road. The out-of-control car would have killed him had not the strange glow appeared in its path and diverted it.*

The witnesses got up to walk into the road to see if they could find any reason for this odd sight, such as a stray reflection. There was none. But to Sharon's horror her son was in the middle of the road. He had slipped out of the bedroom, round the back of the house and on to the road. The out-of-control car would have killed him had not the strange glow appeared in its path and diverted it. O

Of course, it would be a fantastic coincidence if these two events were not somehow linked. We have to assume that, whatever the glow was, its appearance was connected to the plight of this child. Someone, or something, apparently knew that danger was imminent and prevented the car from ploughing into the child. Naturally, we cannot be certain that it was a time traveller. But this story seems to suggest a deliberate mission to rescue the child – a mission from somewhere that knew up front what was going to happen.[2]

WALKING WITH TRILOBITES

Anecdotal stories like these are interesting, but not proof of anything. But then how do you look for hard evidence of time travellers – tangible signs that people from the future have visited the past?

Science knows a good deal about the origins of life on earth, through geological methods such as studying rock strata and fossils. Fossils are moulds or casts of bones of animals that died and became covered in mud or sand after which the sediment hardened into rock over very long periods of time. They were then buried under mountains or oceans for millions of years. Eventually, this rock was exposed by geological upheaval and rediscovered. Because we know when each particular rock was formed or geological upheaval occurred, we can calculate when the animals that turned into these fossils must have lived and died.

Life on earth began with primitive cells about four billion years ago, developed into crude life forms much later, and only led to what we could consider real creatures such as insects, reptiles and so on about four hundred million years ago. Humans appeared far more recently still – just a few million years ago – and civilised humans as late as maybe fifteen thousand years ago. So any sign of intelligent human life on earth way back in geological history would be so anomalous that time travellers on a field trip from the future would be one of the few serious options to explain it.

Many strange geological discoveries do suggest this possibility, but some are open to debate. For instance, a sphere like a metal cricket ball has been found in South African rock of almost three billion years ago, when no animal life existed. It looks artificial, but could easily be a natural product created by heat or friction in the same way that small space particles called tektites look man-made but are melted naturally by their entry into the earth's atmosphere.

More difficult to explain is what resembles a sandal shoe print found by a trilobite collector near Antelope Spring, Utah in rock over 500 million years old. The fossil has definite hallmarks of a shoe, including signs of wear and of a heel. There are even crushed trilobites underfoot, suggesting that the wearer walked over them and left the imprint that later became fossilised. No human can have walked over a trilobite without time travel. These once thriving creatures which look like giant woodlice died out hundreds of millions of years ago.

Even more bizarre are various finds of artificial objects inside ancient rock: gold chains in coal seams, a rusty nail recovered from the Kingoodie Quarry near Dundee, Scotland, amidst sandstone rock 400 million years old, and so on. As the report to the British Association for the Advancement of Science revealed, the nail was deep in the rock, not on the surface, and could not have been hammered in after quarrying. Somehow the nail seems to have fallen on to the sand and been trapped in the rock *when it formed*. But how could a nail fall on to sand hundreds of millions of years before any human beings lived?

We always have to be careful with this kind of evidence. For much of the time, other possibilities can be found. For instance, there are what seem to be human footprints interspersed with dinosaur tracks in a magnificent rock exposure by the Paluxy River in Texas. The prints all date to 100 million years ago when dinosaurs thrived but nothing remotely like an ape (let alone a human) did. The 'human' print crosses and indents a recently laid down dinosaur trail, as if the human was following this creature. If the prints are, as they seem, human, then time travel is a serious option because no people really could have been 'walking with dinosaurs' without coming from the future. We can certainly imagine that if time travel is developed, geologists wishing to study dinosaurs will book some of the first tickets. If so, then such footprints may really get created. But recent computer simulations suggest that a form of dinosaur might have walked oddly and created prints that resemble our own. However, this is theoretical and there are sufficient geological riddles to suggest that one day we may leave evidence that is already a part of our past![3]

THE MAN FROM NOWHERE

Throughout history there have been occasional reports of people who seem to appear from nowhere and possess advanced or anomalous knowledge. It is a teasing romantic notion to think of the undoubted genius Leonardo da Vinci as a time traveller, because he invented aircraft and submarines centuries before that technology was available. But we need to bear realism in mind. Human geniuses do get born, and do not require a time machine.

Boston (USA), 1945

However, one of the most extraordinary cases of a man stranded out of time began on 11 February 1945 with the night shift at a Boston hospital. Nurses saw a man get out of an ambulance and wheel a trolley into the foyer. The ambulance driver said only of his patient, 'You will call this man Charles Jamison.' Police searches revealed that no ambulance had been sent to the hospital by any recognised source. Nurses described the ambulance as a blue van with no wording to match that of any ambulance services in the city. The driver was wearing what looked like a high-ranking naval uniform.

When doctors were called, they could see that the patient had shrapnel wounds and seemed to have suffered a mild stroke. They also found fading tattoos that involved both the British and American flags and the words 'US Navy' and 'United Kingdom'. A massive search, using the patient's fingerprints and involving the FBI, produced nothing. 'Charles Jamison' himself was unable to help: he was in a coma, with paralysis and a long-term inability to speak.

In summer 1947, Jamison suddenly sat up in his wheelchair and startled his nurse by saying in a noticeable British accent, 'I simply do not know', as if replying to a question. This led to lengthy sessions in which his doctor, Oliver Williams, and a British naval expert gently tried to coax information from him. He was shown many photographs of ships, naval uniforms and UK facilities in an effort to identify his home. Whenever tricks were pulled (such as showing him an inaccurate naval uniform), he saw right through them.

Jamison described serving on HMS *Bellerophon* in the Battle of Jutland in 1916 and sailing on the *Cutty Sark*, an old sailing vessel now a museum piece on the Thames. This might have been possible before its move to London in the early 1920s. However, he had no recall of any events after then – a quarter of a century was missing, and there was only talk of a 'secret mission' that he declined to discuss. It was unclear whether his amnesia was simply traumatic and had obliterated decades of memory or whether he was keeping a big secret.

The handwritten note in the ship's records baffled the former captain, who was unable to explain why it appeared to have been added later to the typed manifest.

After following a fortuitous lead, it was revealed that Jamison had arrived in Boston on 9 February 1945 aboard the USS *Lejeune*. The handwritten note in the ship's records baffled the former captain, who was unable to explain why it appeared to have been added later to the typed manifest. Nor could he recall Jamison. But the 'doctored' note said he had been born in Boston on 17 July 1895 and had spent four years in a German prisoner-of-war camp before being found inexplicably adrift off the Irish coast. This was during the *Lejeune*'s sixteen-day voyage from Southampton to Boston, repatriating injured troops.

Unfortunately, extensive research including checks on birth certificates failed to find anyone of this name who matched. Then an even stranger sequel came with the discovery of a note in the records of Lloyds shipping. This was a report by the crew of the German submarine U-24 that they had engaged and sunk a wooden ship that fired on them in the North Sea on 10 July 1941. This ship was clearly identified by the name on its side as the *Cutty Sark*. They saw it disappear under a barrage from the U-boat and rescued just one man – Charles William Jamison – who spent the next four years in a German camp in Belgium before being liberated in early 1945.

The *Cutty Sark* was not really sunk by the U-24 in July 1941. It was then berthed in London, and is still on display there now. Jamison was never able to resolve these problems. He did recall that his last posting was indeed on board a vessel sunk by a German U-boat, but gave this ship's name as the *Hinemoa*. The only ship of that name was scrapped in 1945 after being towed out to sea and holed with explosive charges.

After this final claim Jamison relapsed into a catatonic state and during his last twenty years of life never said another word. He died in January 1975 and was buried, with naval honours, in a coffin draped with the British and American flags. We may never know his true story.[4] ○

THE PHYSICS OF TIME TRAVEL

It may be that such cases have other explanations than actual time travel. But let us consider the possibility that they do reflect physical journeys in which people from our future have visited what is already our past. Is there any scientific respect for such a concept?

In fact, both relativity and quantum physics, as you have seen, have demonstrated that time seems not to be a linear progression – that in some senses information can be received from the future. However, sending information, or energy fields, through time is very different from sending people on real voyages. Relativity appears to argue against any material object travelling faster than light (or at least *at* the speed of light), and time travel would seem to require that.

Moreover, there is the thorny issue of the paradox which most physicists rely upon to prove that time travel must be rejected. Indeed, physicist Stephen Hawking has argued that some as yet unidentified law must exist to make the consequence of quantum physics (that time travel seems feasible) somehow untrue, because these paradoxes show that voyages through time defy what is reasonable.

A simple paradox is to argue that you build a time machine tomorrow, travel back in time and shoot yourself as you are being carried from the maternity hospital on the day of your birth. Since you can now never grow up to build that time machine, how could you be here in the past as a result of riding on a time machine that you will now never build? In fact, how can a future you exist since the future you has just ensured that no future you will ever live?

Such is the apparent absurdity of these thought experiments that actual travel through time seems hoist by its own petard, unless you envisage the paradox as forming part of a loop in which these events become a unity. If so, then they only *appear* impossible to us because we are constrained to think of time as a linear progression. Since it is not linear, concepts like 'before' and 'after' do not stop this event from happening because they are simply an illusion.

The other conceivable way to resolve the paradox is via the many worlds theory of quantum physics: the past world to which you travel is not the same reality from which you left. As such, in the above experiment you shoot only one of many near-identical versions of yourself and not the same being that grew up and turned assassin (that is, yourself). The only time travel that may be outlawed by the physics of such parallel universes could be into the past or future of your own reality. Journeys into alternative versions of that universe could happen without creating a paradox.

But when you design a more complex thought experiment, you suspect that even an alternative worlds theory might disallow time travel. Because how can you be shot, even by an alternative version of your future self? If there are many parallel realities, there may be many would-be assassins all conducting similar experiments to yourself. So being immune from your own bullet when you were a child does not mean you are safe from a million other future versions of yourself from some parallel reality.

Clearly there is immense complexity here. But perhaps it does offer one way to explain the story of Charles Jamison. Was he somehow projected into a different version of his own reality, in which most things remained the same but the *Hinemoa* was involved in a secret experiment and *was* sunk by a German U-boat? Did he recall a timeline out of phase with our own because it is not actually our own but simply one of billions of alternative realities that are more or less alike?

As you can see, time travel is a far more risky endeavour than space flight. If it is invented, it would be folly to make actual trips through time without a huge amount of research. Time travel machines will also have to fly like spacecraft. The vacuum of near earth orbit might be the only reasonably safe place to 'jump time zones' without risking suddenly reappearing in your lab fifty years from now right in front of an express train on the new railway line that has been built through your land. So time travel, if perfected, will at first almost certainly involve a simpler, safer method, such as the attempt to harness energy fields and transmit information, and probably not the immediate creation of an actual machine to carry people.

WORMHOLES

Modern physicists who are considering possible ways to build a time machine are beginning to explore such methods of information or energy transfer. To send a human through time, you might even first have to convert their molecules into energy and reconstitute them on the other side. This may naturally involve some possibly insurmountable problems!

But there is a way in which such a transfer could occur, using what

are known as wormholes. These are well supported as a probable consequence of the curved nature of space–time. They are in effect short cuts
through this folded universe caused by the way in which mass and gravity
bend, and may effectively forge a tunnel through space and time.

This effect is best imagined using an apple with two painted spots.
Because the surface of the apple is curved, you can use a tape measure
to gauge the distance between these two spots by the shortest route. Let
us say it is six inches. If you imagine a worm crawling along this line at
six inches per hour it would, of course, take an hour to make the journey.
However, a crafty worm might decide that it is much easier to munch
through the apple and thus burrow from spot to spot via the centre. You
can simulate this using a knife and punching through. If you core out
the hole, creating a tunnel, you can now put your tape measure through
and discover that the new distance between the two spots is much less
– let us say four inches. If the worm travelled at the same speed on this
shorter journey between the two spots it would get there in two-thirds the
time.

. . . if wormholes can be used as a basis for journeys around the universe, they offer a means not just to go from star to star at very fast speeds, but actually to travel through time.

Wormholes offer just such a short
cut between points in the universe.
According to our three-dimensional
perception of space, these two spots
(which might be different stars, for
instance) remain at a fixed distance, but
when you tunnel through like this the
trip can be made in a faster time. A
faster journey on a route that still has the same apparent length means a
more rapid velocity. This can even involve journeys beyond light speed
and in certain circumstances that means you travel in time. So if wormholes can be used as a basis for journeys around the universe, they offer
a means not just to go from star to star at very fast speeds, but actually
to travel through time.

QUANTUM FOAM

Michael Crichton is a master of scientific speculation. From novels and movies concerning futuristic theme parks (*Westworld*) to genetic engineering being used to re-create dinosaurs (*Jurassic Park*), he has researched and written about where science might plausibly go during the coming years. Many of these concepts have been only a little ahead of actual events. We may therefore take seriously his 1999 novel *Timeline* in which he suggests that in the twenty-first century technology may be perfected to send people through time.

Crichton bases his impressively conceived ideas on quantum physics, the many universes theory and the existence of wormholes. His one major progression is the idea that deep within sub-atomic matter the basis of reality will be composed of what he calls 'quantum foam' (first mooted by physicist John Wheeler in 1998). This links the microscopic realm by a whole series of wormholes of such tiny size that no current techniques can detect them.

In a review of this concept, Stephen Reucroft and John Swain, particle physicists from North Eastern University in the USA, find his ideas in keeping with the progress of modern physics. Like many quantum theorists, they seem to accept that the fiction of time travel could become reality as an inevitable consequence of where physics is taking us.[5]

Crichton's fictional scientists could not literally send a person through miniature wormholes, acting as tunnels between the trillions of alternative realities and different times. The enormous gravitational forces involved in wormholes and the black holes that probably spawn them, would be sufficient to tear normal matter apart. This would make their use as conduits for time travel very difficult. But energy waves can be made small enough to pass through such a tunnel which is so tiny that it has thirty-two zeros following its decimal point. So time travellers are broken down, pushed through the microscopic wormholes in the quantum foam and re-created anew in the alternative universe to which they are sent.

This process is more like photocopying than transportation from the *Starship Enterprise*, and begs the question as to whether the 'you' that emerges in the other universe or time zone is the same as the one that was left behind. The energy is the same, the physical matter different, much as the message on a photocopy is the same at either end but the paper on which it is written is not. Such techniques, if ever devised, may even allow us to discover whether body and soul are one and the same.

In fact, crude experiments of this type have already been conducted in quantum physics labs.[6] We can deconstruct single particles, send them as energy across a room and re-create a new identical particle at a 'receiving station'. We cannot ask the particle if it is exactly the same as the one that started out, of course, even if it appears identical. And, as yet, doing this with complex structures such as primitive animals, let alone humans, is way beyond our capabilities. But it is not beyond possibility. The indications are that when we are in a position to conduct plausible time travel experiments, it will involve the use of energy fields and their transfer through the alternative universes within the heart of quantum particles.

David Deutsch, at Oxford, is one quantum physicist who sees possibilities. In 1999 we appeared on a Channel 4 TV documentary discussing time travel. I was presenting real-life cases. He was describing how quantum physics may one day transmit energy through time.[7]

Another physicist seeking to develop time travel methods is Dr Frank Tipler, who says that a very large amount of energy is required. One possible source is the massive potential within the quantum realm, where linear particle accelerators move very tiny objects at large fractions of the speed of light. Once done, they engineer collisions and generate rare particles whilst releasing huge bursts of energy. Ever more sophisticated and powerful particle accelerators (super-colliders, as they are termed because they are used to smash particles together and generate short-lived subparticles) are being designed and will be built, probably as a result of international co-operation. Current examples of smaller experimental programmes exist near Stanford in California, Geneva in Switzerland and

Daresbury in England, although a new UK accelerator was agreed in March 2000 and will relocate to Oxfordshire.

Tipler has even calculated the form of a time travel energy field. Apart from having a huge output, it would consist of a cylindrical vortex and contain very dense matter that would create a gravity well. This might act like a black hole, causing light to get trapped and forming an apparent zone of darkness.

All of this data is useful because it offers clues when seeking the consequences of any time travel experiment or side-effects accidentally created through quantum experiments. From Tipler's research we might expect cylinders, vortices, huge glowing energy fields, gravity distortion effects, zones of darkness and apparent disruptions in space and time where people or things suddenly 'jump track'.

As you may have realised, these are exactly what we were uncovering in case after case during the first half of this book.

TIME AND A WORD

As we saw, Gregory Benford used energy transfer through time as the plot for his excellent novel *Timescape*. Here messages were picked up by early computers forty years before they got transmitted. A real-life case duplicates some aspects of Benford's speculations. I had some contact with the witnesses at the time and they have stood by their story in all their reports. Researcher Gary Rowe, who spent some time working with them, has reported that he was impressed.

Dodleston (UK), 1984

In October 1984, Ken Webster, his girlfriend and a college friend experienced odd events whilst living in an old cottage in the village of Dodleston near Chester. The events consisted of disruptive poltergeist attacks, with furniture being violently overturned and marks scrawled on to walls. This is similar to many other cases alleged from around the world, thought by researchers to be an energy discharge generated by emotional 'tantrums' – perhaps triggering quantum disruptions.

The violence diminished when messages began appearing on a primitive home computer. These memos were initially dismissed as a hoax played on the witnesses by unknown people remotely accessing their system. But a different computer brought to the cottage produced more messages. And when – almost as a whim – answers were offered on screen, the poltergeist attacks ceased and the messages increased in number. For nearly a year and a half, text was received on these tiny machines (by today's power standards) with no such thing as easy remote access, networking or an internet to make it simple for someone to 'hack in'. Webster and his colleague Peter Trinder, an English language expert seeking answers, contacted my local group in their attempts to discover what was going on. We tried to get scientists interested but, as Webster reports, this was never easy as people were at a loss to understand this case.

For nearly a year and a half, text was received on these tiny machines (by today's power standards) with no such thing as easy remote access, networking or an internet to make it simple for someone to 'hack in'.

The messages received are rather difficult to evaluate. They were rambling accounts ascribed to various sources, some claiming to be from the Middle Ages. One of these was a long-dead villager, Tomas Harden. Trinder was never happy with the phraseology in these messages, but one problem was that Tomas often commented that he was not *writing* them. The implication was that somehow his 'thoughts' were being captured by a 'light box' that transmitted his impressions through time. For obvious reasons, many people prefer to think that this whole thing has to be some sort of elaborate hoax. But no evidence of a hoax was uncovered. Most visitors ended up thoroughly perplexed and satisfied with the sincerity of the people involved.

Aside from the bizarre messages that might be regarded as some sort of communication from the past, there were also baffling ones that seemed to be from the future. What might be a date (2109) was sometimes attached. Although opinion is divided as to exactly what these meant, one definite interpretation is that some kind of consciousness was communicating across six hundred years and linking the past, present and future whilst interacting with this simple computer. So if there was indeed a hacker, it was from the future!

Such an idea seems absurd, of course. But if time travel experiments do occur, we might anticipate that some odd 'interference' effects could show up from them and that, by their nature, such interference would affect the past. For any future experimenters, the past would be our present.[8] O

SCRABBLE TIME

Although most people who have studied the Dodleston case suspect some playful hacker from the twentieth century at work, none of those living in the cottage is considered guilty because messages appeared when all were present or all were absent. However, what I find most intriguing is that at the same time as this case, October 1984, when nobody outside the Webster house knew about it, a very similar and not publicly reported case was taking place. Intriguingly, this too happened in Cheshire, this time at Altrincham. We might wonder if this was further 'interference'.

Altrincham (UK), 1984

In this second case, a graphic designer called Roy told me about odd things that had started to happen at home. I went to see him and was totally satisfied that he was reporting incidents that had occurred. Just as at Dodleston, some thirty miles away, it began with poltergeist effects. Roy would find coat hangers lined up on his bed in a neat pattern. He also claimed, just as Tomas Harden did, that he saw 'visions', as if someone were feeding images directly into his brain. This caused Roy to lapse into a state of reverie and lose contact with reality. In these images he saw a human-like figure wearing futuristic seamless clothing. He even once awoke from sleep to watch this figure (or a projection) as it stood at the end of his bed seemingly fascinated by his alarm clock. The figure appeared real (he had to screw up his eyes to see it properly because he was not wearing his glasses in bed), and yet when it suddenly vanished it made no noise. As the rational witness told me, 'If this was a physically real person in my bedroom, then air would have to rush to plug the gap left behind by its instant disappearance. That would have made a noise, but there was none.' This conflicting evidence most resembles a video replay – like those crashing bomber planes or the Butterflies 'ghost' – which would need to be viewed by the eyes but had no physical substance.

At Altrincham, too, there were problems with Roy's computer. He did not get lengthy messages across time. Instead, he had an intelligence that took over the memory and answered his questions. If he played Scrabble, the computer's artificial intelligence used randomly allocated letters to communicate with him. This seems to deny the idea of a hacker accessing his simple computer (a different model from that at Dodleston). It really seemed as if some force was controlling the computer memory and using it to correspond with Roy, exactly as it appeared at Dodleston. ○

WONDERLAND

One thing that is odd about the Dodleston and Altrincham cases is their location. This may be a coincidence, but it is intriguing. Almost in the centre of a line between these two places, the M56 motorway passes Helsby Hill, a quartz-rich sandstone outcrop that rises from the otherwise flat landscape. It contains a smattering of villages such as Preston Brook and Daresbury to the south of the Warrington–Runcorn new town.

This area has become a focal point for researchers into the paranormal who have been drawn by the remarkable number of bizarre events reported here. This area has not featured on TV or in the press as a 'haunted' location, yet dozens of people have independently described odd goings-on there. I have looked into many cases and even featured directly in one. Here is just a small summary of a few of the incidents; there are many others.

In the nineteenth century there were several reports of green glows and floating curtains of light seen over the region south of Runcorn. These are like the energy fields seen in time storm cases.

In October 1952 a violent Dodleston-style poltergeist attack occurred near the Mersey Estuary, tossing furniture about. The police staked out the house, but were unable to catch anyone causing the pandemonium.

In 1957 a man claimed to experience missing time and to 'go for a journey into space' after walking on a hill near Preston Brook. This was one of the first such cases reported in the UK.

In 1973 building contractor Peter Taylor told me how his brand-new car failed three times on separate days as he drove through Daresbury village. He had to get out and push it for some distance before the engine and lights came on. On the third occasion, he also blacked out and 'awoke' an hour later and forty miles away without any understanding of how he had been shifted like this through time and space.

Near Moore, in autumn 1977, two night security guards protecting a building site hid under a table as a huge white glow filled the air and a high-pitched humming was heard. They were later found by colleagues after they failed to make a radio check. An hour of time had just 'disappeared' from recall. On the ground outside their hut an odd 'frost' was scattered, despite the fact that the temperature was well above zero. This white powder appeared nowhere else (see also other cases recording this effect, for instance p. 36).

I have on record six other cases of glowing lights creating similar time and space distortions within this same small area. They include one from September 1983 in which a motorcyclist ended up not far from Dodleston after being 'transported' in some mysterious fashion from his last remembered position.

In March 1988 a terrified office worker described to me how she was driving on the slip road off the M56 between Preston Brook and Daresbury when she lost all awareness of time after seeing a 'glow' over the village ahead. The next thing she knew she was stumbling from her car and it was six hours later. She and her vehicle were covered in strange dark muddy spots, even though it had not rained locally.

Three months later I discovered that two TV reporters, Steve Winstanley and Fred Talbot, had had a strange experience when filming a local news item on canal barges. Passing through a tunnel, they had heard a strange noise and two tin cans floated up off their barge, hovered and fell into the water. They assumed it to be the result of a freak suction effect, but at the time they were passing under the very field beside which – unknown to them – the above time loss case had just occurred.

The owner of this land, Bill Whitlow, told me many stories of canal visitors hearing strange noises in the tunnel, which had spawned a legend that it was haunted. In August 1990 Bill himself was at the centre of yet another mystery. A crop circle appeared on his land within a hundred yards of where the 1988 time loss event and the floating cans incident had taken place. The swirled area of crop seemed to have resulted from some freak wind vortex striking from above. Locals told me they had heard a high-pitched screech or wailing noise during the night that it appeared.

The circle attracted no publicity, but I spent some time taking photographs before Bill Whitlow harvested the crop to prevent the media from finding it. As I stood in the field, my parents were parked off the road in their brand-new car behind a hedge a hundred feet away. Suddenly, a car climbing the hill normally from Preston Brook towards Daresbury crashed into them at speed. My mother was seriously injured and had to be cut free from the wreckage while our car was a total write-off. The driver of the other vehicle claimed he was pulled across the road on to the pavement towards the field (in which he could not see the crop circle because of the hedgerow). He assumed a tyre must have burst. But police accident investigators revealed to me later that his car was in perfect order and they could find no evidence of dangerous driving. It was, they said, just baffling, as if some force had just tugged him off the road.

CURIOUSER AND CURIOUSER

These stories have continued right up to today. They often feature similar themes – for instance, in 1995 a glowing light above the estuary off Runcorn was seen to suck a tube of water into the air. I received a report in the early hours of 25 August 2000 via Jodrell Bank Science Centre, which featured a glowing orange mass 'like an aircraft on fire' drifting from the outcrop atop Helsby Hill towards the Mersey

There is something truly remarkable about this part of northern Cheshire. It features many reports of glowing lights, strange noises, energy fields, gravity-defying incidents and, most specifically, distortions in the flow of time and space.

Estuary. But the point is surely made.[9] There is something truly remarkable about this part of northern Cheshire. It features many reports of glowing lights, strange noises, energy fields, gravity-defying incidents and, most specifically, distortions in the flow of time and space. There are too many of these relatively rare phenomena in such a small area to dismiss them all with comfort.

One woman told me in 1988 that her car had failed on the road between Moore and Daresbury and she was sure it was because of something that 'local scientists' were up to. She was told that this was nonsense. I got the same reaction when I contacted the nuclear research facility near Daresbury, where sub-atomic experiments have been conducted. This research centre is one of Europe's leading particle accelerators and in the late 1970s developed a pioneering 'synchrotron' that emits broad spectrum radiation to probe the structure of matter. 'Nothing we are doing here could cause such things,' I was assured, I am sure perfectly sincerely. But the woman whose car had failed told me later that a friend who worked at the plant had admitted that they received other phone calls from people who had suffered electrical interference or car failure, or saw strange glowing lights as they passed by. Whilst the facility could not see how it could be responsible, it was no doubt wise to avoid inviting public controversy.

It is worth pondering how this pattern seems to come together. We do know that if you accelerate quantum particles at extremely fast speeds various things occur. The fragility of the linear concept of time and space is exposed and possible doorways into alternative realities or spatial and temporal anomalies are revealed. It is not inconceivable that, unknown to the nuclear physicists working at any such research site, their experiments are producing unexpected side-effects in the local space–time environment. Do these involve disruptions in the framework and flow of space and time? Are rifts being opened up that lead to glows in the sky, humming noises, gravity distortions, electromagnetic interference, altered states of consciousness and bizarre trips through time and space? The evidence is provocative.

Perhaps this is merely a coincidence. I have no way of knowing if the

Daresbury facility could have accidentally created these anomalous events that seem to swarm around it. But we should look closely at the immediate area of other particle research laboratories. If similar patterns emerge, we really would have to consider the possibility that quantum experiments are providing the possible keys to real time travel.

What is also interesting about Daresbury is that the village has one other major claim to fame – it was the birthplace of Charles Dodgson, later to become well known as the writer Lewis Carroll. Biographer, Karoline Leach, tells me that Dodgson seems to have had a long-term interest in the paranormal, may even have had some strange experiences as a child in Daresbury and was intrigued by the mathematical theories that led after his death to the discovery of quantum physics. Several of his stories feature mysterious elements such as time lapses and, of course, *Alice's Adventures in Wonderland* and *Through the Looking Glass* have even been seen by some commentators as allegories of quantum physics. They do feature the strange distorted reality, discontinuities in time and space and semi-magical behaviour so typical of modern physics (see p.118).[10]

It is difficult to imagine that Lewis Carroll could have known about the scientific revelations, because these came years after he wrote his tales. And, of course, the remarkable experiments that would be undertaken by physicists right on his doorstep did not happen until far into his future. But as we have seen, there are two caveats to apply to our understandable presumption that there can be no significance here.

As Jung and Pauli noted, coincidences need not be as meaningless as they seem. And if pushing back the frontiers of quantum physics does distort the local space–time environment at Daresbury, the fact that this occurred a century into the future is not the insurmountable barrier it might appear. Just because these experiments did not happen until long after Dodgson's death is not necessarily to say that those experiments had no effect on him before they were actually carried out – for time is relative, do not forget.

Curiouser and curiouser, Alice might say.

16
Chasing Rainbows

In this book I have attempted to build a reasonable argument for what might be happening. I feel the pattern that emerges points the way towards the need for further study. The signs suggest that these cases may contain a hidden ability for time and space to be disrupted, not in some black hole in the far reaches of the cosmos but right here on earth in everyday circumstances.

What has to happen next is simple. More people need to take on the task of chasing rainbows – seeking out these anomalous cases. If this work independently duplicates my findings, we can reasonably conclude that we are on to something. I believe that we are, but if I am wrong then some other answer must exist. That is the challenge that we now face.

But just how do we set about finding new time storm cases?

A GRAND DELUSION

We live in an age in which the supernatural has been turned into a highly profitable circus. Tall tales frequently prop up flagging newspapers, and TV shows know they can improve their ratings by featuring aliens. Star witnesses perform a well-practised routine about mystery and government cover-ups. Most are just swept along by the rush to judgement that descends over these subjects like a tidal wave.

Our world has fallen for a massive delusion. Yes, there are reports of strange things going on, but that's all they are – reports, with lots of wild speculation. The idea that they reflect aliens probing us like lab rats is very weak on evidence. But many people perceive possibility as certainty and explain the lack of credible proof (such as extraterrestrial DNA) as part of some global conspiracy.

> *Our world has fallen for a massive delusion. Yes, there are reports of strange things going on, but that's all they are – reports, with lots of wild speculation. The idea that they reflect aliens probing us like lab rats is very weak on evidence.*

Witnesses to a time anomaly must perceive it in culturally relevant terms. Distortions to space and time rarely get seen in their own right but rather as symptoms of a greater cause. Story-hungry media and impassioned UFO enthusiasts fight over a case as they try to force out hidden truths about other-worldly visitors. By the time they move on, some tale about little grey men has taken root, been made into a movie and sold all over the world. There is no way back towards the truth.

THE FIRST TIME STORM

Probably the first time storm case that I encountered happened in October 1974.

Aveley (UK), 1974

The Days (husband, wife and young children) were returning home to Aveley in Essex when they rounded a bend and encountered a very localised patch of glowing green mist. As they drove right into it, their car radio started to spark with electricity, so the father pulled out the wires in case it caught fire. Then there was a bump, as if their car had bounced on to the road from mid-air, and everything had changed. They were inexplicably nearer home, and when they hurried in to watch a favourite TV programme not only had it ended, but the TV channel had gone off air for the night. Frantic calls to confirm the impossible revealed that it was true. In a blink, as they drove through the mist, they had lost over two hours of time. O

As you can see, this story is a fairly consistent example of the time storm. It has nothing to suggest aliens or spaceships. Unfortunately, by 1977, when it was investigated, that was no longer true. Two colleagues, Andy Collins and Barry King, both UFOlogists, decided to follow it up – as they did honestly – and in early 1978 I went with them to Aveley and met the witnesses. They were sincere, but by now the consciously reported facts had taken off for Mars because the two adults had been hypnotically regressed on several occasions. I sat in one one such session with Sue, the wife, and was stunned.[1]

The hypnosis had followed for several reasons. After the experience, the family suffered some common physiological changes (nausea, inability to eat certain foods, sleeplessness and so forth). They also had nightmares featuring strange lights and monsters (which may have been unconsciously based upon the then popular science fiction TV series *Dr Who*). Understandably baffled by what had happened, the Days were desperate to discover the truth about where they had 'gone' during the missing hours. It was never considered by anyone (myself then included) that they need not have gone anywhere (a time anomaly might have simply pulled them into the future). I was conditioned to think in terms of UFOs and aliens, just as they were, and indeed even now half the world is still deeply conditioned.

So we presume there was an actual event to explain what happened during any missing time. The hypnosis offered an escape route from confusion and created an account of being 'beamed' into a UFO inside the mist. It was satisfying to the witnesses. It explained where they had been. It helped them to cope. For a while it satisfied me too, although as I came upon more and more cases the doubts grew.

In truth, we have zero evidence for the reality of a UFO trap hiding inside green mist waiting to snare this family in their car. But that is how the 'Aveley abduction' is now known as a star case in British UFO lore. Of course, we also have only the sincere witness testimony for the initial incident. But they all concur and there is a logical consistency. The puzzling time gap makes it more, not less, credible, given what we know about the very similar time storms from this book.

This is not so with the alien 'memory'. The husband and wife here shared only partly similar stories under hypnosis. Their accounts of the trip into the UFO diverged because they were supposedly led off to different parts of the ship on their extraterrestrial guided tour.

In many abduction cases clues are often visible within the added hypnotic testimony, or through dreams and flashbacks. I have come upon witnesses revealing stories that seem triggered by personal phobias. There were TV shows (the robot out of *Buck Rogers in the 25th Century* or bracelets worn in *Blake's Seven*). And after one witness sincerely told the world on TV about aliens smelling of cinnamon, several cases with this previously unheard of feature soon cropped up.

To me this is pretty conclusive evidence of how we should interpret what is happening. The raw, consciously recalled details of the time storm describe a real event. The glowing mist, electrical effects, sense of floating off the road and the sudden jump through time and space are the actuality. Everything else is visionary and added later as a result of our natural desire to eliminate the gap in recall. Unfortunately, this quest often uses hypnosis – a technique widely known to introduce fantasy just as easily as true recall (which is why it is rarely used in courts of law). Through the widespread myth about alien contact, what began as an intriguing time anomaly can lose all coherence amidst 'padding' from the subconscious.[2]

CASE HUNTING

Each case needs to be stripped of all the preconceptions that will surround its reporting. You have to look at the facts as consciously and
reliably reported, and forget speculative, imaginary or visionary add-ons
that grow like barnacles during the public airing of such events. Take this
next case. Here is what the witnesses describe. You will see immediately
why it should be of interest.

Harperrig Reservoir (UK), 1992

On 17 August 1992, Gary Wood and Colin Wright drove across the
moors west of Edinburgh carrying a satellite TV tuner that they were
delivering to a friend at Tarbrax. To reach this very isolated village off
the A70 requires a drive of twenty miles through virtually uninhabited countryside that includes several reservoirs and the Pentland
Hills. Some time after 11 p.m. they were halfway there and not close
to any village, but near the Harperrig Reservoir above the starlit road
on their left.

Suddenly Colin yelled to Gary, who was driving, and instinctively
Gary put his foot down, taking them into the approaching blind corner
at speed. Colin had seen a dark mass ahead of them and only twenty
feet above the road. By accelerating, Gary was seeking to drive under
it and escape. It was an unthinking reaction to the perceived danger.
Within moments they were underneath the mass and several events
rapidly followed. Firstly, the Oz Factor took hold as all sounds disappeared. A strange state of disassociation came over them. The car
radio faded into silence. But the oddest part was how what seemed
like a 'shimmering curtain' of mist had descended along with (or
perhaps now was) the dark mass. There was no way to avoid driving
into this.

Once inside the dark mist there was nothing but blackness. Every
light – from the stars, from their headlamps – was swallowed up in

an inky void. Colin reports: 'I kept thinking that we were going to crash into a field, because there was another tight bend after this first one. But for some reason we did not do so.'[3]

What happened next utterly stunned these two men but will not surprise readers of this book. As if it had been sucked up off the road and then dropped (although they do not recall this happening), their car hit the tarmac with a heavy jolt. The 'black curtain' had gone and the stars were visible again. Somehow they had gone through the tight bends without catastrophe and were correctly aligned on the A70 some distance further along, driving as if nothing had happened. They were perplexed, but continued to Tarbrax – arriving, to their astonishment, in the early morning. Some hours had seemingly just vanished.

At their friend's house, the expressions on their faces told the story. The two men also began to exhibit symptoms such as pounding headaches and muscular aches, and described feeling in a very weird state of consciousness as if their minds were not quite in phase with their bodies. They likened it to being on powerful medication. Some of these after-effects lasted well into the next day. ○

This story in its conscious form is a fine example of the time storm phenomenon, featuring most of the symptoms we have met often in this book. Unfortunately, but typically, it did not stop there. In their understandable search for answers, these men saw publicity for a Scottish UFO group. Inevitably, the idea that the dark mass was a UFO (and so, in popular conception, an alien craft) and the need to plug the missing time was eagerly grasped by some commentators. Hypnotherapist Helen Walters began to eke out further 'recall', and a story emerged from the two men (with some similarities and some differences) in which spindly aliens conducted 'tests' on these witnesses.

Once again, we face a case that now appears as an alien abduction. However, in my opinion it is again doubtful that this is what happened. The parts of this case of which we can be reasonably confident are a near-perfect match for the time storm. All the aspects that involve aliens emerged later, not consciously, through hypnosis and visions. At the very least we would have to treat this 'recall' on a totally different footing from more solid parts of the testimony.

When seeking evidence of time storms, the trick is to know which facets of a case to put aside as potentially misleading. Again and again you will find these to be the details that suggest alien involvement, leaving behind remarkably familiar events.

EXPLORATION

Researcher Ron Halliday cites a case from just outside Armadale in Scotland – in fact just north of Harperrig Reservoir and near the site of other similar events.[4]

Armadale (UK), 1994

On 30 July 1994 there was an electrical storm near Armadale. Andrew Swan, a power worker who laid cables, was sufficiently interested in this phenomenon to drive to a suitable out-of-town spot and watch. He went there at about 11.45 p.m. Once in a good position, he caught sight of a dark, pyramid-shaped mass near the ground. Andrew decided to drive closer, because he thought it was a helicopter in trouble. As he closed in, he called the police on his mobile phone to warn of danger. Then there was a strange noise and sensation as if his car was being bumped. Concerned, he remembered a halogen spot lamp he kept in the vehicle for night work and set this up to shine towards the dark mass. As soon as he did so, it seemed to reflect the beam back and the halogen bulb exploded through an overload.

Andrew decided to escape the scene, but to his horror his car engine would not start. Moments afterwards there was a rush of air and something sped past. Frustrated at the slowness of the police

response, Andrew called them again. When they arrived soon afterwards, he reported what had happened and insisted that they give
him a breath test (which he passed) so that they could be sure he
was serious. All that they could
do was call out the AA to rescue
the stranded driver.

> *When the AA patrolman
> arrived he was puzzled by
> the failure of the car engine
> and lights. Baffled, the AA
> told Andrew they would tow
> him home. But as the two
> men stood talking, the car
> lights came back on.*

When the AA patrolman
arrived he was puzzled by the
failure of the car engine and
lights. Baffled, the AA told
Andrew they would tow him
home. But as the two men stood
talking, the car lights came back
on. Donald Macandrew, the
patrolman, was traced by Ron
Halliday and says that he had no explanation for such an electrical
effect as it did not 'make technical sense'. In fact, Macandrew told
Halliday that after towing the car home (the engine still would not
start) he was sufficiently intrigued to return to Swan's house a couple
of days later and take another look at the vehicle in his own time. By
now it was working fine.

So far we have a dark mass, an energy discharge and odd electrical effects on a vehicle. But Ron Halliday's careful investigation with
the AA and police revealed another problem. The storm took place
before midnight. Swan was on site about twenty minutes and called
the police just after midnight, then a second time maybe half an hour
later, and they called the AA – bringing Macandrew on site at an estimated 1.15 a.m. That is not what the official records show.

The police computer logged the mobile phone calls at just after 2
and at 2.42 a.m. The AA records show Macandrew radioing his arrival
at 3.36 a.m. This is consistent with the perceived gaps between these
events, but may suggest an apparent time discontinuity that Andrew

Swan never recognised. He told Halliday that the computer records
must be wrong because there was no way he was out there for hours.
Yet if he did not make the first call until well after 2 a.m., at least
two hours disappeared around the time when his car was 'bumped'
and the halogen light exploded. ○

How often do other such time anomalies go unrecognised because no
jump in time is obvious?[5]

OTHER VISIONS

Another phenomenon that can be mistaken for a time storm is the NDE
(near-death experience). Here people who have a car accident, for example,
find themselves floating in dissociated states 'out of the body'. They see
strange beings and glowing lights and interpret them as visions of heaven
(rather than as an alien kidnap). But as you can see, the similarities are
notable.

In reality the NDE features the sudden onset of an altered state, the
sense of floating, disassociation, and sometimes the presence of a mist or
glow. Less common are reports of tubes and tunnels and encountering
strange shapes milling about inside the glow or mist. So the comparisons
with a time storm are even closer.[6]

Research has shown that many of the symptoms described during an
NDE occur as a result of hormonal changes and the firing of neurones in
the brain. Indeed, proximity to death is not even necessary. Often indi-
viduals only need to *fear* they may be dying to trigger the experience (for
instance, falling off a cliff into soft snow that breaks their fall). Again the
links with time storms are evident.[7]

There is a possibility that in some cases we simply misconstrue what
takes place. Expectation and circumstance dictate the form that the experience takes (and of any dreams, visions or hallucinations that follow). If

you think the glowing mass is an alien craft, the experience may become overlaid with imagery which supports that conclusion. If you believe you are close to death, any anomalous imagery might get swept along with that false interpretation.

Some NDEs have features of the time storm, although I have found far fewer of them reported in this context than as alien craft. Also, many records of NDEs do not seem likely to fit the time storm (for instance, cases in which a witness is undergoing medical treatment and is therefore surrounded by medical staff). This is not true of misreported alien contacts – a very large number of such reports, in my experience, seem to fit neatly into the pattern of the time storm when you strip away their façade.

So I would caution against stretching the evidence to make cases fit a time storm. In the Isle of Mull events, for example (see p. 80), if Dwight had driven the hire car off the road would the affair have been perceived as an NDE? Would the witnesses have lost consciousness in the accident and perceived their later recall of these events as a result of hovering between earth and heaven? Recall the 'something' swirling inside the mist. It is easy to see how witnesses might interpret that as a flying saucer, aliens, angels or dead relatives, according to circumstance.

TIME TRIPPING

Of course, we should also pay attention to time slips as some could mask – or even be a consequence of – time storm activity. Although such cases are rare, there are about a hundred well-documented incidents in the annals of paranormal research and I suspect there are more that take place but never get reported because witnesses simply do not know how to report them. Canvassing for information is one way forward.[8] This case illustrates some clues to look for.

Montélimar (France), 1979

In October 1979 the Simpson and Gisby families went on holiday together, driving from Kent to Spain via France. As I have learned from meeting three of the four witnesses, they had an odd experience when seeking overnight accommodation near Montélimar. As they drove along a back road, the Oz Factor took hold, with all sounds muting and traffic disappearing. They then found an isolated small hotel and stayed the night but faced three big problems. Problem one was that it was like a hotel out of time. The staff and guests all wore old-fashioned clothes. A policeman whom they asked for directions did not recognise the word *autoroute* (motorway) and the bill was ridiculously cheap. Problem two was that several photos they took at the hotel do not exist. When the film was processed, despite them all remembering taking these shots, they were just not there. The final problem was that on their return journey an attempt to stay again in this quaint 'theme hotel' failed as they could not find it. Extensive research, including return trips to France, have also failed to find any hotel on this dusty rural road. O

> *They found an isolated small hotel and stayed the night . . . The staff and guests all wore old-fashioned clothes . . . and the bill was ridiculously cheap.*

Did these four people enter another reality where they literally spent the night? If so, this would be the most fantastic case of a time slip on record. There are difficulties, such as why nobody noticed their modern car parked outside all night. But apart from such temporal absurdities (pretty much a way of life with time slips anyhow) the witnesses tell a consistent tale and seem sincere. What I also found interesting when I quizzed them in detail was the fact that they described a strange 'feel' to the weather just before the anomaly. It was sticky, with heavy pressure and a lot of static electricity in the air. This more than anything made me pay attention. It is the sort of clue to be on the lookout for.[9]

17
What Is Going On?

THE TIME HAS COME TO SEEK OUT POSSIBLE ANSWERS TO THIS MYSTERY. Because this is a new phenomenon, there is likely to be far more evidence than we have yet discovered, so such conclusions must be tentative. I offer thoughts and ideas for your consideration. But if you think you can unravel the truth, I would be fascinated to hear your views.

TALL STORIES

A few cases clearly owe more to imagination than to physics, and I have excluded several from this book because I felt them dubious. One famous incident involves the alleged journey of a doctor and his wife in their car across South America – arriving in an instant half a continent away in Mexico. The case contains some suggestions of reality (features like the sudden bank of mist), but local researchers whom I consulted consider it to be a hoax. This scepticism has never been proven, but was enough for me to exclude it.

There are likely to be tall stories that get reported as time storms. Human nature being what it is, a few people will invent things for whatever reason. We must always consider such a possibility, but it cannot be used to dismiss the whole phenomenon. Time storm evidence is built on widespread and consistent data from witnesses who have nothing obvious to gain and often much to lose. Most, I believe, are reporting what they have honestly experienced.

MISPERCEPTION

When dealing with strange phenomena as I have now for many years, you quickly realise some home truths. One is that only about 1 per cent of all cases are fabricated. However, the vast majority of claims turn out to be examples of misperception. People may take a video of a balloon and think it is a spaceship, but they do not commonly see meteors blazing across the sky and claim to be transported through time by them. Nevertheless, you do have to beware the over-zealous investigator.

Here is a typical cautionary example (a few facts changed to protect the guilty). Whilst doing a nature study in a park, Mrs Smith saw a golden misty glow. A local UFO team became involved and made a reconstruction of her case (deconstruction might be a more appropriate term). The glow turned into an alien craft as the questioning became more intense. Soon the witness was 'persuaded' that she got home later than expected (probably by up to an hour). In UFO group parlance that did not only mean that a time anomaly had occurred and was seen as this golden glow. Aliens were assumed to have kidnapped her and stolen a chunk of her memory. In order to 'help' resolve the dilemma that they created, this group set up hypnosis sessions with a 'qualified dentist'! After several attempts nothing much was remembered – I asked a UFOlogist why and was told that the aliens had put up a very effective barrier to stop recall of the trauma. Then the 'breakthrough' followed. Apparently, dentists offering hypnotic regression are not in the plans of super-advanced aliens who block memory recall. This woman now described sitting in a chair next to a being dressed in a silver suit. Quickly this golden glow in the park had become a full-scale alien kidnap that Mrs Smith believed was utterly real and the UFO group made the lead item for years in their lectures.

There are, however, a few difficulties. There was good evidence that the golden glow was just the landing light on a low-flying aircraft in a holding pattern caused by holiday traffic. More worrying still, before the hypnosis I checked with a neighbour who happened to be able to confirm the time that Mrs Smith had got home that night. It was not an hour later, as the eager UFOlogists had concluded. At best it was a few minutes later than expected. Nobody takes much notice of watches when having an experience like this, so who can be sure that a few minutes of time was unaccounted for? But it is very tempting to seek out alien contact because these exciting cases form reputations in the paranormal pecking order.

Of course, if the golden glow is not an anomaly and the missing time does not exist, the case falls apart as nothing more than a cautionary tale of believing too much. Hypnosis uncorked a genie and reality was the first casualty of this investigation, as it so often is within the paranormal.

This is not because the witness lied (she was sincere and would have passed a lie detector test). It was not because the UFO group was dishonest (merely out to prove a cause believed in so passionately that they found evidence that was not truly there). This case became more than it ever was through social forces and a widespread desire to find exciting aliens instead of 'boring' misty glows.

I have seen this sort of thing happen often. Of course, whilst sometimes (as here) there was probably never a mystery beyond the one manufactured by over-enthusiasm, on other occasions the same process follows a genuine anomaly. A time storm generating real effects is just as amenable to unconscious manipulation by those who seek – and find – what they want.

So there will be cases that have mundane explanations. And we do need to take care to look for them. There are recognised natural physical phenomena that have some attributes of the time storm. In this book, atmospheric vortices (a sort of mini-tornado), electrical storms, atmospheric ionisation possibly induced by changes to the climate and rare meteorological events like ball lightning could create some of the features being reported. If witnesses exaggerate other aspects of the case, we may have to consider time storms as being rare (but known) phenomena that do not require the laws of physics to be stretched.

I do suspect that some cases fit into this category. Check out what seems like an unusual whirlwind effect (p. 61) or highly peculiar ball lightning (p. 57). Scientists studying these phenomena can gain much from examining such evidence, and I believe that many interesting natural events do get misreported as supernatural. But will all cases have an explanation in terms of social pressure, misperception and rare atmospheric processes?

Perhaps, in the end, they will. If so, the apparent edifice of this mystery will erode like a sand dune on a windy day. However, what argues against this to me is the cumulative evidence. A picture has emerged of scientifically credible physical effects. These point towards a cohesive reality, as do the various clues about bunching of events (as around Daresbury) or clustering with certain people (visually creative and with interesting clues about brain chemistry). Then there are the altered states, reality blinks and other well-reported patterns to this phenomenon. All of it fits so well with the cutting edge of known science about the nature of time.

Overall, I feel we still do have more going on than hoaxing or misperception.

COSMIC CAUSES

Science has long sought evidence for black holes in the deepest reaches of space. As yet they remain theoretical, but are well predicted by modern physics. By their nature (they stop light emerging) they are hard to find and need to be discovered via their side-effects. A few possible candidates have appeared, lurking behind astronomical phenomena a very long way from earth. But it has generally been agreed that you will not find black holes nearby. If you did, their consequences would be obvious. Indeed, arguably the earth could not survive even in close proximity to a small black hole because of its voracious appetite for matter and its enormous destructive potential.

However, perhaps mini-black holes can occur as bridges between the parallel universes suggested by quantum physics. If so, the position changes.

Scientists will argue that such mini-black holes would also be evident. The presence of that kind of spectacular phenomenon on earth would betray its existence by virtue of severe effects on light, gravity, space and time. All that is true, but we might say that such evidence *is* out there and science is simply not paying attention to it. Understandably science is sceptical, because this evidence is well disguised amidst jungle weeds of paranormal sensationalism. But hack them away as we have tried to do, and what gets left? Interesting data suggesting something that science may even now be seeking in all the wrong places.

We have seen cases (p. 14) where light appears to be absorbed to the point of total blackness, or where distortions on light create prismatic effects (p. 232), impossible 'bends' to light rays (p. 40) and a mysterious lack of shadows (p. 37). So mini-black holes may be occurring close to earth. I am qualified to ask such a question, but not to answer it. I leave that up to expert readers of this book. However, I do find it intriguing that we might reasonably predict the very effects that we seem to have found.

If mini-black holes are occurring, can they literally take people out of our reality, or drop them here from some other reality? Are they being dismissed because we judge the fantasies, visions and hallucinations that they provoke rather than the physical reality that is their cause? And can we find a way to harness the power within to develop propulsion, transportation or even time travelling mechanisms?

SIDE EFFECTS

Whatever time storms are, they take the form of a natural phenomenon – in effect a storm in the fabric of space–time. This may occur due to the forces of nature in the same way that a thunderstorm results from air flow or atmospheric electricity. But lightning conductors can influence the pattern of strikes during a storm. It is even now possible to create an artificial storm in a laboratory and mirror nature.

So can time storms be given a helping hand in their formation? Are they accidental side-effects of our own quest for scientific knowledge? Research into EM fields, the energy that swarms around us in the universe, has been continuing for more than a century. Occasionally, science has stumbled upon chance discoveries. In the early years of the twentieth century, the great electrical engineer Nikola Tesla was trying to perfect a way of sending information across large distances. He had a laboratory near Colorado Springs and local horses sometimes got electric shocks through their hooves, animals such as birds that used magnetism to guide them flew disorientated, in circles, and nearby electric bulbs glowed even when switched off.

By 1908 Tesla was seeking finance for an energy torpedo. He believed that he had a way to send massive pulses that would cause the air to glow and create explosions through energy transfer. Although he was widely acknowledged as a genius (he gave his name to a basic unit of physical measurement), most scientists thought such ideas cranky. But he may have been on to something.[1]

Tesla's great rival, Marconi, was commercially more successful as he stuck to practical applications such as communications. But he too appears to have come upon unexpected side-effects as a consequence of dabbling with EM fields. During the 1930s, he was in the employ of the Italian dictator Mussolini, and there are reports of complications from his research just outside Rome. Many sheep were found dead in their fields with no apparent cause. Mussolini's wife was once held up when car after car in a line ahead of her lost power. It was as if they had all entered some invisible curtain of energy. This story has a very familiar ring, given the data in this book.

In fact, Marconi was close to discovering radar in this work with VLF (very low frequency) radiation. Had he stuck to that task, World War II might have gone rather differently. But Mussolini saw the military potential of a weapon that could render electrical power useless and urged Marconi in this direction. He was considering defecting to the UK in July 1937 when he died from a heart attack.[2]

In Britain, Robert Watson-Watt's experimental physics team were covertly working in Rendlesham Forest in Suffolk (around what is now RAF Bawdsey and the Orford Ness nature reserve) when they too stumbled upon the destructive potential of EM fields. Many people in this rural area east of Ipswich spoke of car engines failing, of disruption to their electrical power, of strange buzzing noises and odd green glows. Fishermen off Orford Ness claimed that they got strange red marks on their skin when they went out on certain days.[3]

However, in 1935 the possibility of reflecting images of solid objects like invading aircraft was priority. As a result radar was perfected instead of a weapon. After the war, allied research continued in Rendlesham Forest. Even Marconi Industries set up a plant there. A facility on Orford Ness experimented with powerful over-the-horizon (OTH) radar because traditional radar is useless against high-velocity missiles through its physically restricted range (which gives no useful warning at high speeds). OTH radar bounces off the upper atmosphere and can see past the horizon formed by the curvature of the earth. But it is powerful, has side-effects and can ionise the surrounding air.

Much of this OTH research is still top-secret, locked away by the Ministry of Defence, but one codename used for the work was 'Cobra Mist'. So far as we know it had ended in Rendlesham forest by the mid-1970s, but a remarkable series of events occurred in this area that might be related and it ought to be no surprise that this area is now one of the world's most celebrated UFO sites.[4] Green glows have been seen emerging from the sea off the Ness (see p. 44). But most remarkable of all were the events of 26 December 1980, when a team of USAF security officers from the base at Woodbridge chased a weird glow through the trees towards

Orford Ness. This famous incident is usually portrayed as an 'alien landing' (it made front page headlines in 1983 after a Freedom of Information document was released in the USA).

The American servicemen who got close to the glowing mass have described it in familiar terms. They report how, as they closed in, the air was filled with a static charge, causing their hair to stand on end. They began to lose all sense of reality and reported classic Oz Factor symptoms. The closer they got, the more time slowed down. It was as if they were 'walking through treacle'. Then there was a blink in reality and they were somewhere else in the forest an hour or so later. They also seem to have misperceived a local lighthouse in very strange ways, even though they knew it was a beacon. They saw a prismatic mirage created by the glow splitting light rays, and shadows on the side acted 'out of phase' as if in a different time frame from the world beyond. Did they meet a rift in space–time triggered by the energy field research?[5]

Research into OTH radar still goes on at other sites such as Pine Gap in Australia. Geologist Harry Mason explored the cause of a mystery explosion in the Western Australian bush and found exactly what has been described in this book: electrical interference, green glows, all sorts of energy anomalies and even effects filmed from the orbiting space shuttle as it passed overhead. Without knowing anything about the events in Rendlesham Forest or the data from this book, Mason has argued that the alleged OTH radar work at Pine Gap may cause atmospheric side-effects.[6]

TIME RIFTS

It may be that experiments of this sort (or at particle accelerators) are unwittingly producing side-effects, which are not spotted because they are reported as being paranormal in nature and are therefore widely dismissed by naturally cautious scientists. However, the government of nearly every major power maintains an interest in UFOs, despite their argument (with which I largely concur) that most are misperceptions and none is evidence of some sort of alien invasion. We could ask why.[7]

The French government sponsors research involving atmospheric scientists at the space centre in Toulouse. The UK has three official departments collating data even in our money-conscious times. One of these is the DSTI (Directorate of Scientific and Technical Intelligence), a unit that employs Ministry of Defence scientists to study information under the Official Secrets Act. If there are no spaceships invading earth, why bother – ask the UFOlogist. Then assume there clearly *must* be spaceships that the powers-that-be are hiding.

I disagree, and say why else would it be worth monitoring UFO data? Here is one good reason. Natural energies in the atmosphere may be provoking some sightings and defence authorities (aware of the possibility from their own weapons research) would want to harness that power before any other country does. So they monitor the data. Indeed, if covert experiments produce these phenomena they would need to follow up what the public perceive of them. We might be unwitting guinea pigs in an energy 'cold war'.

Aside from the proximity to particle accelerators (where reported effects are accidental), it is fascinating to look at how UFO events cluster. We have seen strange activity around the research sites in Rendlesham Forest (UK) and Pine Gap (Australia). In the USA in 1948, the CIA and NSA (National Security Agency) were deeply concerned about green glows appearing with alarming regularity in one particular region – New Mexico. This area contained some of the country's top physicists (once secret files reveal the involvement of physicists such as Teller and Oppenheimer, who had been instrumental in building the atom bomb). The centre of attention was the physics laboratories around Los Alamos, then the most sensitive on earth.

The idea that aliens were invading these covert locations did not stand much scrutiny. I suspect it was realised very quickly that these events clustered around such research sites not because aliens were spying on them, but because the glows were the consequence of research conducted there by humans. We were accidentally manufacturing UFOs ourselves, in the form of atmospheric distortions. That is the real reason for a 'cover-up'. It has nothing to do with little green men and a lot to do with big green currency – the financial repercussions of commercial leadership in energy research. The aim is not just to understand these forces, but to control them, so as to develop from them new propulsion systems and some sort of weapon.[8]

It is impossible to say how much progress might have been made, but I dare say the ideas that we have explored within this book have not been lost on the brilliant minds in the employ of governments. The science may as yet be beyond us. The technology might not yet be achievable. But if there is a cover-up (rather than an expedient decision to let the UFO advocates cause chaos for them by their own credulity), it probably results from the unfulfilled possibilities of this phenomenon. Protracted secrecy would probably only follow failure. World domination might follow success.

TIME MACHINES

Although it is possible to view some UFO evidence as time machines coming back from the future, that is dangerous. So much of it is clearly very misleading. Just how do you decide if a case is really a time machine from the year 2050 or a misperception of a Boeing 737 from Heathrow?

None the less we have come upon some possible cases. Mrs Sage's futuristic helicopter is one that springs to mind as a possible time machine visiting its past (see p. 85). I would not eliminate the possibility that this EM research will one day lead us towards a machine that can travel through time. From all we have learned about the structure of quantum physics, we must see that as feasible.

One prototype time machine has allegedly been built. London inventor Tony Basset created a device that generates a large static electrical field and ionises the surrounding air. It is on a far smaller scale than those apparently used in OTH radar work at places like Orford Ness or Pine Gap or in the vicinity of particle accelerators, but Basset claims it has time-warping effects. This small box emits the faint humming and buzzing noise that I have often heard described by time storm witnesses. According to Basset, if you sit by this machine it can project you through time. He has conducted experiments in which people have been able to 'go outside and read car number plates that are not yet parked there' – presumably by visiting the future.

I sat in this box's presence in London for two hours, but nothing happened to me except a headache. Right next to it – touching it, even – was one of the four people who claimed to have experienced a time slip in a French hotel (see p. 224). Cynthia Gisby remarked that she felt a tingling and light-headedness in its proximity (possible symptoms of the onset of the Oz Factor), but no new time anomaly resulted.

Basset advised me that it was difficult to perform this experiment to order, but he could probably do so if he prepared carefully at home later. So I suggested that he go home, get it to work and then travel back to this moment as we attempted this experiment. If so, we should be able to witness the results! But as you might imagine, nothing happened. Tony Basset did not come back from the future. I suspect his device – assuming it actually does anything significant – creates visionary experiences (possibly by inducing the Oz Factors in susceptible people). During the resulting altered state it causes hallucinations. I doubt that literal time travel is happening here.

Of course, the most likely explanation for the failure of this test is that his device is not a real time machine – just a box that creates a static charge. Any success claimed by its inventor may result from an induced altered state and visions/imagination (take your pick), although I would be delighted to be proven wrong.

However, it is intriguing that the basis for this sincere experiment seems similar to the method adopted by Dr Michael Persinger, who creates electrical fields that can generate visionary experiences. The altered states and EM energy involved in Basset's 'time machine' are also not far removed from reported effects during the real cases discussed in this book.

THE PHILADELPHIA STORY

The best-known time travel experiment is so bizarre that it is a legend. It has spawned movies and a novel, all science fiction-based very loosely on alleged fact. I have talked at length to one witness who swears he took part in this experiment and was beamed decades through time by it, although I was not impressed by his suggestion that he recalled it only after seeing one of the movies which jogged his recall!

The case does not start with promise. It owes a great deal to an oddball. This man, Carl Allen or Carlos Allende (both names were used), first told the story to a UFO writer named Maurice Jessup in 1956. It is very probable that this witness made up much of his story. However, there are also some grounds to suspect that it was based upon real events far less dramatic than portrayed in the movies about the so-called Philadelphia Experiment.

One important established fact not down to Allende or Jessup is that in late July 1904 something odd happened off the Delaware breakwater near Philadelphia. It was recorded *after* the ship set sail for Romania, possibly as a result of a promise made to its captain not to draw sightseers whilst the vessel was still in port. This happened during a few days of unusual local atmospheric conditions that included a tornado, electrical disruptions and ball lightning – in other words, a flurry of electrical energy phenomena concentrated on this coastal area at the appropriate time. From the data in this book, these phenomena could be seen as a form of corroborative evidence.

Philadelphia (USA), 1904

The *Mohican*, a British vessel commanded by Captain Urquhart, encountered something that he said 'was beyond me . . . [I] never saw anything so terrifying in the years I have been at sea.' As they sailed in a dead calm, a 'strange grey cloud' appeared with 'bright glowing spots in the mass'. This made straight for the ship and quickly surrounded it, just as so many car drivers have reported happening.

Once within the cloud, the entire ship was filled with a 'strange glow' and the sailors watched in terror as their beards 'stuck out like bristles on a pig'. The compasses were spinning wildly. Some of the crew were on their knees praying and Urquhart tried to distract them by giving them things to do. But nobody could move the metal chains or anchors. They were magnetised to the hull, or perhaps weighed so much that nobody could lift them (it is unclear). A strange altered state descended on the crew (the Oz Factor once again). The captain described a 'great silence over everything that only added to the terror.' Time lost all meaning, but eventually the cloud disappeared and everything returned to normal.[9] ○

So much for established fact. We switch now to July 1943, thirty-nine years (possibly to the day) into the future and at the same location. Oddly, Philadelphia Experiment discussions do not mention the 1904 incident, though it is more verifiable than the alleged experiment itself and involves recognisable time storm phenomena in the same part of the western Atlantic.[10]

The story about what happened in 1943 relies on far more doubtful testimony. It started with annotations made by Allende in a copy of Maurice Jessup's book and sent to Jessup. In correspondence Allende related a tale of covert experiments carried out off the Delaware breakwater with a naval vessel, the USS *Eldridge*. Allende was proven to be a real sailor and could theoretically have been aboard a nearby ship watching, as he alleged. He explained that he had seen the *Eldridge* surrounded by an eerie green cloud that caused its hull to become semi-transparent. The legend usually expands on this to say that the ship disappeared or was teleported to a different part of the Atlantic (very near the scene of the 1904 *Mohican* incident). Some of the crew are supposed to have burst into flames while others ended up buried inside the steel hull.

Much of this sounds like a very tall tale. It is not clear that Jessup took Allende's ramblings seriously, but what was definitely curious (and still unexplained) is that the UFO writer was invited to the Office of Naval Research (the ONR) in Washington. This research unit had also been sent copies of Allende's allegations in one of Jessup's books, and a senior officer there decided to follow them up. A small reprint containing the marginal notes sent to the ONR was even paid for by this unit and distributed to their staff. The navy describe this move as 'a private venture' by the officer in question, but it seems hard to fathom why it should have been done unless someone thought there could be something to Allende's story. This is another hint that at the heart of the exaggerated stories there might exist a kernel of truth.

Not much has emerged about this meeting. Jessup was in a depressed state and committed suicide soon afterwards. The ONR, of course, were not keen to say much either. Allende disappeared.

This left the claims about the Philadelphia Experiment to grow wildly out of proportion and lead to the eventual fictions by which it is now best known. It was not widely discussed even in paranormal circles until a novel (*Thin Air*), the two movies (*The Philadelphia Experiment I* and *II*) and another movie (*The Final Countdown*), all loosely based on the same premise but with a twist, appeared between 1979 and 1993. None of these made any pretence to be true. Oddly, none referred to the 1904 incident.

An interesting feature of the more recent retellings (usually utterly unsupportable) is the claim that the *Eldridge's* crew were projected about forty years into the future. If this is anything beyond imagination, it is interesting to wonder if the side-effects of the experiment might also have projected thirty-nine years *back* in time as well (if we ascribe the *Mohican* incident in 1904 to such side-effects manifesting off the Delaware coast at that time).

Moreover, some of these latest witness claims allege that Project Rainbow (the name allegedly applied to the Philadelphia experiment) was continued after World War II right up until early January 1981 – in fact just days after the events in Rendlesham Forest (see p. 231), when it was allegedly abandoned. The work used abandoned equipment at a former OTH radar site on Long Island. If this is invention, it has coincidentally chosen highly appropriate hooks to build upon.

THE INVISIBLE MEN

It is hard to know if there ever really was a Philadelphia Experiment. My suspicion is that there probably was some sort of EM field test of a far less dramatic form than in the legend. According to Allende, Tesla's research (see p. 230) was the stimulus (the inventor was then working for the US government war effort, and it is likely that his EM field experiments were all part of this). The initial idea was to try to combat radar by finding a way to make objects such as aircraft or ships invisible to it – something that Stealth technology now achieves. The work involved creating a massive EM field in an attempt to deflect radar waves.

The idea seems to have been an extension of experiments known to have been conducted at this time, which used huge EM fields to try to detonate mines from a distance. This would allow an advance 'sweep' of the otherwise dangerous Atlantic shipping lanes that were constantly mined by the Germans.

The *Eldridge*, too, was a real US Navy ship. She was officially tested in the Delaware River in August 1943, so in July that year she would have been in the final stages of construction and could conceivably have been used for covert testing before being fully fitted out. Interestingly, all her records exist apart from those covering the period July to December 1943. So there is some credibility behind the basic fact that this ship could have been used as a test bed.

It is possible that experiments did seek to use EM fields to deflect radar waves, and that when conducted these had unexpected side-effects. Some of these effects fit remarkably well with the witnesses' testimony reported in this book (a misty cloud with a green glow, for example). We have also seen cases in which cars allegedly become semi-transparent during time storms (see, for example p. 91). So Allende's claim that this occurred to the *Eldridge*, whilst fantastic, is not without support from our own findings.

But did the ship 'disappear' and 'reappear' some miles across the ocean, as Allende suggested? Again, this rather surprisingly fits with time storm cases in this book. So does the most fantastic claim of all – that a hole in space–time created a vortex to project sailors into the future. Even this neatly matches reports that we have discovered in the course of this book.

So it is very difficult to know what parts of the Philadelphia Experiment might be true. But I think this book offers a sound argument for not being as dismissive as we surely otherwise would have to be.

I doubt whether naval experiments into time travel resulted from this attempt to aid the war effort, but EM field tests on the *Eldridge* might have inspired the OTH radar work that followed. At Rendlesham Forest, Los Alamos and Pine Gap, massive electrical fields, green glows and atmospheric disturbances have again been reported, seemingly by people who had never heard of the Philadelphia Experiment, because prior to 1979 few had. By then, many events tied to the alleged OTH research were already on record.

In the end, we can only consider such possibilities and wonder. There are some aspects to these events that we can be reasonably sure about, some that are more open to question, and others that are highly speculative.

I think time storms are an established phenomenon with a very consistent set of features. Something very interesting seems to be going on here. I believe we can accept that they occur through energy fields that trigger rifts in space–time. As a consequence they produce some extraordinary possibilities.

Open to debate is what causes these things to occur. Perhaps there is a natural disturbance in the atmosphere that can disrupt time and takes the form of a mini-black hole. Perhaps these events are by-products of our own long research into the use of EM fields, started for other reasons and leading to these anomalies quite unexpectedly.

Bear in mind that in New Mexico in 1945 the results of research at the Los Alamos labs massively disrupted atomic structure and brought nuclear reactions into being. These led to the local testing of the first atomic weapons. It seems unlikely that such energy could be unleashed into our atmosphere without some unforeseen consequences. Indeed, the lingering damage caused by radiation was not fully understood, so the scientists were not prepared for all eventualities. We may still be discovering an even more unnerving side-effect of our arrogant efforts to emulate God and, as Einstein put it, play cosmic dice.

It would be a remarkable irony if these two 'triumphs' of scientific endeavour – radar and nuclear weapons – were born to protect the world through unleashing nature's fury and yet had unexpected consequences that echo round the universe today. Did they expose the fragility of time and space, demonstrating a possible way to prise open the doorways between quantum universes? Have they pioneered what may ultimately prove to be success in time travel?

Certainly the evidence in this book, the ideas we have about the nature of time and the chilling pattern to the concentration of these events in and around such research centres is powerful. It may even be persuasive. At the least it is sufficient to require further exploration, because the prize – time travel – is so fascinating.

If we continue to chase those rainbows and research the evidence for time storms we may discover whatever truth lurks behind our disturbing questions. Then we can start in earnest to search for evidence. What will it mean to discover that our own descendants may be covertly moving amongst us, to know that they might be using whatever legacy we are building today through these strange experiments with space and time? How will our world change if the illusions of time are shattered for ever?

One of the great dreams of science fiction could soon be coming true. Proof of that extraordinary moment could be out there right now, waiting for us to find it. Indeed, in many ways the concept of time travel may already be true, and we might have to seek tomorrow's answers by looking in the past. Because in terms of time travel, tomorrow really is today.

References

Chapter 1

1. NUFON archives, Manchester
2. BUFORA case 77–444, *BUFORA Bulletin*, July 1978
3. Carole Thomas in *FSR Case Histories 10*, June 1972
4. Letter to *FSR*, Vol. 12, No. 6, 1966
5. *Northern Daily Leader*, NSW, Australia, 8 April 1976. Subsequent investigation by Bill Chalker
6. Chrysis investigation by Brian Straight
7. *Wings over Africa*, Durban, 1969
8. Investigation by J. Randles and R. Sandbach
9. Interview with the sister, 1988
10. Letters to author. Interviews by Ken Phillips
11. Information gathered on site in Hungary, September 1992
12. UFO research of *Finland Quarterly Report*, 2, 1981
13. Lecture by A. Huneeus, MUFON, Washington, June 1987, plus subsequent discussion with author

Chapter 2

1. See many examples in J. Randles, D. Clarke and A. Roberts, *The UFOs That Never Were*, London House, 2000
2. Statistics in *Vehicle Interference Report*, BUFORA
3. See articles on temporal lobe epilepsy and fantasy-prone personality in J. Randles, *The Complete Book of Aliens and Abductions*, Piatkus, 1999

Chapter 3

1. Song-Zi Xian county annals, researched by Lin Wen Wei
2. Letter in *Fortean Times* 79, February 1995
3. M. Caidin, discussion with author, Nebraska, May 1992
4. B. Chalker, *The OZ Files*, Duffy & Snellgrove, 1997

Chapter 4

1. Letter to author, 29 July 1990, followed by interview
2. *FSR*, Vol. 2, No. 5, 1956
3. Investigation for BUFORA by Peter Johnson
4. NICAP study, *Strange Effects from UFOs*, 1969
5. *FSR*, Vol. 13, No. 6, 1967

Chapter 5

1. *FSR*, Vol. 21, No. 5, 1976
2. J. Vallée, *A Challenge to Science*, Spearman, 1967, pp. 194–7
3. *Project Blue Book*, USAF, Dayton, Ohio
4. Experiments on two cars – one involved in a car stop in Essex, the other its sister hire car – did show minor variations, but not sufficient to enable clear statements to be made
5. D. Group, *Evidence for the Bermuda Triangle*, Aquarian Press, 1984, p. 98
6. *International UFO Reporter*, July 1983

Chapter 6

1. M. Persinger in *Perceptual and Motor Skills Bulletin*. Many digests in *Bulletin of Anomalous Experience* (available on CD-Rom)
2. 'Mind Phantoms', *New Scientist*, 8 July 2000
3. S. Roney-Dougal, *Where Science and Magic Meet*, Element, 1991
4. *New Scientist*, 19 November 1994
5. Letter to author from witness, February 1978
6. Brigit Salgstron, *UFO Sweden*
7. Letter to author, 26 October 1990

Chapter 7

1. On-site investigation by J. Randles and R. Sandbach
2. D. Clarke and A. Roberts, *Phantoms of the Skies*, Hale, 1990
3. D. Group, *Evidence for the Bermuda Triangle*
4. *FSR*, Vol. 32, No. 3, 1987
5. B. Chalker, *The Oz Files*, pp. 183–9

Chapter 8

1. K. Basterfield, *UFO*, Reed, 1997, pp. 89–103
2. BUFORA case investigation by K. Phillips and J. Jafaar, 1992
3. Letter from witness to author, 1987
4. *FSR*, Vol. 22, No. 2, 1976
5. Investigation by Dr Richard Sigismonde, discussion with author November 1983

Chapter 9

1. Investigation for BUFORA by D. Dixon, 1999
2. Letters from witness to author, various dates in 1980
3. C. Parsons, *Encounters with the Unknown*, Hale, 1990, pp. 139–40
4. R. Davies, *Supernatural Disappearances*, Hale, 1995
5. *FSR*, Vol. 27, No. 2, 1981
6. *FSR*, Vol. 21, No. 3, 1975

Chapter 10

1. G. Whitrow, *The Natural Philosophy of Time*, OUP, 1980
2. The Zeno paradox was named after the Greek philosopher who asked how long it takes to catch an arrow in flight. You move towards it, but in the same time it moves away from you. How do you ever catch it? he wondered.
3. J. B. Priestley, *Man and Time*, Aldus, 1964
4. Sir A. Eddington, *The Nature of the Physical World*, Cambridge University Press, 1928

5.   P. Caveney and R. Highfield, *The Arrow of Time*, W. H. Allen, 1990

6.   A. Einstein, *Relativity: The Special and General Theory*, Methuen, 1920

7.   S. Hawking, *A Brief History of Time*, Bantam, 1995

8.   J. Gribbin, *Timewarps*, Dent, 1979

9.   P. Davies, *God and the New Physics*, Penguin, 1983

10.   L. Fagg, *The Two Faces of Time*, Quest, 1985

11.   M. Born, *Atomic Physics*, Blackie, 1969

12.   G. Zukav, *The Dancing Wu-Li Masters,* Hutchinson, 1979

13.   R. Brennan, *Heisenberg Probably Slept Here*, Wiley, 1997

14.   D. Bohm, *Wholeness and the Implicate Order*, Routledge & Kegan Paul, 1980

Chapter 11

1.   D. Bohm, *Wholeness and the Implicate Order*

2.   A. Faraday, *The Dream Game*, Harper & Row, 1976

3.   Manoharan, Lutz and Eigler, 'Quantum Mirages Formed', *Nature*, Vol. 403, February 2000, p. 512

4.   *Daily Telegraph*, 12 April 1997

5.   *Daily Telegraph*, 26 June 1997

6.   J. Randles, *Sixth Sense*, Hale, 1986, p. 62

7.   J. Sarfatti, *The Roots of Consciousness*, Random House, 1975

8.   D. Bohm, *Wholeness and the Implicate Order*

9.   E. Taylor and J. Wheeler, *Space–Time Physics*, Freeman, 1966

Chapter 12

1.   C. Jung with W. Pauli, *Synchronicity*, Routledge & Kegan Paul, 1953

2.   C. Jung, *Flying Saucers: A Modern Myth*, Routledge & Kegan Paul, 1959

3.   J. Randles, *The Paranormal Sourcebook*, Piatkus, 1999, pp. 79 and 217

4.   The complete books of Charles Fort, available through John Brown Publishing. Available in simple volumes or as collected works

5. *London Evening Standard*, 23 July 1997

6. 'Falls from the Sky' in J. Randles, *The Paranormal Sourcebook*

Chapter 13

1. *Sixth Sense*, p 18, op cit

2. J. Randles, *Phantoms of the Soap Operas*, Hale, 1989

3. D. Zohar, *Through the Time Barrier*, Heinemann, 1982, Chapter 10

4. G. Rattray Taylor, *The Natural History of the Mind*, Secker & Warburg, 1979

5. H. Saltmarsh, *Foreknowledge*, Bell, 1938

6. A. Baddeley, *Your Memory*, Avery Inc., 1993, p. 61

7. Private communication from witness

8. J. Grant, *Dreamers*, Ashgrove, 1984

9. Anamnesis life profile research by K. Phillips and A. Keul for BUFORA

10. Letter in *Fate*, July 1986

11. J. Randles, *Time Travel*, Blandford, 1994

12. Ninian Marshall in *British Journal for Philosophy of Science*, 1960

Chapter 14

1. Letter in *Exploring the Supernatural*, October 1986

2. J. Randles and P. Hough, *The Afterlife*, Piatkus, 1994

3. 'Cursed Crossroads' in J. Randles' *Truly Weird*, Collins & Brown, 1998

4. J. Forman, *The Mask of Time*, Macdonald & Janes, 1978, p. 62

5. J. Forman, *The Mask of Time*

6. J. Randles, *Star Children*, Hale, 1994. J. Randles and P. Hough, *Life after Death and the World Beyond*, Piatkus, 1996

7. J. Randles, 'Slip in Time'. *Strange but True? Casebook*, Piatkus, 1995

8. J. Randles, *Intruder on the Shore. The Truth about the MIB*, Piatkus, 1997

9. *Merseymart*, 10 June 1999

10. J. Randles and P. Whetnall, *Alien Contact*, Neville Spearman, 1981

11. D. Clarke, *Supernatural Peak District*, Hale, 2001

12. Letter in *Strange* magazine, 12, 1993
13. P. Devereux, *Earthlights*, Turnstone, 1982
14. M. Persinger and G. Lafreniere, *Space–Time Transients*, Nelson-Hall, 1977
15. Letter in *Fortean Times*, 83, 1995
16. 'Phantom Intruder,' in J. Randles' *Truly Weird*
17. George Filer files, January 2000
18. J. Randles, *The Complete Book of Aliens and Abductions*, Piatkus, 1999
19. John Carpenter in *MUFON Journal*, May 1999

Chapter 15

1. *Fate*, June 1978
2. Letter in *Fate*, June 1985
3. M. Cremo and R. Thompson, *Forbidden Archaeology*, Bhaktivedanta, 1997
4. See research by Ron Edwards in *Fate*, March 1997
5. 'Rip in time', *Boston Globe*, 3 January 2000
6. Work was conducted in 1998 by physicists at Cal Tech, as reported in *Science*, 23 October 1998
7. D. Deutsch and M. Lockwood, 'Quantum Physics of Time Travel,' *Scientific American*, March 1994
8. K. Webster, *The Vertical Plane*, Grafton, 1989
9. J. Randles and P. Hough, *Mysteries of the Mersey Valley*, Sigma, 1992
10. K. Leach, *In the Shadow of the Dreamchild*, Peter Owen, 1999

Chapter 16

1. UFOIN investigation by A. Collins and B. King
2. See 'Hypnosis Problems' in J. Randles' *The Complete Book of Aliens and Abductions*
3. J. Randles, and P. Hough, *Strange But True?*, Piatkus, 1994
4. UFOIN investigation by M. Keatman
5. R. Halliday, *UFO Scotland*, B & W publishing, 1998, pp. 210–13

6. See J. Randles, and P. Hough, *The Afterlife*
7. S. Blackmore, *Dying to Live*, Grafton, 1994
8. J. Randles, *Time Travel in Fiction and Possibility*, Blandford, 1994
9. J. Randles, *Strange but True? Casebook*

Chapter 17

1. O. Nichelsen, 'The Death Ray of Nikola Tesla,' *Fate*, January 1990
2. D. Marconi, *My Father Marconi*, McGraw-Hill, 1962
3. B. Butler, J. Randles and D. Street, *Sky Crash*, Grafton, 1986
4. J. Randles, *UFO Crash Landing: Friend or Foe?*, Blandford, 1998
5. J. Randles, *UFO Study*, Hale, 1981
6. P. Hough and J Randles, *Supernatural Causes* (unpublished manuscript), 2000
7. J. Randles, *Intruder on the Shore. The Truth about the MIB*
8. D. Clake, J. Randles and A. Roberts, *The UFOs That Never Were*, London House, 2000
9. M. Shokemaker in *Fortean Times*, 48, 1997
10. 'Disappearing Act', *Fortean Times*, 128, 1999

Useful Addresses

BUFORA (British UFO Research Association)
BM BUFORA, London WC1N 3XX
www.bufora.org.uk

Fate
PO Box 1940, 170 Future Way, Marion, OH 43305–1940, USA

Fortean Times
PO Box 2409, London NW5 4NP
www.fortean-times.com

FSR
PO Box 12, Snodland, Kent, ME6 5HJ

International UFO Reporter
2457 West Peterson Ave, Chicag, IL 60659, USA

MUFON (Mutual UFO Network)
103 Oldtowne Rd, Seguin, TX 78155, USA
www.mufon.com

NUFON (Northern UFO Network)
6 Silsden Ave, Lowton, Warrington, WA3 1EN, UK

Strange
PO Box 2246, Rockville, MD 20847, USA
www.strangemag.com

UFOIN (UFO Investigators Network)
www.ufoin.org.uk

Any readers who wish to report experiences or pass on suggestions can contact the author at 1 Hallsteads Close, Dove Holes, Buxton, Derbyshire, SK17 8BS (e-mail: nufon@currantbun.com)

Index

THE COMPLETE BOOK OF ALIENS AND ABDUCTIONS

By Jenny Randles

The Complete Book of Aliens and Abductions is the definitive reference guide to the most extraordinary phenomenon of our time. Jenny Randles, Britain's leading expert in the scientific investigation of the paranormal, chronicles the evidence for the perplexing mystery of human contact with aliens.

Read about:

- The British businessman who was attacked by a UFO on his way home from a meeting
- Three unrelated groups of witnesses who encountered the same aliens within minutes on a lonely Australian mountain road
- A New York woman who was 'floated' through the window of her high-rise apartment and whose abduction was observed by secret-service bodyguards
- And much more.

Jenny Randles served as Director of Investigations of the British UFO Research Association for 12 years and is a founding member of the Association for the Scientific Study of Anomalous Phenomena. She has sold over a million copies of her books.

GOD'S EQUATION

Einstein, Relativity and the Expanding Universe

By Amir Aczel

Amir Aczel made higher mathematics intelligible to us in his ground-breaking *Fermat's Last Theorem*. Now, he does the same with a book of truly awesome scope: *God's Equation*. Based on worldwide research and interviews with dozens of prominent scientists, this book chronicles one of the most exciting scientific detective stories ever told.

God's Equation also discusses:

- The latest development in cosmology
- Studies of the nature of the universe
- The most fundamental truths about our larger environment
- Einstein's Theories which help to explain the links between relativity and cosmology

Amir D. Aczel, Ph.D. is the author of several books, among them *Fermat's Last Theorem* and *Probability 1*. He is an internationally known mathematician.

INVESTIGATING THE UNEXPLAINED

Explorations into ancient mysteries, the paranormal and
strange phenomena

By Paul Roland

Investigative journalist and paranormal researcher Paul Roland assesses
the evidence and suggests possible explanations for some of the most
curious and disturbing mysteries and phenomena of our time.

Read about:

- The evidence for alien intervention in human affairs, including
  a new investigation into the Roswell incident
- A range of disturbing scientific experiments including an exam-
  ination of the secret CIA psychic spy programme, the 'Philadelphia
  Experiment', and the incredible work of Nikola Tesla
- Some of the great unsolved mysteries of archaeology, including
  advanced civilisations around the world lost to history
- Phenomena such as out-of-body experiences, ghosts, guides and
  angels, and the reality of spiritual healing.

Packed with spell-binding eyewitness accounts and interviews with world
authorities including Robert Temple, Betty Shine and psychic spy David
Morehouse, *Investigating the Unexplained* will perplex, provoke and haunt
every reader.